EUROPEAN STUDIES ON CHRISTIAN ORIGINS

Editor
Michael Labahn

Published Under
↘ LIBRARY OF NEW TESTAMENT STUDIES

↘ **352**

Formerly The Journal For The Study Of The New Testament Supplement Series

Editor
Mark Goodacre

JESUS FROM JUDAISM TO CHRISTIANITY

Continuum Approaches to the Historical Jesus

EDITED BY TOM HOLMÉN

t&t clark

Published by T&T Clark
A Continuum imprint
The Tower Building, 11 York Road, London SE1 7NX
80 Maiden Lane, Suite 704, New York, NY 10038

www.tandtclark.com

British Library Cataloguing-in-Publication Data
A catalogue record for this book is available from the British Library.

ISBN-10: 0567042146 (hardback)
ISBN-13: 9780567042149 (hardback)

Typeset by Data Standards Limited, Frome, Somerset, UK
Printed on acid-free paper in Great Britain by Biddles Ltd, King's Lynn,
Norfolk

CONTENTS

PREFACE

This volume is largely based on papers presented at the seminars of the Study of the Historical Jesus Research Programme arranged during the Dresden meeting of the European Association of Biblical Studies in the summer of 2005. These seminars, held under the title *Jesus in Continuum*, served to launch a research project known by the very same name. Gatherings of the project continued at the EABS Budapest meeting in the summer of 2006.

I am grateful to all contributors to this volume and to all participants in the seminars, both those who partook in the discussion and those who presented their work. Gratitude is also due to the organizers of the Dresden meeting, especially to Philip R. Davies from the EABS for his support in the different phases of commencing and arranging the Study of the Historical Jesus Research Programme. Further, I wish to thank T&T Clark for accepting this volume for publication – in particular Rebecca Vaughan-Williams from the staff of the Press.

Turku (Åbo), 2006
Tom Holmén

THE CONTRIBUTORS

Edwin K. Broadhead is Associate Professor, Berea College, Berea, Kentucky, USA.

Ingo Broer is Professor of New Testament, University of Siegen, Department of Social Sciences, Theology, Siegen, Germany.

Bruce Chilton is Bernard Iddings Bell Professor of Religion and Executive Director of the Institute of Advanced Theology at Bard College, Annandale, New York, USA.

Sean Freyne is Emeritus Professor of Theology and Director of the Joint Programme for Mediterranean and Near Eastern Studies, Trinity College, Dublin, Ireland.

Tom Holmén is Academy Research Fellow of the Academy of Finland and Adjunct Professor, Åbo Akademi University, Department of Exegetics, Turku, Finland.

Thomas Kazen is Senior Lecturer in New Testament Exegesis, Stockholm School of Theology, Stockholm, Sweden.

William Loader is Australian Research Council Professorial Fellow at Murdoch University, Perth, Australia.

Annette Merz is Professor of Culture and Literature of Earliest Christianity at the University of Utrecht, Department of Theology, Utrecht, the Netherlands.

ABBREVIATIONS

AB	Anchor Bible
ABD	David Noel Freedman (ed.), *The Anchor Bible Dictionary* (New York: Doubleday, 1992)
ABRL	Anchor Bible Reference Library
AGJU	Arbeiten zur Geschichte des antiken Judentums und des Urchristentums
AMNSU	Arbeiten und Mitteilungen aus dem neutestamentlichen Seminar zu Uppsala
ANRW	Hildegard Temporini and Wolfgang Haase (eds.), *Aufstieg und Niedergang der römischen Welt: Geschichte und Kultur Roms im Spiegel der neueren Forschung* (Berlin: W. de Gruyter, 1972–)
ASTI	*Annual of the Swedish Theological Institute*
ATANT	Abhandlungen zur Theologie des Alten und Neuen Testaments
BBR	*Bulletin for Biblical Research*
BETL	Bibliotheca ephemeridum theologicarum lovaniensium
Bib	*Biblica*
BIS	Biblical Interpretation Series
BLS	Bible and Literature Series
BR	*Bible Review*
BS	The Biblical Seminar
BSR	Biblioteca di scienze religiose
BTB	*Biblical Theology Bulletin*
BZ	*Biblische Zeitschrift*
BZNW	Beihefte zur *ZNW*
CBQ	*Catholic Biblical Quarterly*
CCR	Cambridge Companions to Religion
ConBNT	Coniectanea biblica, New Testament
CRINT	Compendia rerum iudaicarum ad Novum Testamentum
CSR	*Christian Scholars Review*
EBib	Etudes bibliques
EF	Erträge der Forschung
EKKNT	Evangelisch-Katholischer Kommentar zum Neuen Testament
EncJud	*Encyclopaedia Judaica*

EvT	*Evangelische Theologie*
ExpTim	*Expository Times*
FCB	Feminist Companion to the Bible
FRLANT	Forschungen zur Religion und Literatur des Alten und Neuen Testaments
HTKNT	Herders theologischer Kommentar zum Neuen Testament
HTR	*Harvard Theological Review*
ICC	International Critical Commentary
IEJ	*Israel Exploration Journal*
JAC	*Jahrbuch für Antike und Christentum*
JBL	*Journal of Biblical Literature*
JH	*Jewish History*
JSHJ	*Journal for the Study of the Historical Jesus*
JSHRZ	Jüdische Schriften aus hellenistisch-römischer Zeit
JSNT	*Journal for the Study of the New Testament*
JSNTSup	*Journal for the Study of the New Testament*, Supplement Series
JSOTSup	*Journal for the Study of the Old Testament*, Supplement Series
JTS	*Journal of Theological Studies*
KNTTM	Kommentar zum Neuen Testament aus Talmud und Midrasch
KuI	*Kirche und Israel*
LCL	Loeb Classical Library
NEchtB	Neue Echter Bible
NHS	Nag Hammadi Studies
NovTSup	*Novum Testamentum*, Supplements
NTAbh	Neutestamentliche Abhandlungen
NTOA	Novum Testamentum et orbis antiquus
NTS	*New Testament Studies*
NTTS	New Testament Tools and Studies
QD	Quaestiones Disputatae
RB	*Revue biblique*
RGG	*Religion in Geschichte und Gegenwart*
RHPR	*Revue d'histoire et de philosophie religieuses*
SAC	Studies in Antiquity and Christianity
SANT	Studien zum Alten und Neuen Testament
SBLMS	SBL Monograph Series
SBS	Stuttgarter Bibelstudien
SBT	Studies in Biblical Theology
SFSHJ	South Florida Studies in the History of Judaism
SGJC	Shared Ground among Jews and Christians
SNTSMS	Society for New Testament Studies Monograph Series

SNTU	Studien zum Neuen Testament und seiner Umwelt
SP	Sacra pagina
ST	*Studia theologica*
STK	*Svensk teologisk kvartalskrift*
TANZ	Texte und Arbeiten zum neutestamentlichen Zeitalter
TBü	Theologische Bücherei
TDNT	Gerhard Kittel and Gerhard Friedrich (eds.), *Theological Dictionary of the New Testament* (trans. Geoffrey W. Bromiley; 10 vols.; Grand Rapids: Eerdmans, 1964–)
TGl	*Theologie und Glaube*
TheolBeitr	*Theologische Beiträge*
TLZ	*Theologische Literaturzeitung*
TWNT	Gerhard Kittel and Gerhard Friedrich (eds.), *Theologisches Wörterbuch zum Neuen Testament* (11 vols.; Stuttgart: Kohlhammer, 1932–79)
TynBul	*Tyndale Bulletin*
TZ	*Theologische Zeitschrift*
VTSup	*Vetus Testamentum*, Supplements
WMANT	Wissenschaftliche Monographien zum Alten und Neuen Testament
WUNT	Wissenschaftliche Untersuchungen zum Neuen Testament
ZDPV	*Zeitschrift des deutschen Palästina-Vereins*
ZNW	*Zeitschrift für die neutestamentliche Wissenschaft*
ZTK	*Zeitschrift für Theologie und Kirche*

Ancient Sources

(Abbreviations of the names of books of the Bible and of the Dead Sea Scrolls are not included.)

1–2 Clem.	*1–2 Clement*
Ant.	Josephus, *Antiquities of the Jews*
Apion	Josephus, *Against Apion, or Contra Apion*
Apoc. Mos.	*Apocalypse of Moses*
b.	Babylonian Talmud
Did.	*Didache*
Gen. R	*Genesis Rabbah*
Gos. Thom.	*Gospel of Thomas*
Hypoth.	Philo, *Hypothetica*
Jos.	Philo, *De Josepho*
Jub.	*Jubilees*
Ket.	Kethuboth

Kid.	Kiddushin
LAB	*Liber Antiquitatum Biblicarum*
Leg. Gai.	Philo, *Legatio ad Gaium*
m.	Mishnah
Mid.	Middoth
Nid.	Niddah
Pliny, *Hist. Nat.*	Pliny, *Historia Naturalis*
Ps.-Phoc.	*Pseudo-Phocylides*
Sanh.	Sanhedrin
Shab.	Shabbath
Sot.	Sotah
Spec. Leg.	Philo, *De specialibus legibus*
t.	Tosefta
T. Iss.	*Testament of Issachar*
T. Levi	*Testament of Levi*
T. Naph.	*Testament of Naphtali*
T. Reub.	*Testament of Reuben*
Vit. Mos.	Philo, *De vita Mosis*
War	Josephus, *The Jewish War, or De Bello Judaico*
Yeb.	Yebamoth
Yom.	Yoma

AN INTRODUCTION TO THE CONTINUUM APPROACH

Tom Holmén

The purpose of this volume is to outline a continuum approach to the historical Jesus. To this end, some individual studies are presented which in practice, rather than in theory, examine the possible contours of such an approach. Hence, there is to date no normative or established description of the continuum approach, and much of its agenda remains open. For this reason, too, only some rather general characteristics of the approach were given to the present writers as guidelines. Rather than being set some specific rules to work with, each writer was encouraged to explore what the continuum perspective to the historical Jesus could be, and how it should be pursued. In other words, the volume pretty much starts from scratch.

One of the characteristic pursuits of the latest phase of Jesus-of-history research, namely the so-called Third Quest, has been the serious attempt to locate Jesus within first-century AD Judaism, to seek a Jesus who would be plausible within his Jewish context.[1] Comparatively less emphasis has been put on the question as to whether or how, if at all, the picture of Jesus plausible within the Jewish context also suits and accounts for the Jesuanic *Wirkungsgeschichte*, the history of the influence and reception of Jesus in early Christianity. Still, it stands to reason that a historically accurate description of Jesus should prove itself plausible even in this respect. By integrating the Jewish context, the teaching of Jesus and the Christian reception history into one account, the continuum perspective seeks to uncover a Jesus who is both fitting within his Jewish context

---

1. See, for example, G. Theissen, A. Merz, *Der historische Jesus* (Göttingen: Vandenhoeck & Ruprecht, 1996), p. 29; N. T. Wright, *Jesus and the Victory of God* (Christian Origins and the Question of God, 2; Minneapolis: Fortress, 1996), pp. 119–20; T. Holmén, 'The Jewishness of Jesus in the "Third Quest"', in M. Labahn, A. Schmidt (eds.), *Jesus, Mark and Q: The Teaching of Jesus and its Earliest Records* (JSNTSup, 214; Sheffield: Sheffield Academic Press, 2001), pp. 143–62. Cf. also the titles of, for instance, J. H. Charlesworth, *Jesus within Judaism: New Light from Exciting Archaeological Discoveries* (London: SPCK, 2nd impr., 1990); C. A. Evans, *Jesus and His Contemporaries: Comparative Studies* (AGJU, 25; Leiden: Brill, 1995); B. Chilton, 'Jesus within Judaism', in B. Chilton, C. A. Evans (eds.), *Jesus in Context: Temple, Purity, and Restoration* (AGJU, 39; Leiden: Brill, 1997), pp. 179–201.

and in a comprehensible relation to early Christian attitudes. Thus, according to this perspective, a historically plausible picture of Jesus is one that can be placed in the Judaism–Christianity continuum. This is the decisive characteristic of the continuum approach.

'Continuum' should not be understood as focusing on continuity alone. On the contrary, both continuity and discontinuity are involved as modes of historical *évènement*. On various issues Jesus may have departed from or adhered to Judaism, and again, early Christianity may have departed from or adhered to the Jesuanic proclamation. In each case, however, scholarship is obliged to account for the elements of discontinuity and continuity. The continuum approach challenges scholars to explain 'why', and this applies to each phase of transition, whether Judaism–Jesus or Jesus–Christianity, as well as to both the continuity and discontinuity modes of transition. 'Continuum' thus denotes the attempt to take note of the interaction and interdependence of the various phenomena of history, and to avoid treating them as isolated from each other. In particular, the continuum approach maintains that a phenomenon is seriously determinable only in the light of its anterior *and* posterior history.

With respect to historical Jesus research, the continuum approach means that extra attention is paid to nascent Christianity. In a continuum perspective to the historical Jesus, early Christianity and its writings, both canonical and extra-canonical, do much more than merely provide the material for ascertaining historically reliable information about Jesus. Early Christianity must be considered on its own terms. So too the relation between Jesus and Christianity should be given a conscious and systematic consideration. Accordingly, the tentative explication of the continuum approach that will not follow concentrates to a substantial degree on assessing the Jesus–Christianity phase or dimension.

One might ask what is new in an approach to the historical Jesus conforming to the above outline. A rather close analogy can be drawn to the 'Third Quest's' emphasis on the Jewishness of Jesus. The recognition of the fact that Jesus was a Jew was of course not an innovation of the 'Third Quest'. A. Schweitzer had stressed, in opposition to the liberal and modernized Jesuses, the Jewish background of Jesus and the necessity of understanding Jesus as within the Judaism of his time.[2] Similarly, the scholars of the history of religions school emphasized understanding Jesus in his religious and cultural context.[3] Shortly after Schweitzer there was a

---

2. See, for instance, A. Schweitzer, *Geschichte der Paulinischen Forschung von der Reformation bis auf die Gegenwart* (Tübingen: Mohr Siebeck, 1911), p. vii.

3. See, for example, J. Weiss, *Die Predigt Jesu vom Reiche Gottes* (Göttingen: Vandenhoeck & Ruprecht, 1892); W. Bousset, *Kyrios Christos: Geschichte des Christusglaubens von den Anfängen des Christentums bis Irenäus* (FRLANT, 21; Göttingen: Vandenhoeck & Ruprecht, 2nd edn, 1913). The early Church had (Hellenizingly) altered the simple Judaism of Jesus.

flux of Jewish scholars who portrayed a profoundly Jewish Jesus.[4] The New Quest for the historical Jesus,[5] again, explicitly acknowledged Jesus' Jewishness. It maintained that a plausible picture of the historical Jesus 'should be "at home" within first-century Palestinian Judaism'.[6]

Despite such good principles and intentions, only with the commencement of the 'Third Quest' has there emerged a serious and mainstream, instead of merely marginal, attempt to understand Jesus in a continuum with the Judaism of his time and not in contrast with it. Jesus was not a different Jew, as such standing on the verge of becoming non-Jewish. Instead, with all his differences he inherently formed part of the diverse and heterogeneous Jewish religiosity also called early 'Judaisms'.[7] Although there are in the 'Third Quest's' aspiration to find Jesus the Jew some important aspects that still deserve fuller recognition – and here, as I shall soon point out, the continuum approach is a significant help – the consistent emphasis on Jesus' Jewishness has thoroughly altered the outlook of scholarly work on the historical Jesus. Scholars who nowadays want to find Jesus will, as J. H. Charlesworth has put it, keep bumping into pre-70 Palestinian phenomena.[8] Being in this way immersed in the first-century world, scholars' depictions of Jesus will not only be enriched with some colourful details of the Jewish context but will elementally grow from it.

The 'Third Quest' agenda has significantly affected methodological thinking as well. As to the criteria of authenticity of Jesus research, the

4. See G. Lindeskog, *Die Jesusfrage im neuzeitlichen Judentum: Ein Beitrag zur Geschichte der Leben-Jesu-Forschung* (AMNSU, 8; Leipzig: Almqvist & Wiksells, 1938); S. Ben-Chorin, *Jesus im Judentum* (Wuppertal: Theologischer Verlag Brockhaus, 1970); D. A. Hagner, *The Jewish Reclamation of Jesus: An Analysis and Critique of the Modern Jewish Study of Jesus* (Grand Rapids: Zondervan, 1988).

5. See, for example, E. Käsemann, 'Das Problem des historischen Jesus', *ZTK* 51 (1954), pp. 125–53; H. Conzelmann, 'Jesus Christus', *RGG* 3 (1959), pp. 619–53; J. M. Robinson, *A New Quest of the Historical Jesus* (SBT, 25; London: SCM Press, 1959).

6. So precisely M. D. Hooker, 'Christology and Methodology', *NTS* 17 (1970–71), pp. 480–87 (482). Cf. also, for instance, E. Käsemann, *Exegetische Versuche und Besinnungen: Erster Band* (Göttingen: Vandenhoeck & Ruprecht, 2nd edn, 1960), p. 206; N. Perrin, *Rediscovering the Teaching of Jesus* (New York: Harper, 1967), p. 51.

7. For the term 'Judaisms' see J. Neusner, 'Preface', in J. Neusner, W. Scott Green, E. S. Frerichs (eds.), *Judaisms and their Messiahs at the Turn of the Christian Era* (New York: Cambridge University Press, 1987), pp. ix–xiv. The plural form of the word had naturally been introduced earlier; see, for instance, the title 'Palestinian Judaisms' in S. Sandmel, *The First Christian Century in Judaism and Christianity: Certainties and Uncertainties* (New York: Oxford University Press, 1969), pp. 58–106.

8. J. H. Charlesworth, 'The Foreground of Christian Origins and the Commencement of Jesus Research', in J. H. Charlesworth (ed.), *Jesus' Jewishness: Exploring the Place of Jesus in Early Judaism* (SGJC, 2; New York: Crossroad, 1996), pp. 63–83 (82). Further on the characteristics of the recent study on Jesus, see T. Holmén, 'A Theologically Disinterested Quest? On the Origins of the "Third Quest" for the Historical Jesus', *ST* 55 (2001), pp. 1–23.

criterion of dissimilarity has been deprived of its two-dimensional character. An increasing number of scholars have recognized that the early Christians would not have gratuitously adopted elements of Judaism dissimilar to their views and ascribed them to Jesus. It is therefore unnecessary to seek to establish dissimilarity to Judaism in order to put together an argument for authenticity.[9] However, the criterion has quite rightly persisted as a probe of possible dissimilarity to Christianity.[10] This simple change of methodology has clearly affected the concrete pictures of Jesus arrived at by scholars in their investigations. For example, no more can a Jesus tradition's authenticity be questioned for the mere reason that it presents Jesus as quoting or referring to the Old Testament.[11]

Similarly, then, in stressing the importance of the Jesuanic *Wirkungsgeschichte* in early Christianity, the message of the continuum approach is not unheard of. *Wirkungsgeschichte* is being taken into account in historical Jesus research already for the reason that it is this process that produced the Jesus tradition, the only accessible route to Jesus. However, a kind of conscious adjustment and localization of the picture of the historical figure of Jesus in relation to the subsequent 'Christianities', similar to that pursued in relation to the 'Judaisms' contemporaneous to Jesus, has remained absent. I would argue that, if applied seriously and systematically, the continuum approach could occasion dramatic changes in the scholarly outlook on Jesus as comparable as those effectuated by the 'Third Quest's' consistent pursuit of seeing Jesus within Judaism. The changes would certainly also promote earnest historical description. After all, a Jesus who can be placed within early Judaism but who cannot be understood in relation to early Christianity is no more historically plausible than a Jesus who can be combined with nascent Christianity while remaining an enigma as a Jew of his time. Both dimensions should receive enough attention and be explained satisfactorily. The main overall purpose of the *Jesus in Continuum* project, to which

---

9.   The notion was put forward by B. F. Meyer in several studies. See his *The Aims of Jesus* (London: SCM Press, 1979), p. 86; 'Objectivity and Subjectivity in Historical Criticism of the Gospels', in D. L. Dungan (ed.), *The Interrelations of the Gospels* (BETL, 95; Leuven: Leuven University Press, 1990), pp. 546–65 (547–48). My most detailed treatment of the issue can be found in T. Holmén, 'Doubts about Double Dissimilarity: Restructuring the main criterion of Jesus-of-history research', in B. Chilton, C. A. Evans (eds.), *Authenticating the Words of Jesus* (NTTS, 28.1; Leiden: Brill, 1999), pp. 47–80; idem, *Jesus and Jewish Covenant Thinking* (BIS, 55; Leiden: Brill, 2001), pp. 27–32. See even T. Holmén, 'Knowing about Q and Knowing about Jesus: Mutually Exclusive Undertakings?', in A. Lindemann (ed.), *The Sayings Source Q and the Historical Jesus* (BETL, 158; Leuven: Peeters, 2001), pp. 497–514.

10.   See below.

11.   Only occasionally can one still find such reasoning; see, for instance, R. W. Funk, R. W. Hoover, *The Five Gospels: The Search for the Authentic Words of Jesus* (New York: Scribner, 1996), pp. 177–78.

the present volume belongs,[12] is to try to establish this mode of thinking in scholarly discourse.

Conscious efforts to extend the attention of Jesus research to Christian reception history – in the vein of the continuum approach – remain few and far between, although the extended perspective can be seen as emerging in some recent works. Macro-scale applications of a continuum approach can be seen in N. T. Wright's and J. D. G. Dunn's multi-volume investigations.[13] Both Wright's *Christian Origins and the Question of God* and Dunn's *Christianity in the Making*, comprising volume-length studies on the historical Jesus as well as on early Christianity, seek to accommodate 'this Christianity' with 'that Jesus'. Naturally, finding Jesus a place within Judaism also belongs to Wright's and Dunn's research programs. However, while Jesus' position within Judaism – let us call it the Judaism–Jesus dimension – is worked out by them within the confines of one distinct investigation, the Jesus–Christianity dimension falls into separate studies written successively. This mode of procedure cannot properly allow the kind of interplay or movements within the hermeneutical circle that would be necessary to let the Jesus–Christianity dimension affect the emerging picture of the historical Jesus in a way that corresponds to how the Judaism–Jesus dimension has been applied. Instead, Jesus the Jew has already been portrayed when Wright and Dunn proceed to present their views of the subsequent early Christianity. Thus Jesus cannot be further adjusted in relation to the unfolding picture of early Christianity. In other words, there appears to be less than a satisfactory opportunity to accommodate 'this Jesus' with 'that Christianity'.

Of course, studies of this length must concede to practical demands. Both writers may also readjust earlier portraits at the end of their projects.[14] Still, a point worth consideration is whether the continuum

---

12. The *Jesus in Continuum* project was launched by the historical Jesus seminar held during the 2005 Dresden meeting of the European Association of Biblical Studies (EABS). Papers read at that seminar are now gathered in this volume. The project continued in the Budapest 2006 EABS meeting.

13. The first three volumes of Wright's planned five-volume enterprise are: *The New Testament and the People of God* (Christian Origins and the Question of God, 1; Minneapolis: Fortress, 1992); *Jesus and the Victory of God* (Christian Origins and the Question of God, 2; Minneapolis: Fortress, 1996); *The Resurrection of the Son of God* (Christian Origins and the Question of God, 3; London: SPCK, 2003). Dunn has planned a three-volume series of which the first one has appeared: *Jesus Remembered* (Christianity in the Making, 1; Grand Rapids: Eerdmans, 2003). At the time of writing this, his preliminary title for the second volume was *Beginning from Jerusalem*.

14. Perhaps this is one of the purposes of Wright's planned fifth monograph he mentions in the commencing volume; see Wright, *People of God* (13), p. xiii. Also, in this first volume Wright does a preliminary review of early Christianity.

perspective indeed calls for rethinking common working practices and orders. I shall return to these thoughts later on.

On the methodological side, a clear example of a continuum approach is certainly G. Theissen's and D. Winter's *The Quest for the Plausible Jesus*.[15] Together with many other scholars, they abandon the dissimilarity to Judaism part of the criterion of dissimilarity,[16] which they replace with the criterion of contextual plausibility, that is, establishing an independent profile within the context of first-century Judaism.[17] The dissimilarity to Christianity part they, however, retain, and combine with the criteria of multiple attestation and coherence, which together form the criterion of plausibility of effects.[18] By doing this Theissen and Winter

---

15. G. Theissen, D. Winter, *The Quest for the Plausible Jesus: The Question of Criteria* (trans. M. E. Boring; Louisville: John Knox Press, 2002).

16. Among scholars who discard the dissimilarity to Judaism part and support what could be called the criterion of dissimilarity to Christianity are, for example, S.-O. Back, *Jesus of Nazareth and the Sabbath Commandment* (Åbo: Åbo Akademi University Press, 1995), p. 18; Charlesworth, *Jesus within Judaism*, pp. 5–6; C. A. Evans, 'Authenticity Criteria in Life of Jesus Research', *CSR* 19 (1989), pp. 6–31 (24–27); Holmén (see references in n. 9 above); Meyer (see references in n. 9 above); S. E. Porter, *The Criteria for Authenticity in Historical-Jesus Research: Previous Discussion and New Proposals* (JSNTSup, 191; Sheffield: Sheffield Academic Press, 2000), pp. 70–76; A. F. Segal, *Rebecca's Children: Judaism and Christianity in the Roman World* (Cambridge, Mass.: Harvard University Press, 1986), pp. 68–69; Theissen, Merz, *Der historische Jesus* (1), pp. 118–20; Theissen, Winter, *Plausible Jesus* (15), pp. 169, 179; and C. Tuckett, 'Sources and Methods', in M. Bockmuehl (ed.), *The Cambridge Companion to Jesus* (CCR; Cambridge: Cambridge University Press, 2001), pp. 121–37 (132–33). Those who uphold the so-called criterion of embarrassment can also be included in this group of scholars (see, for instance, J. Breech, *The Silence of Jesus: The Authentic Voice of the Historical Man* [Philadelphia: Fortress, 1983], pp. 22–26, and J. P. Meier, *A Marginal Jew: Rethinking the Historical Jesus*, vol. 1: *The Roots of the Problem and the Person* [ABRL; New York: Doubleday, 1991], pp. 168–71), since embarrassment is a special case of the criterion of dissimilarity to Christianity; see Holmén, 'Double Dissimilarity' (9), pp. 75–76; Theissen, Winter, *Plausible Jesus* (15), p. 156. Already J. Jeremias complained about the significant methodological failure of the criterion of dissimilarity in detaching Jesus from his true historical context, Judaism; see J. Jeremias, *Neutestamentliche Theologie. Erster Teil: Die Verkündigung Jesu* (Gütersloh: Mohn, 1971), p. 14. This has now become a common complaint of the 'Third Quest'; see, for instance, R. T. Osborn, 'The Christian Blasphemy: A Non-Jewish Jesus', in J. H. Charlesworth (ed.), *Jews and Christians: Exploring the Past, Present, and Future* (SGJC, 1; New York: Crossroad, 1990), pp. 211–38 (218–21); D. J. Harrington, 'The Jewishness of Jesus: Facing Some Problems', in J. H. Charlesworth (ed.), *Jesus' Jewishness: Exploring the Place of Jesus in Early Judaism* (SGJC, 2; New York: Crossroad, 1996), pp. 123–36 (132–33).

17. See Theissen, Winter, *Plausible Jesus* (15), pp. 179–88.

18. Indeed, this comes as a surprise after reading that the intention of the writers is to *replace* the criterion of dissimilarity (see, for instance, Theissen, Winter, *Plausible Jesus* [15], pp. xv, 172, 251). For the sake of clarity I offer the following direct quotations: 'The two aspects of the criterion of the plausibility of historical effects take up two traditional criteria (or three, depending on one's categories): on the one hand, *the "criterion of dissimilarity" in its application to early Christianity (here called "resistance to tendencies of the tradition")*,

come to emphasize the explicability of the contextually plausible (i.e., with respect to early Judaism) Jesus in relation to the subsequent Christianity much in the way of the continuum approach as delineated at the beginning of this Introduction: one should expect to find both continuity (criteria of multiple attestation and coherence) and discontinuity (the criterion of dissimilarity to Christianity) between Jesus and early Christianity.

Theissen's and Winter's study remains quite strictly on a theoretical level. It is intended to be a presentation of methodology of Jesus research, a criteriology, and, except for some stock examples, it does not pursue the methodology in practice. Conversely, S. Freyne sees his recent volume on Jesus (*Jesus, a Jewish Galilean*) as an application of the contextual plausibility criterion.[19] In Freyne's view, the criterion assures coherence between the Jewish matrix, Jesus himself and the Jesus movement. This should be taken into account in order to do justice to the historical relationships involved in the rise of early Christianity. In articulating the concrete significance of the relationships, Freyne points out that, on the one hand, Jesus' having a place within early Judaism does not necessarily presuppose that he would have conformed to any one of the known groups. On the other hand, accounts of Jesus which can explain the origins of a movement in his name are more plausible than accounts which cannot do that.[20]

Finally, a combination of conscious methodological thinking and concrete application along the lines of a continuum approach can be found in B. Chilton's studies, in which he employs what he calls a 'generative exegesis'. According to Chilton,

> canon is a function and expression of those meanings which communities gave their scriptural materials during the course of their composition. Generative exegesis is designed to trace those meanings within the social and cultural contexts in which the materials of

---

and, on the other hand, aspects of the criteria of "coherence" and "multiple attestation" (here combined under the heading "coherence of sources")' (Theissen, Winter, *Plausible Jesus* [15], p. 179; emphasis mine.) Further, resistance to tendencies of the tradition (that is, dissimilarity to Christianity) 'remains an important criterion' and it holds 'the first place' (Theissen, Winter, *Plausible Jesus* [15], pp. 179, 211). See further in T. Holmén, 'Review Article of G. Theissen & D. Winter: *The Quest for the Plausible Jesus*', *JTS* 55 (2004), pp. 216–28. Cf. my overall estimation there: 'The Quest for the Plausible Jesus is … a convincing and valid presentation of the authenticating method of historical Jesus research. It contains numerous brilliant and important observations' (p. 227).

19. S. Freyne, *Jesus, a Jewish Galilean: A New Reading of the Jesus-Story* (repr., London: T&T Clark International, 2005), pp. 22–23, 171. Freyne refers to the discussion of the criterion in G. Theissen, A. Merz, *The Historical Jesus: A Comprehensive Guide* (trans. J. Bowden; London: SCM Press, 1996).

20. See Freyne, *Jesus, a Jewish Galilean* (19), pp. 171–72.

Scripture were produced. It is a matter of inference from the given, received form of the text, back to the circles of tradents and redactors who shaped the material. The inferences involved include what are usually called source-criticism, rhetorical criticism, and social history, all within the coordinated attempt to explain how the received form of the text came to be as it is before us.[21]

The generative exegesis paradigm shares some central elements with the continuum approach, for example the emphasized awareness of the interdependence of historical phenomena, the consistent attempt to explain and understand these dependencies, and the aim to study early Christianity more on its own terms.[22]

But what then could be the 'dramatic changes' in the scholarly outlook on Jesus that a serious and systematic pursuit of the continuum approach could bring about, for which I argued above? Some of them are best characterized as following through with some aspects already highlighted by the 'Third Quest's' emphasis of the Jewishness of Jesus. For example, by positing Jesus as a real and central link between early Judaism and early Christianity, the continuum perspective is apt for seeing in him a true acting force in the Judaism of his time. Jesus not only gathered influences and reacted upon them but gathered reactions by influencing others. This is also the characteristic the 'Third Quest' portraits of Jesus should evince if Jesus is indeed regarded as thoroughly Jewish, thus as 'both symptom and result' of the Judaism where 'radical pluralism' was the 'order of the day'.[23] Often Jesus is portrayed almost as a mere collage of various views that we know existed at the time. The fact that one takes seriously the possibility that Jesus, too, contributed to the 'radical pluralism' manifests itself in how scholars decide on such questions as: Would only the existing modes of messianic thinking have been relevant to Jesus or could he have developed a messianism of his own? Or should only the existing views of the Jewish law be considered applicable when

21. B. Chilton, 'A Generative Exegesis of Mark 7.1-23', in B. Chilton, C. A. Evans (eds.), *Jesus in Context: Temple, Purity, and Restoration* (AGJU, 39; Leiden: Brill, 1997), pp. 297–317 (299–300). See also, for example, B. Chilton, *A Feast of Meanings: Eucharistic Theologies from Jesus through Johannine Circles* (NovTSup, 72; Leiden: Brill, 1994); *idem, Rabbi Jesus: An Intimate Biography* (New York: Doubleday, 2000).

22. See, for instance, Chilton, *A Feast of Meanings* (21), where he discusses the circles of Peter, James, Paul and John.

23. So B. Chilton, *The Temple of Jesus: His Sacrificial Program Within a Cultural History of Sacrifice* (University Park: Pennsylvania State University Press, 1992), p. 181. Cf. also J. H. Charlesworth's characterization of the Judaism of the time as a 'swirling dynamo full of life'; J. H. Charlesworth, 'From Jewish Messianology to Christian Christology: Some Caveats and Perspectives', in J. Neusner, W. Scott Green, E. S. Frerichs (eds.), *Judaisms and their Messiahs at the Turn of the Christian Era* (New York: Cambridge University Press, 1987), pp. 225–64 (227).

constructing a portrait of Jesus? Could he instead be seen as having advanced some new and original variations thereof? Bringing effectively the Jesuanic *Wirkungsgeschichte* in view and systematically seeking an understanding of it from the viewpoint of Jesus' mission and message, the continuum approach bestows an active and creative role even upon Jesus the Jew, a role that is already taken for granted with respect to Jesus' Jewish contemporaries as well as his followers.

Likewise, the continuum approach will lead to a disposal of what is left of the tendency in the 'Third Quest' to artificially dissociate Jesus from his historical context. I already remarked that many 'Third Quest' scholars discard the dissimilarity to Judaism aspect of the criterion of dissimilarity.[24] This aspect provides no cogent arguments concerning the question of authenticity but will generate a methodical separation of Jesus from Judaism. A tendency remains, however, which works like the dissimilarity to Judaism aspect but in another direction, namely in regard to the Jesus–Christianity dimension. This is the systematic calling into question of the authenticity of traditions which are similar to Christian thinking. From time to time there has even emerged a kind of 'criterion of similarity to Christianity' which functions negatively to suggest inauthenticity. A rule amounting to such a criterion can be found in the reports of the Jesus Seminar: 'Features of stories that serve Christian convictions directly are likely to be the product of the Christian imagination.'[25] As pointed out by M. Casey, this way of reasoning excludes *a priori* the existence of accurate information about Jesus that would have supported the ideas of the Christian writers.[26] The views of the early Christians are thus by definition regarded as deviating from the genuinely Jesuanic ones.

Due to the 'Third Quest's' attempt to study Jesus as a figure within Judaism, scholars nowadays generally disapprove an in-principle detachment of Jesus from the Judaism of his time. The continuum approach now promulgates a similar outspoken disapproval of an in-principle detachment of Jesus from his *Wirkungsgeschichte* in early Christianity. Just as when we seek out Jesus' place within Judaism and accept only such accounts of Jesus as can be situated plausibly in contemporary Judaism, so too we need to think carefully and express precisely how the suggested

---

24. See n. 16 above. Cf. also Theissen, Winter, *Plausible Jesus* (15), p. 169: 'In the Third Quest, the CDJ [*sc.* criterion of dissimilarity to Judaism] is fundamentally rejected ... and the CDC [*sc.* criterion of dissimilarity to Christianity] is applied in a controlled manner.'

25. R. W. Funk, *The Acts of Jesus: What did Jesus Really Do? The Search for the Authentic Deeds of Jesus. Translation and Commentary by Robert W. Funk and The Jesus Seminar* (San Francisco: HarperSanFrancisco, 1998), p. 35. See also, for example, R. J. Miller, 'Historical Method and the Deeds of Jesus: The Test Case of the Temple Demonstration', *Forum* 8 (1992), pp. 5–30 (22).

26. M. Casey, 'Culture and Historicity: The Cleansing of the Temple', *CBQ* 59 (1997), pp. 306–32 (330–31).

picture of Jesus can plausibly be related to what became of Jesus and his teaching in early Christianity. Artificial means of creating discontinuity between Jesus' and his followers' convictions, such as the above 'criterion of similarity', operative on a methodological level, or any other *a priori* shortcuts, are effectively precluded by the continuum approach's demand that discontinuities should be satisfactorily explained. A short example should help illustrate this.

A regular challenge that the hypothesis of a non-eschatological Jesus,[27] a finding perhaps supported in some part of the Jesus tradition, tries to cope with is to explain somehow those traditions that clearly propose that Jesus came with an outspoken eschatological programme. Obviously, one solution here has been to declare the eschatological Jesus traditions as products of or misinterpretations by early Christianity. The continuum approach, however, reveals such a solution to be rather problematic by entrusting the non-eschatological Jesus hypothesis with a further chal- lenge: the hypothesis should include an explanation of why and how, assuming Jesus' non-eschatological proclamation, early Christianity turned out so eschatological. It then happens that the more one ascribes the eschatological Jesus traditions to early Christianity – as if solving the first challenge – the more pointed the eschatological picture of early Christianity one arrives at, thus making the second challenge more severe. Moreover, taking into account the full continuum perspective, the continuity from John the Baptist's emphatic eschatology to the early Christian eschatology should also be observed. Jesus the non-eschatolo- gist, the former disciple of John and the Master of the early Christians, appears then strikingly alone and disconnected from both his anterior and posterior history. Those wishing to sustain the non-eschatological Jesus hypothesis should then ponder whether and by what means this dual discontinuity can be satisfactorily explained or whether it would rather be better to opt for another kind of picture of Jesus which can more readily be made understandable in the continuum perspective.

Further changes occasioned by a systematic application of the continuum approach could concern the scholarly treatment of a special case of Jesus traditions cohering with early Christian ideas. When such a tradition displays an original variation of known Jewish ideas, there often appears in scholarship an especially strong tendency to ascribe without further ado the tradition to early Christians. However, recognizing in Jesus someone who truly made a difference in the continuum of early Judaism and Christianity – a characterization in accordance with the picture of Jesus as a Jew of his time – one must become critically disposed to such automatic ascriptions as well. Even when promoting a view

27. See, for example, M. J. Borg, 'A Temperate case for a Non-eschatological Jesus', in M. J. Borg, *Jesus in Contemporary Scholarship* (Philadelphia: Trinity Press, 1986), pp. 47–68.

cherished by Christians and displaying a novel development from Judaism, Jesus traditions presenting the view do not need to be seen as Christian retrojections into Jesus' life. The possibility that the novel development derives from Jesus himself should always be given fair consideration. This is what applying the continuum perspective and acknowledging Jesus as a Jew of his day means in practice.

If all this results in scholars dismissing drastic discontinuities between Jesus and early Christianity more than before, so be it. It is, in general, probable that instead of a clear-cut creation of the Christian imagination or a slavish repetition of the given, concepts that can most often account for the relation between Jesus and early Christianity are development and unfoldment. Indeed, these work in all directions. Jesus did not repetitively borrow from his contemporaries nor did he appear to be coming from outside his context, but he showed originality in applying ideas that were familiar to the Jewish tradition. Similarly, early Christianity did not simply copy what Jesus had proclaimed nor did they go into a large-scale manufacture of Jesus traditions *ex nihilo*. Therefore, it should be legitimate to begin with the assumption that, by being explained, discontinuities between Jesus and early Christianity usually turn out to exhibit development and unfoldment rather than detachment, and that a genuine starting point in Jesus' mission and message still often underlies them.

With these remarks we come to observe a certain corollary that the continuum perspective has in its view of early Christianity. It is of course generally acknowledged that Christianity did not emerge in a vacuum but was affected, in different ways, by the settings of Palestinian and Diaspora Judaism as well as the Hellenistic Graeco-Roman world.[28] Considerably less often, however, scholars of early Christianity seek to allow for the role that Jesus' proclamation would have played in the shaping of early Christian views and convictions. Understandably, by minimizing Jesus' influence one avoids much laborious study and also speculation. The question is whether such minimizing is warranted; my remarks above suggest that it is not. The continuum perspective now challenges even this branch of scholarship, more than it has done up to this point, in an acknowledgment of Jesus as a real and significant factor in the emergence of the early Christian traditions. If accounts of early Christianity cannot accommodate a plausible picture of Jesus the Jew, active, innovative and carrying out a mission of consequence to early Christianity, the accounts are themselves implausible.

Finally, I would like to raise the following question: Should we consider

---

28. In a way, while Judaism largely constituted the cradle of the message of the early followers of Jesus, the Graeco-Roman world came into view mainly by being the receiver of the message.

a certain concrete change in the common working order of the historical Jesus study? The continuum approach is here presented mainly as a means of studying Jesus. As is plainly clear, we can learn about early Judaism and Christianity directly from the respective sources, but Jesus is, in a way, an 'unknown variable'.[29] Thinking of the continuum Judaism–Jesus–Christianity, we approach from opposite ends and target Jesus at the centre. On the one hand, then, learning about Jesus affects – or as has been argued in this chapter, indeed should affect – our understanding of early Christianity. On the other hand, we must also recognize that, although somewhat differently and perhaps to some lesser degree, the pictures of both Jesus and early Christianity that follow again reflect and prompt a reconsideration of early Judaism, and so on and on. In other words, a full appreciation of the continuum perspective also requires an appreciation of some delicate and intricate swings in the hermeneutical circle, and the problem is how most effectively and properly this can be done in practice.

Perhaps the commonest mode of procedure when studying Jesus has been to deal first with 'the Jewish background' of Jesus (or the selected aspects of Jesus' mission and message) and then to try to understand him (the selected aspects) in this light. The observations concerning the continuum approach put forward in the present chapter, however, should have made it clear that this mode of procedure does not usually guarantee that sufficient weight is given to the Jesus–Christianity dimension. On the contrary, it is obvious that the mode of procedure can be applied while escaping quite easily from giving any more consistent account of the relation of the portrayed historical Jesus to his posterior history. Instead, therefore, I would propose that like the Jewish background, the Christian *Wirkungsgeschichte* should be dealt with on its own *before* turning to a consideration of Jesus. Of course, in performing the actual investigation work scholars are in principle free to realize the hermeneutical processes involved. Nonetheless, the concrete presentation of the investigation and its results will need to take place in some solid and easily accessible form. Appearing in print, the study must follow a mode of procedure which is necessarily a simplified and solidified form of the actual investigation process. My point is that, in general, the choice of that procedure can either further or thwart our efforts to give proper consideration to the requirements of the hermeneutical circle in the preceding investigation work. I also contend that, in particular, the commonest mode of procedure, the two-part 'Judaism → Jesus', is quite discouraging with respect to allowing for swings between Jesus and early Christianity. For

---

29. Naturally, there is much unknown about several aspects of early Judaism and early Christianity too. In comparison with them, however, Jesus is mostly a matter of inference and conjecture.

this reason, if it can be agreed that the Jesus–Christianity dimension indeed deserves more attention than is usually paid to it, the working and presentation order that should be applied is 'Judaism → early Christianity (the Jesuanic *Wirkungsgeschichte*) → Jesus'.

Obviously, although guaranteeing attention to where it is often lacking in current Jesus studies, this form of presenting one's investigation is not always practical or even possible. For instance, it cannot be applied when writing multi-volume studies such as those of Wright and Dunn already referred to above. A true three-part mode of procedure requires that all parts, Judaism, Jesus and his *Wirkungsgeschichte*, are discussed within one and the same presentation, not divided into two or more successive and separate studies. This is due to the fact that dividing the presentation in such a way would in all probability also mean that the investigation itself would take place substantially in successive and separate phases, thus without proper opportunity for interaction and movements within the hermeneutical circle. Most readily such a mode of procedure could be applied when dealing with some particular aspects of Jesus' teaching and/ or life. Thus, if one seeks to find out, for example, Jesus' views of the Sabbath, after the usual discussion of the Sabbath in early Judaism, one should review early Christian conceptions of the issue. Only then would a treatment of Jesus' views follow. The treatment would in this way be necessarily subjected to the critical appraisal of the plausibility of the relation between Jesus' proclamation and what came after and of it.

I would think the three-part mode of procedure is at least worth trying, perhaps as a part of the future agenda of the *Jesus in Continuum* project.

Much more could naturally be said about the continuum approach. I will, however, stop here and let the other writers of the present volume continue. Unlike my theoretical and general discussion in this Introduction, they will deal with the approach from a more practical standpoint. The views on the continuum approach expressed above are my own and will not necessarily be subscribed to by the other writers. And even though some of the views do appear to be acknowledged in the following essays as well, these will each come – in accordance with the starting point of this project – with their own ways of exploring the possibilities of the continuum perspective to the historical Jesus. This is the thread running through the somewhat diverse topics discussed in the volume.

B. Chilton's essay, '*Mamzerut* and Jesus', is an investigation that focuses on traditions pertaining to the birth and descent of Jesus. Chilton's central question reflects the core idea of the continuum approach: How, considering the setting of first-century Judaism, should we explain the emergence of the different views of Jesus' birth in the New Testament? Chilton discerns three New Testament theories of Jesus' conception: consequence of an intervention of holy spirit, Jesus as the son of Joseph, and Jesus as being born of fornication. In order to find a solution to this diversity of views, Chilton studies the rabbinic concept of *mamzerut* or mixed genealogy. By scrutinizing how the status of a *mamzer* could have been applied to Jesus, Chilton seeks to present a plausible social reality that would have given rise to the birth narratives and other New Testament explanations of Jesus' origin.

W. Loader's essay discusses the issue of sexuality in Jesus' life and teaching. The fact that the data pertaining to the issue of sexuality is quite limited puts the continuum perspective in a central role. Thus, Loader seeks to discover features of the early tradition which would be 'explicable on the assumption of attitudes of the historical Jesus which in turn make sense in the light of his precedents'. Such features are, in Loader's opinion, views of sexuality and holiness, which he contends are based on Jesus' particular understanding of eschatology and his own calling, Jesus' generally strict attitude in relation to matters of sexuality, as well as the fact that he remained unmarried by intention. Jesus did not put forward a general denial of sexuality, exhort not to marry or the like. Nonetheless, that some people espoused these kinds of restrictive views on sexuality is well conceivable as a later development of the attitudes of Jesus mentioned.

A. Merz regards the parable of the widow and the judge in Lk. 18.1–8 as an excellent test case for studying the transmission of Jesus' teaching from the viewpoint of observing continuity and discontinuity. She draws on the criteriology of G. Theissen and D. Winter (discussed above), and sets out to 'investigate the most plausible meaning of the parable in the framework of a proclamation by Jesus addressed to Palestinian Jews (*contextual plausibility*), and how it is possible to understand historically the genesis of the tradition as a whole, in its contradictory unity, on the basis of the original parable (*plausibility of effects*)'. With respect to this parable, Merz argues, Jesus' continuity with the Judaism of his day can be traced in a narrative tradition which deviates from the main trend of the Bible and pictures widows who transgress the conventional boundaries set for them and fight for their rights or for their people. Already in pre-Lukan Christianity, however, the parable was interpreted in the light of Sir. 35.12–23. This text facilitated the recasting of the quite subversive point of the Jesuanic parable in the form of the dominant biblical perspective where widows kept to their social and gender roles.

T. Kazen sets out to examine the expression 'Son of Man', a truly perennial question of the historical Jesus research. According to Kazen, scholarship has to date not labelled all 'Son of Man' words put in the mouth of Jesus as inauthentic. Kazen's aim is now 'to examine whether a particular understanding of the expression "Son of Man" can plausibly explain the gist of the Son of Man sayings belonging to the Jesus tradition, without exaggerating the aspects of discontinuity between Jesus and early

Christians, i.e. by employing a continuum perspective'. To this end, Kazen studies a corporate understanding of the expression 'Son of Man', construable in particular on the basis of Daniel 7. In Kazen's view, the corporate interpretation of the expression, *including* Jesus, would explain how in the post-Easter Christological 'explosion' the expression could be made to denote Jesus *individually*. In this way – unlike, for instance, when applying the generic understanding of the expression ('man', 'a human being') – the early Christian development can be seen as both possible and comprehensible.

S. Freyne's article 'Jesus and the "Servant" Community in Zion' expands upon his recent monograph on the historical Jesus (referred to above) to contemplate links between Jesus and early Christianity. Freyne argues 'for continuity between a minority Jewish movement that finds a clear expression in Isaiah and the Jesus movement, both in its pre- and post-Easter phases'. He thinks that the minority version of Isaian Zion-tradition would also provide the background for Jesus' self-understanding and vision. In part as a reaction to a purely social explanation of Jesus' life and ministry, Freyne underlines the power of symbols and religious motivation in shaping historical processes. An example of such power is, according to Freyne, the fact that soon after Jesus' violent death a group of his followers assembled in Jerusalem. This daring and even provocative act would make sense if one assumes that the group aspired to stay in continuity with Jesus' vision of the Zion-tradition. Freyne discusses in particular the group identified by James the brother of the Lord.

E. Broadhead aims to analyse a certain piece of the Judaism–Christianity continuum, namely attitudes to the Israelite priesthood. While an understanding of Jesus has been sought in relation to many different groups of early Judaism – such as Essenes, Pharisees and Zealots – the priestly leadership of Israel could, according to Broadhead, offer a more fruitful approach. Besides applying the continuum that stretches from Israel's faith to the early Church, Broadhead defines a continuum of analysis which moves from possibility through plausibility to probability. As to the priesthood, Broadhead finds the following placing of Jesus within the continuum Judaism–Christianity as plausible: Jesus was a disgruntled Galilaean, a former follower of John the Baptist, and a proclaimer of the eschatological kingdom of God. These characteristics and, in particular, Jesus' condemnation of the temple, posed a critical challenge to the Jerusalem priests and temple worship. The fall of the temple in AD 70 required, in general, a reinterpretation of the role of the priesthood. Followers of Jesus who in the temple's destruction saw the fulfilment of Jesus' prophecy gradually moved from his conflict with the ruling priests to an application of the priestly traditions to the community of the followers.

In his article, I. Broer asks if the execution of Jesus could have been an exclusively Roman deed or whether we should rather think of some interaction between Jewish and Roman authorities. Since the Jewish involvement has by some scholars been discarded as a fabrication of the early Christian tradition, Broer sets out to examine whether Jesus' death would be understandable without recourse to the Gospels' descriptions thereof. Here he mainly applies the historical principle of analogy drawn on the basis of contemporary sources that in general tell about Roman executions and ways of handling Jews. In Broer's view, Jesus' teaching had no transparent political dimension. This being so, it is difficult to explain a purely Roman interest in executing Jesus by crucifixion. Jewish participation in some form is a more plausible assumption. This establishes, according to Broer, a perspective of continuum between the Jesus phenomenon, now in particular his execution, and early Christianity. Despite obvious historical inaccuracies, in seeing the crucifixion as a manoeuvre of both Romans and Jews the Christian descriptions of Jesus' death also display continuity with what actually happened to Jesus. Broer also enquires into why scholars argue so vehemently over the issue of Jewish participation in the action against Jesus – both when affirming and when denying it.

Hopefully readers will find the continuum approach, explicated and concretized in this Introduction and in what follows, useful.

MAMZERUT AND JESUS

Bruce Chilton

1. Introduction

What this volume calls a continuum approach to Jesus, a deliberate advance in the scholarly 'Third Quest' for the historical Jesus, aims to make connections among three fields of meaning. These three fields involve organic links among them, but the specialization typical of academic enquiry during the modern period, especially since the end of the Second World War, has artificially separated them. The importance of these links, and the damage to historical enquiry inflicted by separating them, become obvious as soon as the three fields of meaning are identified: (1) the development of teachings and narratives in early Judaism, (2) the distinctive appropriation and shaping of those traditions by Jesus as a Jewish teacher or rabbi, and (3) the reception of Jesus' perspectives within earliest Christianity.

The first and the third of these fields are attested in literatures (albeit literatures whose composition histories are often fraught, and laced with stages of oral development): the Pseudepigrapha, including the Dead Sea Scrolls, and Rabbinica attest early Judaism, while the New Testament, the Apostolic Fathers, the earliest Apologists, and several of the discoveries at Nag Hammadi illuminate Christianity.[1] But the second field of meaning – 'the historical Jesus' – is a long-standing and much disputed variable in research, because 'the historical Jesus' is primarily a matter of inference. Jesus himself did not write any of the materials attributed to him; they were transmitted successively prior to their incorporation within the Gospels decades after his death.

Writing in a book published in 1992, I commented that, although various allegedly deductive norms or 'criteria of authenticity' have been used in the study of Jesus, deductions from the Gospels can never pass the critical test as history, because the Gospels do not represent public and

---

1. This applies both to its primitive stages (prior to any conscious autonomy from Judaism) and at its early stages (when, although conceived as being autonomous, the movement lacked coherence in the view of both observers and practitioners).

verifiable historical sources. An appraisal of the overall hermeneutical –
and therefore historical – task requires investigators to deploy their
methods in a different way:

> In the case to hand, we only have access to Jesus insofar as the texts
> which claim to convey him in fact do so. There is no 'primitive,'
> 'historical,' 'authentic,' or otherwise real Jesus apart from what texts
> promulgate. In the first instance, therefore, Jesus is only knowable as a
> literarily historical phenomenon: what the Gospels point to as their
> source. ... Yet the Gospels are historical in effect, albeit not by
> intention. In the process of the synoptic catechesis, the Johannine
> reflection, and the Thomaean revision of traditions, those traditions,
> some deriving from Jesus and his first followers, are permitted to come
> to speech. Moreover, the Gospels refer back to Jesus as their source: the
> literarily historical Jesus is a fact of which any reading of the Gospels
> must take account, even if the question of the historical Jesus remains
> problematic. That is to say, we cannot understand the documents at all,
> unless we can identify what they believe they are referring to (whether or
> not we accept that they in fact do so). That reference constitutes the
> literarily historical Jesus for a particular document, and the community
> of tradents which produced the document. ... There are, then, precisely
> two indices of Jesus as he may be known historically: (1) what may be
> said of him in aggregate as the presupposition of the canonical Gospels
> and Thomas; and (2) within a critical understanding of Judaism prior to
> the destruction of the Temple. Other alleged measures, such as his
> distinction or dissimilarity from Judaism, or the alleged primitivity of a
> given source, are examples of ideology masquerading as science,
> attempts to define the Jesus to be discovered in advance of investigation.
> As the Gospels are read, it is crucial that they be assumed at no point
> (and at no hypothetical level) to convey a historical perspective directly.
> Rather, we may infer the literarily historical Jesus to which a given
> source refers on exegetical grounds, and then further conceive by
> abstract reasoning of the historical Jesus who presumably gave rise
> within early Judaism to that source and the others.[2]

My interest in this generative exegesis, linking early Judaism and early
Christianity through Jesus, has resulted in both textual and narrative
investigations,[3] which treat the Gospels as materials from which Jesus'
teaching and experience may be inferred (not deduced), provided they are
read within the context of early Judaism.

Throughout my work I have rejected a deductive approach, which

---

2. B. Chilton, *The Temple of Jesus: His Sacrificial Program Within a Cultural History of
Sacrifice* (University Park: Pennsylvania State University Press, 1992), pp. 114–20.

3. For example, *A Feast of Meanings: Eucharistic Theologies from Jesus through
Johannine Circles* (NovTSup, 72; Leiden: Brill, 1994); *Rabbi Jesus: An Intimate Biography*
(New York: Doubleday, 2000).

treats the Gospels as if they had been produced with the same historical sensibilities that we bring to study. The shift from deduction to inference in the historical study of Jesus is simply necessary, given the state of the sources involved. The fact of that matter is that we have no direct access to contemporaneous, verifiable accounts of what Jesus said, did, thought and felt. But increased awareness of the development of early Judaism and of early Christianity does permit us to locate Jesus in the arc of meaning that originates with the first field of meaning, results in the second field, and produces the third.

This approach is particularly fruitful in dealing with the question of Jesus' birth, because a reading of the New Testament itself reveals a surprising degree of complexity, compared to received opinion. This invites the question: how can we explain how different views of his birth arose within the setting of first-century Judaism?

The New Testament offers not one, but three theories of Jesus' conception. This pluralism of meaning undermines any approach that assumes that the texts simply reflect facts, *or* that they invent a single doctrinal proposition which they present as fact. All three theories need to be accounted for, if an appreciation of the Gospels is to be attained. The generative concern, which establishes a continuum among early Judaism, Jesus and early Christianity, moves away from the assertion or denial of fact, to the assessment of how texts arose and with what understandings. That shift, under way in Europe since the 1940s, is still not complete in the study of the New Testament in North America today. Groups such as 'The Jesus Seminar' continue to treat texts on the assumption that they falsify history, while conservative Evangelicals assume that their historical value is a given.[4] This essay is offered as an exercise in permitting the Gospels to be read within the same, constructive view of history that has become standard in the humanities, although this perspective still struggles to receive its place in the study of the Bible.

One New Testament theory presents Jesus' birth as the consequence of an intervention of holy spirit (by an unspecified mechanism), although Mary had not had sexual relations with a man. That is the explanation of Luke's Gospel most emphatically (Lk. 1.34-35), seconded less straight-forwardly by the Gospel according to Matthew (Mt. 1.18-25).

A second explanation, expressed by Philip in John's Gospel after he had become Jesus' disciple, maintains that Jesus was in fact the son of Joseph (Jn 1.45), and it is – emphatically and rather oddly – repeated both by John's 'Jews' in the synagogue at Capernaum (Jn 6.42) and by Luke's congregation in Nazareth (Lk. 4.22). Although the latter references are or

---

4. See B. Chilton, 'Biblical Authority, Canonical Criticism, and Generative Exegesis', in *The Quest for Context and Meaning: Studies in Biblical Intertextuality in Honor of James A. Sanders* (BIS, 28; Leiden: Brill, 1997), pp. 343-55.

may be dismissive, Philip's is not, and it is difficult to see how the genealogies of Jesus, variously presented by Matthew (Mt. 1.1–17) and Luke (Lk. 3.23–38), can have been developed except on the supposition of this second theory. (Mt. 1.16 and Lk. 3.23 try to finesse the issue, but these adjustments seem to be *post hoc*.) Further, Jesus' identity as David's son – recognized by the Gospels (Mt. 1.1; 9.27; 12.23; 15.22; 20.30, 31; 21.9, 15; Mk 10.47, 48; Lk. 18.38, 39) as well as by Paul and later sources (Rom. 1.3; cf. 2 Tim. 2.8; Rev. 5.5; 22.16) – implicitly invokes this theory, since only Joseph (himself called David's son in Mt. 1.20; cf. Lk. 1.27, 32; 2.4) can have mediated that pedigree to Jesus.

Finally, in John's Gospel opponents appear to taunt Jesus with being born of 'fornication' (*porneia*; Jn 8.41), and such an accusation is often seen as standing behind the pointed omission of Joseph, together with reference to his mother and siblings, in the identification of Jesus in Mk 6.3. At that juncture, Matthew's reference to Jesus as the son of the workman (Mt. 13.55) has been construed to imply Joseph's paternity (but also as saying in a Semitic idiom that Jesus belonged to the class of such workers). But Lk. 4.22, the apparent analogue of Mk 6.3 and Mt. 13.55, has the people in Nazareth say unequivocally that Jesus is *Joseph's* son, and this story might lie behind Jn 6.42.

The New Testament can in no sense be said to endorse the charge in Jn 8.41, perhaps implicit in Mk 6.3, although those texts attest to (or are patient of) the existence of such an accusation. Indeed, it seems that Matthew, Luke and John would prefer to imply that Joseph was Jesus' actual father, rather than approach Mark's admission, that people referred to Jesus in a way which gave comfort to those who denigrated his descent. But the second theory of Jesus' conception – the *assertion* of Joseph's paternity, rather than a grudging acceptance – may legitimately be claimed to be more broadly supported in the New Testament than the theory of the virginal conception, and to be assumed in sources earlier than the infancy narratives of Matthew and Luke.

The purpose of this essay is not to make out a case for the superiority of the second theory, arguable though that is on exegetical grounds. Rather, our purpose is to explain how all three theories emerged. What were the conditions under which some of Jesus' followers would acclaim him as David's son and Joseph's, while others would make his birth even more miraculous than the prophet Samuel's (cf. 1 Sam. 1.1–2.11), and opponents would scorn him as the offspring of fornication?

When rabbinic literature has been used at all in order to illuminate this issue, it has typically been cited in connection with the allegation, cited as early as the time of Celsus (see below), that Jesus' mother had had relations with a Roman soldier. As we will see, however, that tradition seems to be a late arrival within a skein of passages that deal with the overall question of *mamzerut*, or mixed genealogy. The first part of the discussion here addresses the issue of *mamzerut* generally. The second part deals with how the suspicion of mixed genealogy might arise in Jesus' case; the third part involves a consideration of circumstances in which the charge of *mamzerut* might have come to be levelled at Jesus in particular.

2. *Defining* Mamzerut

At base, a *mamzer* was the product of a union that was forbidden, because the couple were not permitted to marry and procreate according to the Torah. Whatever became of the man and the woman as the result of their sexual contact, their offspring was what we may call a changeling or mixling (terms which perhaps better convey the sense of *mamzer* than 'bastard' or 'mongrel', the traditional translations).[5] The sense of abhorrence involved, at the mixture of lines which should never be mixed, was such that the stricture of *mamzerut* could also be applied to the offspring of a woman whose sexual partner was not categorically identifiable, and therefore was not known to have been permitted to her.

The practice of attributing the status of mixed genealogy to particular individuals varied over time. That is not surprising, since Deut. 23.2, although specifying that a *mamzer* is to be excluded from the congregation until the tenth generation (see also Yeb. 8.3 in the Mishnah),[6] does not actually define what such a mixed offspring might be. But for all that the definition of *mamzerut* did change, it is striking that the precise description of Mary's pregnancy in Mt. 1.18 (as occurring between the time a contract of marriage was exchanged and the actual cohabitation of the couple) would have put Jesus into the position of being considered a *mamzer* within a principle articulated in the Mishnah.

In what follows, we will cite and explain the major passages at issue, following the line of chronology critically assigned to Rabbinica, first Mishnah (from the second century), then Tosefta (from the third century), and then Talmud (from the fifth century).[7]

Yeb. 4.13 in the Mishnah[8] attests an established consensus by the

5. This is well expressed in m.Kid. 3.12: 'And in any situation in which a woman has no right to enter betrothal with this man but has the right to enter into betrothal with others, the offspring is a *mamzer*.'

6. Here the exclusion is as explicit as one could ask: 'The male Ammonite and Moabite are prohibited [from entering the congregation of the Lord], and the prohibition concerning them is forever ... *Mamzerim* and *Netin* are prohibited, and the prohibition concerning them is forever, all the same being males and females.'

7. See the now classic treatment of J. Neusner, *Introduction to Rabbinic Literature* (ABRL; New York: Doubleday, 1994).

8. See the translations of P. Blackman, *Mishnayoth* (Gateshead: Judaica, 1983) and J. Neusner, *The Mishnah: A New Translation* (New Haven: Yale University Press, 1988), which I have here adapted.

second century that incest – under the terms of reference of Leviticus (which of course were more rigorous than in the Hellenistic world) – would produce a *mamzer*. At the same time, a rabbi named Joshua supported by Simeon ben Azzai (allegedly citing written evidence) broadens the definition, by including adultery as grounds for finding *mamzerut*:

> How is one a mamzer (Deut. 23.2)? Any case of near of kin which is forbidden, the words of Rabbi Aqiba. Simeon of Teman says, Any case where they [that is, the parents] were liable to extirpation by heaven (Lev. 18.29). And the *halakhah* is according to his words. Rabbi Joshua says, Any case where they were liable to death by a court. Said Rabbi Simeon ben Azzai, I found a scroll of descents in Jerusalem, and there was written in it: A certain man is a *mamzer*, from a man's wife (Lev. 18.20) – confirming the words of Rabbi Joshua.

It is interesting that, in Matthew's Gospel, Joseph is portrayed as having decided to divorce Mary quietly (Mt. 1.19). In the Mishnah, the possibility of such a dissolution of the contract between betrothal and common domicile is mentioned (see m.Sot. 4.1). In the present case, such an act would imply: voiding the contract of marriage without a formal charge of her adultery, and the *mamzerut* of the child. This Mishnaic tractate cites Deut. 23.2 explicitly, moving into a case of adulterous relations by way of application of the statute. The connection of ideas is easy to follow, because the themes of virginity, adultery, rape and incest are developed in Deuteronomy (Deut. 22.13–30) just before the mention of the *mamzer*, and the punishment for such crimes (sometimes expressly demanded in this chapter of Deuteronomy) is stoning.

Ket. 1.9 in the Mishnah, however, is even more to the point, since it corresponds to Mary's predicament as specified in Mt. 1.18:

> She was pregnant, and they said to her, What kind of foetus is this? From a certain man, and he is a priest! Rabban Gamaliel and Rabbi Eliezer say, She is believed. And Rabbi Joshua says, We do not rely on her statement. But she remains in the assumption of having become pregnant by a *Netin* or a *mamzer*, until she brings evidence for her words.

Here we have two opposed policies. In one (Gamaliel's and Eliezer's) the testimony of a mother suffices to establish fatherhood; in the other (Joshua's), evidence – presumably in the shape of knowledge of the couple's common domicile, as we shall see – was required.

Joshua's opinion is consistent with his view in m.Yeb. 4.13, since there a finding of adultery involves a witness (human or supernatural, see Num. 5.11–31), and witnesses are just what he calls for in m.Ket. 1.9. The opposition of Gamaliel and Eliezer in this case, however, draws attention to a severe social problem inherent within Joshua's definition of *mamzerut* and his application of that definition. If the matter turns on being unable to establish a licit father, that extends the number of children who might be considered *mamzers* and opens a large number of women to the charge or the suspicion of adultery.

But the point of view attributed to Gamaliel and Eliezer does not represent all that much progress from the point of view of well-ordered social relations. Since it permits a woman to name a licit father, by the terms of the Torah itself that man would be required to marry her without recourse to divorce (Deut. 22.28–29). What the Mishnah is showing us, in the names of rabbis from the first century, is that *mamzerut* posed social as well as logical problems (see also m.Kid. 4.8).[9] The attributions themselves need not be taken at face value here (although I am struck by the consistency of the views ascribed to Joshua at various junctures in the Mishnah); whether they are accepted or not, the Mishnah's memory that *mamzerut* was a thorny issue remains. Indeed, the most direct proof of that is that the Mishnah not only recollects the problem, but also goes on to resolve it.

This resolution is beautifully represented in m.Kid. 4.1–2 in a passage which will take some explaining, once we have cited it:

> Ten descents came up from Babylonia: (1) priest, (2) Levite, (3) Israelite, (4) impaired priest, (5) convert, and (6) freed slave, (7) *mamzer*, (8) *Netin*, (9) silenced [*shetuqi*], and (10) foundling. Priest, Levite, and Israelite marry among one another. Levite, Israelite, impaired priest, convert, and freed slave intermarry one another. Convert, freed slave, *mamzer*, *Netin*, silenced, and foundling all intermarry among one another. These are silenced – everyone who knows his mother but does not know his father; and foundling – everyone who was retrieved from the market and knows neither his father nor his mother. Abba Saul called a 'silenced' [*shetuqi*] 'to be examined' [*beduqi*].

This passage is a triumph of categorical thinking. Within this list, the status of a *mamzer* is neatly distinguished from that of one put to silence, although the two are also closely associated.

The category of *mamzerut* is evidently reserved for offspring of known instances of adultery, incest or other known instances of illicit intercourse (see m.Kid. 3.12). In contrast, the category of the 'silenced' (*shetuqi*) caste permits mother and child not to be associated with adultery, incest or illicit intercourse and the punishments they occasioned, a compassionate conclusion in the face of the uncertainty of fatherhood. From the point of

---

9. This text states: 'He who says, This, my son, is a *mamzer*, is not believed. And even if both parties say concerning the foetus in the mother's womb, He is a *mamzer*, they are not believed. Rabbi Judah says, They are believed.' Although it may seem odd to wish the status of *mamzerut* upon one's son, that attests the evolution of its meaning, as explored below.

view of mother and child, the *shetuqi* represents a signal advance over Joshua's perspective on the *mamzer* (in m.Ket. 1.9); from the point of view of the alleged father, it also makes life easier than Gamaliel and Eliezer would have it. Even the foundling, whose licit birth could not be attested by a mother or by witnesses (again, under the provisions of m.Ket. 1.9), is protected from the status of *mamzerut* here.

The manifest tolerance of this distinction between *mamzer* and *shetuqi* (or foundling, *mutatis mutandis*), and the elegant social adaptation it facilitated, comport well with the adjustment toward marriage that the passage as a whole conveys. The alignment of the differing castes is articulated in two senses. The first sense of this alignment is the association of one caste with several others. Levites and Israelites can intermarry with one another and with priests. Proselytes and freed slaves can intermarry with impaired priests one notch further down the list, but also with the Levites and Israelites higher in the list. In much the same way, the *mamzer*, *Netin*, silenced, and foundling classes can intermarry with one another and with proselytes and freed slaves.

If this strong association is surprising in view of the treatment of *mamzerut* elsewhere in the Mishnah (and the Hebrew Bible, come to that), it is far from unambiguous. That brings us to the second sense of the articulation of caste alignment of the list. It is hierarchical – and literally so – because priests are assigned a unique position, without a higher association in the list, and emphatically without links to the other categories lower in the list which are not expressly Israelite. Taken together with the associative articulation, the hierarchical articulation conveys an ideal structure of marital preferences.[10] A given arrangement is less desirable the more one moves down the list, so that any sense of preference all but disappears within the varying degrees of *mamzerut* cited (except in implicit contrast to a Gentile without any affiliation with Israel).

This relative disapprobation of the *mamzer* was such that, well after the Mishnah, it provoked the rule that when a Gentile or a slave had sexual relations with an Israelite woman, the result was a *mamzer* (b.Kid. 70a). This was the root of the growing sense that maternity rather than paternity governed one's identity as an Israelite, and also provided for a place for proselytes in procreation, even as it maintained their status as outsiders.[11]

The means by which *mamzerut* is attributed to those of non-Israelite paternity in the Talmudic passage is instructive. In two ways, the attempt

10. So that relatively speaking the status of *mamzerut* lifted (hence the apparently odd stance of m.Kid. 4.8, cited above).

11. Cf. S. J. D. Cohen, *The Beginnings of Jewishness: Boundaries, Varieties, Uncertainties* (Berkeley: University of California Press, 1999), pp. 273–307.

is made to link the Mishnaic category referred to in m.Kid. 4.1 firmly to Scripture:

> *Mamzers*: from where do we know? From where it is written, And Sanballat the Horonite and Tobiah the slave, the Ammonite heard it (Neh. 2.10); and it is written, for there were many in Judah sworn unto him, because he was the son-in-law of Shechaniah the son of Arah, and his son Jehohanan had taken the daughter of Meshullam the son of Berechiah to wife (Neh. 6.17–18). This holds that when a gentile or a slave has sexual relations with an Israelite woman – the offspring is a *mamzer*. That is convenient for him who maintains that the offspring is a *mamzer*, but from the viewpoint of him who holds that the offspring is licit, what can be said? Furthermore, how do you know that they had children? Maybe they didn't have children? And furthermore, how do you know that they were originally here but then went up? Perhaps they were located there. Rather, from this: And these are the ones who went up from Tel-melah, Tel-harsha, Cherub, Addon, and Immer, but they could not show their fathers' houses nor their seed, whether they were of Israel (Neh. 7.61). Tel-melah: This refers to people whose deeds are like those of Sodom, which was turned into a salt heap. Tel-harsha: This refers to those who call 'father,' whom their mothers silence. But they could not show their fathers' houses nor their seed, whether they were of Israel: This refers to a foundling, retrieved from the market. Cherub, Addon, and Immer: Said Rabbi Abbahu, Said the Lord, I said that the Israelites would be valued before me as a cherub, but they have made themselves into a leopard. There are those who say, said Rabbi Abbahu, Said the Lord, Even though they have made themselves into a leopard, nonetheless, the Israelites are valued before me as a cherub.[12]

In the first case, Tobiah's status as an Ammonite and a slave is used to attribute *mamzerut* to his children. But then, the objection is raised that not enough is known about the status of these children for the prescription of Deut. 23.2 to have been known to be applied. Instead, Neh. 7.61 is invoked, on the assumption that the inability to specify one's father's house involved *mamzerut*. Not only does the Talmudic passage maintain this basic point as the straightforward reading of the Mishnah (m.Ket. 1.9); it also associates slaves, silenced ones and foundlings within the general category of the *mamzer*, as the list in the Mishnah does (m.Kid. 4.1).

Once this new Talmudic definition has fully made its way, it was a short step to the tradition that Jesus' father had been a Gentile, and a Roman soldier at that (b.Shab. 104b and b.Sanh. 67a according to manuscripts in Munich and Oxford). It had once been possible to accuse him of

---

12. B.Kid. 70a. Cf. H. Freedman, *Kiddushin: The Babylonian Talmud* (London: Soncino, 1936); J. Neusner, *Bavli Tractate Qiddushin: The Talmud of Babylonia* (Atlanta: Scholars, 1996); *Qiddushin min Talmud Bavli* (Jerusalem: Vagshal, 1980).

mamzerut in a Mishnaic sense, because the identity of his father was not established; according to the Talmudic tradition, his father was known, and known as non-Israelite, and for that reason he was a *mamzer*. Whatever the current definition, it could be and was applied to Jesus.[13]

3. *Proximity and Sexual Contact*

That then brings us to the question of how the status of a *mamzer* can have been applied to Jesus.

Well before the Talmud a commonly cited tradition affirmed that Jesus' father was called 'Panther', a Roman soldier with whom Mary had an adulterous affair (Origen, *Cels.* 1.2).[14] This is a cunning *haggadah*, because it doubles Jesus' *mamzerut*: he is the product of adultery (and therefore a *mamzer* according to the definition of the Mishnah), and the offspring of a non-Israelite father (and therefore a *mamzer* according to the definition which later emerged in the Talmud).

This story is as hybrid as Jesus' birth is made out to be, but the idea has been taken up in recent discussion of Jesus' 'illegitimacy': his irregular birth is explained by the rape of his mother in Sepphoris during the civil strife of 4 BC.[15] Although this hypothesis has helped to move us along the right track, into a consideration of birth status in Judaism, in my opinion it demands more supposition about tight contact between Sepphoris and the hamlets which surrounded it than recent discussion warrants (see

---

13. I owe this formulation to William Horbury, during discussions in the seminar on the Gospels and Rabbinic Literature which I chaired for the *Studiorum Novi Testamenti Societas* (August 2000 in Tel Aviv). I am grateful for the encouraging, engaged discussion that took place; my presentation there is available as B. Chilton, 'Jésus, le *mamzer* (Mt 1.18)', *NTS* 46 (2001), pp. 222–27.

14. Dismissed by J. Maier in *idem, Jesus von Nazareth in der talmudischen Überlieferung* (EF, 82; Darmstadt: Wissenschaftliche Buchgesellschaft, 1978), this legend which Celsus circulated c. AD 178 has recently been championed by J. J. Rousseau, R. Arav, *Jesus and His World: An Archaeological and Cultural Dictionary* (Minneapolis: Fortress, 1995), pp. 223–25. They maintain that an epitaph in Bingerbück, probably from the time of Germanicus and bearing the name of a soldier whose sobriquet was 'Panther', attests the identity of Jesus' real father. But if 'Panther' was a common cognomen, that better explains the phraseology of the Talmudic legend than anything about Jesus' paternity. Otherwise, why not ask whether Milne's Tigger might be the true progenitor of Tiger Woods?

15. See M. Sawicki, *Crossing Galilee: Architectures of Contact in the Occupied Land of Jesus* (Harrisburg: Trinity Press International, 2000), pp. 171–73; J. Schaberg, *The Illegitimacy of Jesus: A Feminist Theological Interpretation of the Infancy Narratives* (San Francisco: Harper & Row, 1987).

below). Further, the 'Panther' tale suits the Mishnaic and Talmudic definition of *mamzerut* so well as to suggest it is a fiction.[16]

So why did some people accuse Jesus of being born of fornication (*porneia*, Jn 8.41)? Was it for the same reason he was called 'son of Mary' in his own town (Mk 6.3) rather than 'son of Joseph'? What emerges from both rabbinic literature (supplemented by Origen) and the New Testament is that Jesus' mother was clearly known, and that the identity of his father was contested. Whoever his natural father was, Joseph, another man to whom Mary was not married while Joseph was her husband (a soldier or not, a Gentile or not), or the power of the most high (if some procreative event really is implied in Lk. 1.35), Jesus was a *mamzer* within the terms of reference established by the Mishnah in its discussion of traditional definitions (m.Ket. 1.9 above all). This category provoked the disparate views of Jesus' birth attested in the New Testament (and, to a lesser extent, in rabbinic discussion).

Although the relevance of *mamzerut* to the evaluation of Jesus might be held to be as much as rabbinic literature can teach us, there is another step to take. The simple fact of proximity between a man and a woman is well attested with halakhic discussion as a cause for concluding that sexual contact has occurred. The most famous instance of that is the Mishnaic tractate Sotah, where having been with a man other than her husband in a private place obliges a married woman to drink the bitter water of Num. 5.11–31 (m.Sot. 1.1–7).[17] In this case, Eliezer and Joshua are said to disagree, as in the question of believing a pregnant woman about the paternity of her child. Joshua demands two witnesses before she is required to drink, while Eliezer is content with the testimony of one witness, even the husband himself (m.Sot. 1.1).

Just as proximity invokes the suspicion of forbidden sexual contact, so it may be used to suggest that permitted contact has occurred. This brings us to a discussion of the *halakhah* most frequently discussed in connection with Mt. 1.18.

R. E. Brown supported the argument of many commentators that there was a difference in marital custom between Galilee and Judaea: he claims that in Galilee no sexual relation was tolerated between a woman and her

---

16. See Cohen, *The Beginnings of Jewishness* (11), pp. 276–80. But he goes too far when he says on p. 276, 'M. Yevamot 7.5 states that the offspring of a Jewish mother and a gentile or slave father is a *mamzer*.' This text in fact relates to a woman of priestly descent: 'An Israelite girl married to a priest, a priestly girl married to an Israelite, when she produced a daughter with him, and the daughter went and married a slave or a gentile and produced a son from him, this son is a *mamzer*.' This may well have been a precedent for the later, broader rule, but the two should not be confused. The pertinent text, which Cohen cites and explains on pp. 277–80, is Talmudic, b.Yeb. 45b.

17. M.Sot. 2.6 establishes by consensus that this only applied between the time of betrothal and divorce, not before or after.

husband before they lived together in their marital home, while in Judaea intimate relations were not excluded in the interim between the agreement of contract and the couple's public cohabitation.[18] J. P. Meier demurs, observing that 'later rabbinic distinctions about differences of customs in Judea and Galilee are of questionable relevance'.[19]

Yet Meier persists in the supposition that Mt. 1.18 reflects a controversy over Mary's virginity, and for him rabbinic literature shows at least that virginity as such was such an important issue that the dispute over Jesus' birth should be seen as one over his mother's sexual experience at the time of her marriage. In this, Meier is far from alone, because the discussion about virginity was prompted by the widely cited compendium of P. Billerbeck.[20] But the texts cited from that source have often been taken out of context in my view, and in any case their relevance for an understanding of Mt. 1.18 seems only indirect.

18.   R. E. Brown, *The Birth of the Messiah: A Commentary on the Infancy Narratives in the Gospels of Matthew and Luke* (ABRL; New York: Doubleday, 2nd edn, 1993), p. 124: 'According to later Jewish commentary [*sic!*] (Mishnah *Ketuboth* 1.5; TalBab *Ketuboth* 9b, 12a), *in parts of Judea* it was not unusual for the husband to be alone with his wife on at least one occasion in the interval between exchange of consent and the move to the home (and so interim marital relations were not absolutely condemned). But *in Galilee* no such leniency was tolerated and the wife had to be taken to her husband's home as a virgin.'

19.   J. P. Meier, *A Marginal Jew: Rethinking the Historical Jesus*, vol. 1: *The Roots of the Problem and the Person* (ABRL; New York: Doubleday, 1991), p. 246.

20.   H. L. Strack, P. Billerbeck, *Das Evangelium nach Matthäus erläutert aus Talmud und Midrasch* (KNTTM, 1; Munich: Beck, 1922); W. D. Davies, D. C. Allison, *A Critical and Exegetical Commentary on The Gospel according to Saint Matthew*, vol. 1: *Introduction and Commentary on Matthew I–VII* (ICC; Edinburgh: T&T Clark, 1988), pp. 199–200 cite comparable texts (m.Yeb. 4.10; m.Ket. 1.5; 4.12; b.Ket. 12a), and draw the same distinction between Galilaean and Judaean custom. See also in C. S. Keener, *A Commentary on the Gospel of Matthew* (Grand Rapids: Eerdmans, 1999), p. 92; he makes reference to S. Safrai, 'Home and Family', in S. Safrai, M. Stern (eds.), *The Jewish People in the First Century* (CRINT, 1.2; Assen: Van Gorcum, 1976), pp. 728–92 (756–57), and to Louis Finkelstein, *The Pharisees: The Sociological Background of Their Faith*, vol. 1 (Philadelphia: Jewish Publication Society of America, 3rd edn, 1962), p. 45. These citations support Billerbeck's observation, but Tosefta remains crucial to any discussion of regional difference. Davies and Allison are less speculative when they observe: 'To judge from the rabbinic sources (which may be late), betrothal or engagement (*'erûsîn* or *qiddûšîm*) in ancient Judaism took place at a very early age, usually at twelve to twelve and a half years (*b. Yeb.* 62b; SB2 [Hermann L. Strack and Paul Billerbeck, *Das Evangelium nach Markus, Lukas und Johannes und die Apostelgeschichte* (KNTTM, 2; Munich: Beck, 1924)], p. 374). Following courtship and the completion of the marriage contract (Tob 7.14), the marriage was considered established: the woman had passed from her father's authority to that of her husband. But about a year typically passed before the woman moved from her parents' house to her husband's house (*m. Ket.* 5.2; *m. Ned.* 10.5; *b. Ket.* 57b). During that time, although marriage was not yet consummated, the woman was "wife" (Deut 20.7; 28.30; Judg 14.15; 15.1; 2 Sam 3.14) and she could become a widow (*m. Yeb.* 4.10; 6.4; *Ket.* 1.2) or be punished for adultery (Deut 22.23–24; 11QTemple 61). Thus betrothal was the legal equivalent of marriage, and its cancellation divorce (*m. Ket.* 1.2; 4.2; *m. Yeb.* 2.6; *m. Git.* 6.2).'

First, the alleged difference in custom cited by Brown and other commentators is not supported by all the texts they cite. It is not the Mishnah (m.Ket. 1.5), but the Talmud (b.Ket. 9b, 12a) which claims a distinction between Galilee and Judaea. The Mishnah speaks only of Judaea, insisting that a man does not have the right, if he had lived with his father-in-law (and therefore with his fiancée) prior to marriage to bring a complaint against his wife after the marriage because she was no longer a virgin. If there is a contrast with Galilee in this case, it is merely by implication. The source of an explicit contrast is the Tosefta (t.Ket. 1.4), whose view the Talmud seems to adapt in this instance.

The significance of the contrast as drawn by Brown[21] – that in Galilee a bride's virginity was demanded, whatever the circumstances of the couple's domicile before their public cohabitation – may also be contested. If the economic development of Jewish Galilee was less elevated and less urban than in Judaea, as contemporary archaeology would suggest,[22] the domicile of a groom with his father-in-law would have been so current that no complaint of the type envisaged in the Mishnah would have been feasible.

Perhaps it was especially in urban Judaea, where more families had the means to offer their children their own marital domiciles, that there was the possibility – real or imagined – of a confusion of the customs of the rich and the poor. Under these circumstances, the Mishnah lays down a rule in m.Ket. 1.5 that brooks no double-dealing: 'He who eats with his father-in-law in Judaea without a witness can not bring a complaint for the cause of non-virginity, because he was alone with her.'

Clearly, then, the rule that proximity allows of the finding of sexual contact (whether permitted or not) seems to have been well established. Just as women were protected against one custom being substituted for another, so there was an explicit caution against moving a woman away from her home (m.Ket. 13.10):

> There are three provinces in what concerns marriage: Judah, Beyond Jordan, and Galilee. They do not remove from town to town or from city to city. But in the same province, they do remove from town to town or from city to city, but not from a town to a city, and not from a city to a town. They remove from a bad dwelling to a pleasant dwelling

---

21. But the formulation is actually that of Finkelstein, *Pharisees* (20), p. 45.

22. See S. Freyne, *Galilee, Jesus and the Gospels* (Philadelphia: Fortress, 1988); R. A. Horsley, *Archaeology, History, and Society in Galilee: The Social Context of Jesus and the Rabbis* (Valley Forge: Trinity Press International, 1996); J. F. Strange, 'First Century Galilee from Archaeology and from the Texts', in D. R. Edwards, C. T. McCollough (eds.), *Archaeology and the Galilee: Texts and Contexts in the Graeco-Roman and Byzantine Periods* (SFSHJ, 143; Atlanta: Scholars Press, 1997), pp. 39–48; Sawicki, *Crossing Galilee* (15); J. L. Reed, *Archaeology and the Galilean Jesus: A Re-examination of the Evidence* (Harrisburg: Trinity Press International, 2000).

but not from a pleasant dwelling to a bad dwelling. Rabban Simeon ben
Gamaliel says, Also not from a bad dwelling to a pleasant one, since the
pleasant dwelling tempts.

Following this rule in a relatively undeveloped area (such as rural
Galilee) would imply that a groom would 'eat with his father-in-law'
after his marriage, as well as before. Although the husband brought a
patriarchal construction of genealogy to the marriage, the location of
household, which was the bride's domain, was determined by where she
lived, and in most cases must actually have been under the control of her
family.

Although m.Ket. 1.5 indirectly indicates how and why one might
conclude that sexual contact had occurred, the fact remains that the
problem specified in Mt. 1.18 is not Mary's virginity, but her pregnancy.
This simple observation, by M.-J. Lagrange,[23] invites another take on
Mt. 1.18. If Joseph and Mary were known not to be living together,
even though they were betrothed, that would account for Jesus' repute
as a *mamzer* in Nazareth. This brings us to the issue of locating
Bethlehem.

4. Bethlehem

'Where Was Jesus Born?' S. Mason and J. Murphy-O'Connor both
answered that question for *Bible Review*,[24] and their remarks landed the
editors with a blizzard of mail. Not surprising, when you consider that
where Jesus was born necessarily involves *how* he was born. The way these
two scholars approached their assigned question takes us into that whole
issue.

Mason represents the position that Nazareth was Jesus' birthplace.
After all, he called it his *patris* (or fatherland; Mk 6.4; Mt. 13.57; Lk.
4.24), although this term might refer to Jesus' region generally more than
to Nazareth in particular (see Jn 4.43–44). More to the point, John's
Gospel has Philip identify Jesus as 'Joseph's son from Nazareth' (Jn 1.45–
46). Murphy-O'Connor, on the other hand, criticizes Mason for suppos-
ing that the messianic prophecy of a son of David (derived from Mic. 5.2)
caused Christians to make up the name 'Bethlehem' as Jesus' natal village.
He insists that Matthew and Luke used different sources that mentioned
the place, so that it is more likely the name was remembered, rather than a
Christian invention.

---

23. M.-J. Lagrange, *Évangile selon Saint Matthieu* (EBib; Paris: Gabalda, 1941), p. 10.
24. *BR* 16 (2000), pp. 31–51.

Both these contributors, for all their differences, follow the principle that an historical 'fact' is an event that we surmise actually happened; discounting all their evidence. But history involves both the chain of events which historians study, and the theories they use to understand them. In this case, our challenge is to see a coherent picture, without just discounting about one half of the evidence (be it about Nazareth or Bethlehem).

But are we even arguing about the right Bethlehem? The Hebrew Bible itself mentions a Bethlehem far to the north of Jerusalem, assigned to Zebulun (Josh. 19.15), and in Jn 7.41–42 some apparently well informed sceptics resist the idea that Jesus is messiah, on the grounds that he comes from Galilee and not from Davidic Bethlehem. In Hebrew the name means 'house of bread', designating a settlement with mills capable of producing fine flour, rather than the coarse grade most people used for their daily needs. In 1975 I learned of a *Galilaean* Bethlehem near Nazareth from study of Talmudic geography published during the nineteenth century. I was disconcerted at the dearth of discussion about this place as the possible site of Jesus' birth.

I was intrigued but wary (conscious of how easily a new idea can be rejected out of hand, just because it *is* new). The Talmud was composed centuries after Jesus lived, so one can't assume it accurately reflects ancient Galilee's geography. I appended my findings to my Ph.D. thesis and let the matter rest. Now, however, archaeological excavations show that Bethlehem in Galilee is a first-century site just seven miles from Nazareth, so my former reserve can be put aside.[25] There is good reason to surmise that the Bethlehem which Matthew and Luke remember dimly and distantly (and through the lenses of Scripture and legend) was actually in Galilee. With the evidence of excavation reports, an idea from the nineteenth century crosses the threshold of probability.

Mt. 1.18, as interpreted here, provides us with a clue to why Jesus' parents were in Galilaean Bethlehem in the first place. Had Joseph been domiciled there, that would explain both why Mary's pregnancy in Nazareth was a scandal, and why Joseph took her away from Nazareth to Bethlehem for Jesus' birth. (Such a change of site is, of course, much more plausible than having Joseph and Mary travelling to Judaea for the birth, a journey which in any case would have violated the custom mentioned in Ket. 13.10 in the Mishnah.) The conditions of Jesus'

---

25. See A. Neubauer, *La Géographie du Talmud* (Paris: Michel Lévy frères, 1868), pp. 189–91, discussed in B. Chilton, *God in Strength: Jesus' Announcement of the Kingdom* (SNTU, 1; Freistadt: Plöchl, 1979), reprinted in B. Chilton, *God in Strength: Jesus' Announcement of the Kingdom* (BS, 8; Sheffield: JSOT Press, 1987), pp. 311–13. For a recent, critical treatment of Bethlehem of Galilee in relation to other Jewish settlements, see Strange, 'First Century Galilee' (22).

conception *as Matthew refers to them* made him a *mamzer* in the eyes of Mary's neighbours in Nazareth. Cultural preoccupation with sex before marriage in the West has caused scholarship to convert the issue of Jesus' status in Israel into the anachronistic question of his legitimacy, and to ignore one of the most powerful influences on his development. Pressed into the caste apart which being a *mamzer* or 'silenced one' (*shetuqi*) made him, Jesus from the beginning of his life negotiated the treacherous terrain between belonging to Israel and the experience of ostracism within his own community. The aspirations of a restored Israel can only have been particularly poignant to those branded with the reputation of *mamzerut*.

5. *Conclusion*

In the case of Jesus' *mamzerut*, then, from the sources of Judaism, literary and anthropological (insofar as archaeological study has evinced Judaic anthropology), a plausible social reality behind the genesis of the birth narratives, as well as other explanations of Jesus' birth in the New Testament, has emerged. In a recent book, I worked the implications of that status into an account of Jesus' life.[26] What is involved in that case is an inferential narrative. The narrative form was selected because it is the sole means by which development may be traced; without tracing development there can be no biography, and no justice can be done to dynamic factors such as *mamzerut* itself.

That this status was understood to carry profound significance is attested by the discussion concerning how exclusion until the tenth generation might be avoided.[27] Because such issues were debated, attempts to suggest that *mamzerut* did not carry much by way of stigma,[28] or that the category did not exist in Jesus' time,[29] appear strained. Indeed, eschatology seems to have been the only cure for *mamzerut*, in the view of Tosefta Kid. (5.4):

> *Netins* and *Mamzers* will be clean in the world to come, the words of Rabbi Yosé. Rabbi Meir says, They will not be clean. Said to him Rabbi Yosé, But has it not truly been said, I will sprinkle clean water upon you, and you shall be clean (Ezek. 36.25)? Said to him Rabbi Meir, And you shall be clean from all your uncleannesses, and from all your idols I

26. Chilton, *Rabbi Jesus* (3).

27. See m.Kid. 3.13: 'Rabbi Tarfon says, *Mamzerim* can be purified. How so? A *mamzer* who married a slave girl – the offspring is a slave. [If] freed, the son turns out to be a free man. Rabbi Eliezer says, This is a slave who also is in the status of a *mamzer*.'

28. See S. McKnight, 'Calling Jesus *Mamzer*', *JSHJ* 1 (2003), pp. 73–103.

29. See C. Quarles, 'Jesus as *Mamzer*: A Response to Bruce Chilton's Reconstruction of the Circumstances Surrounding Jesus' Birth in *Rabbi Jesus*', *BBR* 14 (2004), pp. 243–55.

will cleanse you (Ezek. 36.25). Said to him Rabbi Yosé, Why then does Scripture say, I shall clean you? It means, Even from the *Netins* and the *mamzers*.

Rabbi Jesus would apparently have agreed.[30]

---

30. Since I identified Jesus as a *mamzer* in *Rabbi Jesus* (3), pp. 3–23 a considerable literature on this subject has emerged: M. Bar Ilan, 'The Attitude toward *Mamzerim* in Jewish Society in Late Antiquity', *JH* 14 (2000), pp. 125–70; S. J. D. Cohen, 'Some Thoughts on "The Attitude toward *Mamzerim* in Jewish Society in Late Antiquity"', *JH* 14 (2000), pp. 171–74; Sawicki, *Crossing Galilee* (15), pp. 171–73; A. van Aarde, *Fatherless in Galilee: Jesus as Child of God* (Harrisburg: Trinity Press International, 2001); Chilton, 'Jésus, le *mamzer*' (13); B. Chilton, 'Recovering Jesus' *Mamzerut*', in J. Neusner *et al.* (eds.), *Ancient Israel, Judaism, and Christianity in Contemporary Perspective: Essays in Memory of Karl-Johan Illman* (Studies in Judaism; Lanham: University Press of America, 2006), pp. 81–105.

Sexuality and the Historical Jesus

William Loader

Attitudes towards sexuality are usually deeply embedded in cultures in a way that makes it impossible to isolate any single individual or short period of time as though it could stand on its own. This is especially the case with the historical Jesus where relevant data is limited and where the context of both what precedes and what follows is an essential component of any investigation. This chapter will, therefore, address the issue within the context of such a continuum of culture and influence with a view to reviewing what can and cannot be known.

People approach matters of sexuality in relation to what they see as authoritative texts in a variety of ways. They include wanting the historical Jesus to say and be what the author wants to believe. People who need a biblical mandate for cherished values and seem unable to value them for their own sake can easily skew historical reconstruction. We also encounter the whim to fill gaps with fantasy or spin spurious yarns of conspiracy which become the stuff of novels, instanced most recently by Dan Brown's, *The Da Vinci Code*.[1] The legends of Mary Magdalene's intimacy with Jesus reflected in the gospel which bears her name (*Gos. Mary*) and the *Gospel of Philip* (55b) show Gnostics exploiting marginalized women to legitimize their own sense of marginalization. They claim their secrets go back to that special relationship: a claim of pillow theology against pillar theology.

At one level our resources for understanding the sexuality of Jesus are sparse. At another, our material evidence is such that it could easily fill a monograph. I refer to the fact that beside other claims our documents overwhelmingly assume that Jesus was a male human being. We know a lot about male human beings and by extension a lot about the sexuality of Jesus, the man. While piety sometimes eschews the thought, we must assume Jesus experienced the turbulence of pubescence, produced seminal emissions, and knew sexual desire in dream and reality. We can take all that for granted.

---

1. D. Brown, *The Da Vinci Code* (London: Bantam, 2003).

Beyond that we may seek to derive conclusions from social and cultural norms. Interpreting the silence about marriage[2] leads W. Phipps,[3] for instance, to claim that Jesus probably was married on the basis of the norm and well attested expectation that men must obey Gen. 1.28: 'Be fruitful and multiply!'[4] That case for normalcy is weakened by the fact that some Essenes and others saw celibacy as God's call[5] and more so by the evidence that men married around the age of 30.[6] In the *Testaments of the Twelve Patriarchs* Levi is instructed to marry early (*T. Levi* 9.10) and so marries at 28 (*T. Levi* 11.1; 12.5).[7] The norm and model which we find in the accounts of Issachar (*T. Iss.* 3.5) and Joseph (Gen. 41.45–46; *Jub.* 40.10–11) is to marry at the age of 30. That Jesus was aged 30 when he commenced his ministry according to Lk. 3.23 would probably not have been heard as a random figure by hearers of the gospel story. It was the age when you set up your household – or did something else. Jesus did something else. Instead of receiving a bride from a nuptial bath, so to speak, he submits to John's baptism. Some speculate that rumours of illegitimacy may have made it hard for his family to find him a wife,[8] but this assumes some historicity behind the birth stories which is questionable. Jesus' saying about eunuchs (Mt. 19.12) makes it more likely that he remained unmarried by intention, not default.

2. For what follows see my discussion in W. Loader, *Sexuality and the Jesus Tradition* (Grand Rapids: Eerdmans, 2005), pp. 143–44.

3. W. E. Phipps, *The Sexuality of Jesus: Theological and Literary Perspectives* (New York: Harper & Row, 1993), pp. 40–41.

4. On the duty of procreation in both Jewish and non-Jewish writers from the second century BC and later in the rabbis see M. L. Satlow, *Jewish Marriage in Antiquity* (Princeton: Princeton University Press, 2001), pp. 17–21. He cites Antipater of Tarsus, Pseudo-Phocylides, Philo, Josephus, the Mishnah and Tosefta.

5. On Essenes and celibacy see *Hypothetica.* 11.14–17; Pliny, *Hist. Nat.* 5.73; Josephus, *War* 2.120–21; *Ant.* 18.21; for Essenes who did not choose this option see Josephus, *War* 2.160–61. See also the discussion in Satlow, *Jewish Marriage* (4), pp. 21–24 and P. W. van der Horst, 'Celibacy in Early Judaism', *RB* 109 (2002), pp. 390–402.

6. Satlow, *Jewish Marriage* (4), pp. 108–09: 'Greek and Roman men also tended to marry when they were in their late twenties or early thirties' (p. 108), women in their mid- to late teens (p. 109). 'In Palestine and the West, a man married when he was around thirty to a woman ten to fifteen years younger. By waiting until he was thirty a man was able to establish a household, a crucial assumption underlying Palestinian and Western marital ideology' (p. 132).

7. Similarly the Aramaic *Testament of Levi* 79.

8. D. Instone-Brewer, *Divorce and Remarriage in the Bible: The Social and Literary Context* (Grand Rapids: Eerdmans, 2002), p. 169. On Jesus as actually a *mamzer* see the claims made by B. Chilton, *Rabbi Jesus: An Intimate Biography* (New York: Doubleday, 2000), pp. 6–7 and the discussion in S. McKnight, 'Calling Jesus *Mamzer*', *JSHJ* 1 (2003), pp. 73–103. See also B. Chilton's contribution to this volume in which he delineates three different usages of *mamzer*, noting that at first (applicable to the Jesus story) it referred to someone born to an unknown father.

The silence about Jesus and marriage is best explained by his not having married.[9] We find allusions to disciples being married (Mk 1.30; 1 Cor. 9.5). In discussing his own singleness Paul might have alluded not just to Peter's being married but also Jesus' being married, had he assumed it. One might, however, turn the argument around: he might have justified his own singleness by pointing to the precedent of Jesus. So Paul's silence is ambiguous. Had Jesus been married, however, one might have expected some reference to the fact along with the references to his mother, father, brothers and sisters (e.g. Mk 3.31–35). It is much more likely that he was not. Nothing suggests it was a response reflecting his own advice to excise unruly members (Mt. 5.29–30) nor that it was designed to set women at ease in the mixed company of itinerants, for not all were celibate.[10]

There is more to be said about Jesus and celibacy, but let me return to the broader social and anthropological context. Sexual mores are usually deeply ingrained in established cultures, passed on from generation to generation. Like many cultic practices, such as sacrifice, we are wise not to confuse putative origins of such behaviours and values with how they might have been understood in any later generation. Such values are inherently conservative and have usually evolved to conserve and protect society and its units. Many of these values would have been widely shared with surrounding cultures.[11]

Central to understanding attitudes towards sexuality was the household.[12] Sustaining the household as a stable unit and ensuring stable succession lie behind the perceived need to control women. Marriage belonged within and was subordinate to these household concerns.[13]

---

9. 'The alternatives are not simply whether Jesus was married or not, since it may have been that Jesus had once been married, was now a widower or had abandoned his marriage (which probably would not be seen as divorce, against which he spoke).' Loader, *Sexuality* (2), p. 143.

10. It might have had this effect, nevertheless, as B. Witherington, *Women in the Ministry of Jesus* (SNTSMS, 51; Cambridge: Cambridge University Press, 1984), pp. 31–32, suggests.

11. Satlow, *Jewish Marriage* (4), observes: 'The surviving Jewish marriage documents are very similar to their non-Jewish counterparts' (p. 84), except that in Greek and Roman law daughters could also inherit (p. 85). 'Socially, Hellenistic Jews, for the most part, did not choose marriage as a "boundary marker": when Philo and Josephus try to delineate what is distinctive about Jews, they rarely raise the issue of marriage. Greek-speaking Jews did not use their marriage payments to mark self-identity' (p. 201).

12. For what follows see, for instance, Loader, *Sexuality* (2), pp. 47–54; R. F. Collins, *Sexual Ethics and the New Testament: Behavior and Belief* (New York: Crossroad, 2000), pp. 2–4, who also cites evidence from surrounding cultures; Instone-Brewer, *Divorce and Remarriage* (8), pp. 9–10.

13. 'Marriage took a second seat to consanguinity' (Satlow, *Jewish Marriage* (4), p. 258). Speaking of both rabbinic and epigraphic evidence, Satlow writes: 'Men and women married to form a family, and the family, with its biological ties, was more important than any

Marriage was established by the woman leaving her parents' household[14] and joining a man's within the wider family group.[15] It included at betrothal a festal meal at the wife's parents' house to which the groom contributed and where he gave gifts, some of which were expected to return to him with the bride; on the wedding day a public procession of the bride, dressed up and honoured as royalty, from her father's house to her husband's, sometimes joined by him; and their coming together in sexual intercourse, thus becoming one flesh or kin (Gen. 2.24).[16] The man's father paid the woman's father an amount of money (a bride price) and the latter gave his daughter a dowry which remained hers, but was placed in the hands of her husband.[17] Marriage contracts, where completed, focused on codifying expectations and regulating financial obligations, as they did in the non-Jewish world.[18]

Adultery by wives with other men threatened that stability because it produced illegitimate offspring. For the same reason sexual intercourse before marriage with anyone but the one intended as partner in marriage left the household vulnerable.[19] Female virginity was essential.[20] These

---

conjugal ties within it. Spouses could, and did, die, divorce and remarry – the marital bond was regarded as ultimately unstable' (p. 258). See also S. R. Llewelyn, 'Paul's Advice on Marriage and the Changing Understanding of Marriage in Antiquity', in S. R. Llewelyn (ed.), *New Documents Illustrating Early Christianity 6* (Sydney: Macquarie University Ancient History Documentary Research Centre, 1992), pp. 1–18; and S. R. Llewelyn, 'A Jewish Deed of Marriage: Some Further Observations', in S. R. Llewelyn (ed.), *New Documents Illustrating Early Christianity 9* (Grand Rapids: Eerdmans, 2002), pp. 86–98.

14. The man set up his own household and authority, thus also in that sense leaving his parents as Gen. 2.24 reflects.

15. Endogamous marriage was the norm, not exogamous marriage (with outsiders) as preferred by the Romans and the common pattern in modern Western society. So Satlow, *Jewish Marriage* (4), p. 262.

16. See Satlow, *Jewish Marriage* (4), pp. 163–64, 170–77.

17. Satlow, *Jewish Marriage* (4), writes: 'For Jews of the Greek world, including Palestine (at least in the amoraic period), the dowry was the most important marriage payment ... The most important payment to the tannaim, the *ketubba*, does not reflect any reality, but is instead an idealized payment that was promoted as a preventive to rash divorce but which did not catch on in the rabbinic period' (p. 223).

18. So Satlow, *Jewish Marriage* (4), pp. 84–85.

19. Adultery in marriage was an offence against the husband; during betrothal it was an offence against both the husband and the woman's father.

20. Satlow, *Jewish Marriage* (4): 'Female virginity was widely valued throughout the Mediterranean and New East' (p. 118). 'One reason for this ... was certainly to assure paternity of the progeny' (p. 118). It also 'carried a heavy symbolic value' (p. 118) and was taken as evidence of moral character – the wife likely to remain faithful (p. 119). There is no word in Hebrew or Greek for male virginity. Sexual intercourse was normally acceptable during betrothal, but this was not the case in Galilee. See Satlow, *Jewish Marriage* (4), p. 167; and R. E. Brown, *The Birth of the Messiah: A Commentary on the Infancy Narratives in the Gospels of Matthew and Luke* (ABRL; New York: Doubleday, 2nd edn, 1993), pp. 123–24.

values were espoused or simply assumed in a culture in which polygynous marriage was the norm, reflected not only in the stories of the patriarchs and kings, but also in the provision of Levirate marriage.[21]

At the time of Jesus we find there have been moves towards monogamous marriage, probably in part under the influence of Hellenistic culture.[22] For those who espoused it, divorce and adultery would have emerged as a more acute problem, whereas in polygynous marriages there were more ready solutions: one took another wife or one was simply less attentive to the irritating wife. Where divorce took place, the certificate freed the wife to marry another. Where adultery took place, death was prescribed, but there were milder options as the story of Joseph of Nazareth indicates: public disgrace or private dismissal. Such provisions applied, as this story indicates, not only once married but also when marriage had been agreed.[23] Grounds for divorce included adultery, but

---

21.   Satlow, *Jewish Marriage* (4), p. 189, notes that the attack on it at Qumran assumes its practice. Josephus describes it as a Jewish custom (*War* 1.477), confirmed also by the Babatha archive (early second century AD).

22.   Satlow, *Jewish Marriage* (4): 'The Damascus Document's use of Gen. 1.27 to justify rejection of polygyny combined two different trends within the community. First, there was a rejection of polygyny based originally on Deut. 17.17, as seen in the Temple Scroll. Second, there was from the beginning of the community a notion that contemporary marriage is patterned on the primal marriage. The innovation of the author of this passage in the Damascus Document was to invoke Gen. 1 rather than Gen. 2 to condemn polygyny' (p. 60). Using the creation story to argue for monogamy 'ran against the grain of real marital practice' and 'can be seen as outgrowths of an internal theological development influenced by external factors. Greek and Roman marital ideologies worked well with their practice of monogamy. When Palestinian Jews began to appropriate and adapt these ideologies they were left with a conflict between it and their traditional marital practices. The monogamous trend in our sources is a trace of this conflict' (pp. 190–91). He notes that 'Philo's and Josephus's understanding of concubinage is a standard Greek one. Greek "concubines" were "kept women" who – like their biblical counterparts – were expected to remain faithful to their husbands with no expectation of reciprocity' (p. 193).

23.   The agreement would take place about a year before the wedding, sometimes earlier. Satlow, *Jewish Marriage* (4), observes, contrary to widespread assumptions about betrothal (inchoate marriage) as a normal pattern, that 'the only evidence that Jews practiced a form of inchoate marriage comes from the Gospel of Matthew. Jews outside of Palestine, and perhaps even within the more cosmopolitan areas within Palestine, did not appear to engage in inchoate marriages. But first-century AD Jews in the rural Galilee may have practiced this biblical form of betrothal' (p. 73). He argues that the practice had been abandoned and been replaced by Greek practices and that this is reflected in the LXX's use of φερνή to translate מֹהַר) (bride price), and to translate אָ]רַשׁ , 'to betrothe' with μνηστεύ ω, which is much less legal. Neither Philo nor Josephus nor Qumran writings assume inchoate marriage (pp. 71–72). Satlow argues that the rabbis (re-)introduced betrothal, though probably it was known in Galilee (pp. 75–76).

also neglect of other obligations (Exod. 21.10–11),[24] and could apparently be initiated by either a man or a woman.[25]

Other matters broadly relating to sexuality also had their accompaniment of norms and rituals. For women, childbirth and menstruation were times of uncleanness removed after a set period by simple purification rites (Leviticus 12). Similarly men's sexual emissions rendered them unclean until sunset (Lev. 15.1–6; Num. 5.2). Nakedness was out of place in public and especially in holy places. None of these elements is seen as bad let alone sinful, but they need to be given attention with respect to place and time, and failure to do so constituted sin and could also spread unnecessary contamination. We should not see these as any more burdensome and restrictive than any modern Jew would see them today. The unfamiliar always tends to look burdensome.

As there were movements towards espousing monogamy, so there were movements towards espousing greater strictness with regard to purity in relation to sexuality. The *Damascus Document* which espouses monogamy also warns against having sexual intercourse in the holy city (CD 12.1) and *Jubilees* forbids it on the sabbath (*Jub.* 50.8).[26] 1QM and 4QMMT are especially strict about nakedness, particularly in relation to toileting. People are to go outside the city (1QM 7.7; 11QT 46.12–16; cf. also Deut. 23.10–14). *Jubilees* extends such values to the Garden of Eden which it sees as a temple (*Jub.* 3.8–14, 34–35). Not only is nakedness out of place in God's presence as the knowing couple of the original story illustrates, but sexual intercourse cannot take place in the Garden of Eden.

It is very likely that those Essenes who espoused celibacy reflected such values. In a sense restrictive developments in marriage, i.e. towards monogamy, and restrictive developments on purity put sexuality under pressure. The tension between nakedness and sexuality, on the one hand, and holiness, on the other, will have ancient roots which are beyond the scope of this brief chapter. They doubtless lie in part in Israel's struggle to come to terms with fertility cults. It would be interesting also to know the extent to which the openness of the upper echelons of the priesthood to Hellenistic influence in the third and second centuries became a channel for attitudes which favoured monogamy and perhaps in some instances celibacy. Those most opposed to Hellenism appear to have welcomed its stricter side and the values they saw allied to their own.

Before returning to the historical Jesus, moving further along the continuum, it is striking how these cultural and religious assumptions

---

24. See Instone-Brewer, *Divorce and Remarriage* (8), pp. 93–110.

25. On this see Instone-Brewer, *Divorce and Remarriage* (8), pp. 24–26, 72–80, 85–90, and Satlow, *Jewish Marriage* (4), pp. 214; Loader, *Sexuality* (2), pp. 113–14.

26. Similarly 11QT 45.11–12; 46.16–18.

about sexuality surface in Paul's writings.[27] Just taking 1 Corinthians 7 we find the tension between the sacred and sexual in the advice to abstain from sexual intercourse for a period for the sake of prayer (1 Cor. 7.5),[28] the notion that holiness transfers through union of man and woman to the child (1 Cor. 7.14),[29] and the specific singling out of female virginity as holy (1 Cor. 7.34). In 1 Corinthians 11 we find the tension between uncovered women and the holy place of worship where angels are deemed to be present (1 Cor. 11.10).[30] More broadly we find there assumptions about orders in creation which have their roots in Septuagint Genesis, where we also find the text which Paul uses to ground his argument against prostitution (Gen. 2.24): one becomes one flesh with someone through sexual intercourse (1 Cor. 6.16).

Returning to the historical Jesus, we have noted the likelihood that Jesus was not married and that this was a deliberate choice on his part in the light of his calling. The saying in Mt. 19.11–12 about people who make themselves eunuchs for the kingdom of God in all probability includes a self-reference.[31] Its shocking use of the image of eunuch reflects Jesus' countercultural stance in affirming the marginalized and makes a statement about his own choice to move beyond the traditional masculine domain in the dominant household system.[32] It is striking that it begins and ends with the caution that this is not for everyone but only for those to whom it is given. Paul, independently, offers a similar caution in 1 Cor. 7.7 in espousing his preference for all to be celibate like him (which he keeps doing throughout the chapter): 'but each has his own gift, the

27.   See the discussion of Paul and celibacy in Loader, *Sexuality* (2), pp. 149–92.

28.   Similarly *T. Naph.* 8.7–8. On this see my discussion in W. Loader, 'Sexuality in the Testaments of the Twelve Patriarchs and the New Testament', in R. M. Chennattu, M. L. Coloe (eds.), *Transcending Boundaries: Contemporary Readings of the New Testament. Essays in Honour of Professor Francis J. Moloney* (BSR, 187; Rome: LAS Publications, 2005), pp. 293–309 (295–96).

29.   On this see my discussion in Loader, *Sexuality* (2), pp. 169–71, including the recent suggestion of Y. M. Gillihan, 'Jewish Laws on Illicit Marriage, the Defilement of Offspring, and the Holiness of the Temple: A New Halakic interpretation of 1 Corinthians 7.14', *JBL* 121 (2002), pp. 711–44, that 'sanctify' here means in effect make licit and so legitimize access to the temple – all within the framework of purity thinking (Loader, *Sexuality* [2], p. 170 n. 112).

30.   See the discussion in W. Loader, *The Septuagint, Sexuality, and the New Testament: Case Studies on the Impact of the LXX in Philo and the New Testament* (Grand Rapids: Eerdmans, 2004), pp. 99–104.

31.   So J. Blinzler, 'εἰσὶνεὐνοῦχοι', *ZNW* 48 (1957), pp. 254–70 (269); F. J. Moloney, 'Matthew 19.3-12 and Celibacy', in *idem*, *'A Hard Saying': The Gospel and Culture* (Collegeville: Liturgical, 2001), pp. 35–52 (46–52). See also Loader, *Sexuality* (2), pp. 127–34.

32.   On this see H. Moxnes, *Putting Jesus in His Place: A Radical Vision of Household and Kingdom* (Louisville: Westminster John Knox, 2003), pp. 72–90. I believe he is right in the former but not in the denial.

one so, the other so' – assuming male discourse.[33] Paul may have also been influenced by Stoic–Cynic debates[34] and the Corinthians who needed the caution may also have been influenced by celibacy in the Isis cult,[35] but it is likely that we meet these issues here primarily because we are dealing with the Jesus tradition which will have preserved memory of Jesus' option. The option for celibacy appears to be reflected also in Luke's traditions (Lk. 18.29–30; 14.18–20; 14.25–26),[36] although in Luke there are probably extraneous influences at work as we shall see.

John the Baptist appears also to have been celibate. Similarities between John and the Essenes tempt speculation that in such preferences similar influences are at work.[37] One might put down such celibacy to pragmatism. Some interpret Paul in this way. Marriage is not a good idea when you are facing the end of the world or facing extreme danger.[38] Perhaps Paul was worried more about children than spouses; but he does not put it that way. Was Jesus 'a eunuch for the sake of the kingdom' to enable him to devote more time to his work – a sound and modern-sounding rationale? There may be more to it.

I have not been convinced that Jesus distanced himself from the eschatology which characterized John the Baptist before him and Paul and others after him. While some espouse the 'no time for marriage' explanation, eschatology is relevant to this discussion in other ways. Where values of holiness informed the vision of the eschaton or the image of paradise there were inevitable consequences for whatever was deemed unholy and also unclean. Jesus' response to the smutty attempt at ridicule on the part of the Sadducees about the woman widowed seven times states baldly: 'In the world to come they neither marry nor are given in marriage but are like the angels in heaven' (Mk 12.25).[39]

This is not about a stop on weddings. It is about sexual intercourse. It does not happen. Why? Luke, doubtless under the influence of popular

33. Loader, *Sexuality* (2), pp. 163–64.

34. See the excellent discussion in W. Deming, *Paul on Marriage and Celibacy: The Hellenistic Background of 1 Corinthians 7* (Grand Rapids: Eerdmans, 2nd edn, 2004), pp. 107–27.

35. R. F. Collins, *First Corinthians* (SP, 7; Collegeville: Liturgical, 1999) p. 253; R. E. Oster, 'Use, Misuse and Neglect of Archaeological Evidence in Some Modern Works on 1 Corinthians (1 Cor 7,1–5; 8,10; 11,2–16; 12,14–26)', *ZNW* 83 (1992), pp. 52–73 (60–64).

36. Loader, *Sexuality* (2), pp. 137–39.

37. On the similarities but also significant differences, see J. E. Taylor, *The Immerser: John the Baptist within Second Temple Judaism* (Grand Rapids: Eerdmans, 1997), pp. 15–48.

38. See B. Winter, 'Secular and Christian Responses to Corinthian Famines', *TynBul* 40 (1989), pp. 86–106, who argues that Paul is alluding to the famines that affected Corinth in the period which would seriously affect families.

39. For the discussion of this text see Loader, *Sexuality* (2), pp. 121–26.

philosophy of his day,[40] implies it is because reproduction is no longer necessary – that is the only purpose he sees in sexual intercourse (Lk. 20.34–36). His ideal people abstain from sex even in this life (Anna, Lk. 2.36; Philip's daughters, Acts 21.9).[41] But in Mark's anecdote the focus probably lies elsewhere. This is a different kind of existence and, I suggest, heaven is a holy place, where, as in *Jubilees'* Eden, sex and nakedness have no place.[42]

Whether stemming from the historical Jesus[43] or simply reflecting what was at home in the Jesus tradition, this notion of a holy and therefore sexless life to come probably explains a number of subsequent phenomena. These include the strong move towards celibacy in Corinth and in Paul and arguably the traditions of the *Gospel of Thomas*, and the image of Rev. 14.4, which pictures the elect in two groups: the 144,000 who have not defiled themselves with women, whom I take to be those who chose the celibate state already in this life, and the rest – who as in Mt. 19.12 and 1 Cor. 7.7 are not therefore disparaged.[44]

There is much debate about the extent to which the *Gospel of Thomas* espouses celibacy.[45] The closer one reads the *Gospel of Thomas* in the light of later writings, the more one is inclined to see such statements as

---

40. So Musonius Rufus, *frag.* 12; Plutarch, *Mor.* 144B; Occellus Lucanus, *Nature of the Universe* 45. See Loader, *Sexuality* (2), pp. 219–20. For such influence in Jewish literature see *Spec. Leg.* 3.113; *Jos.* 43; *Vit. Mos.* 1.28; *Spec. Leg.* 3.9; *Apion* 2.25; *Ps.-Phoc.* 186; *T. Reub.* 2.3–4; 4.6; *T. Iss.* 2.3; 3.5 and see D. C. Allison, 'Divorce, Celibacy, and Joseph', *JSNT* 49 (1993), pp. 3–10 (7–9). See, however, *1 En.* 15.3–6, which provides early Jewish testimony to belief that angels have no need of women and sexual relations because they have no need to reproduce.

41. On sexual asceticism in Luke see T. Karlsen Seim, 'The Virgin Mother: Mary and Ascetic Discipleship in Luke', in A.-J. Levine with M. Blickenstaff (eds.), *A Feminist Companion to Luke* (Feminist Companion to the New Testament and Early Christian Writings, 3; London: Sheffield Academic Press, 2002), pp. 89–105 (90–92). She notes also that the reversal of the blessing of Jesus' mother in Lk. 11.27 by Jesus' words to the women of Jerusalem in Lk. 23.27–31 reflects this tendency.

42. The saying attributed to Jesus in Mt. 21.31 about prostitutes entering the kingdom before the chief priests and scribes does not imply that they will continue their profession in the kingdom. It assumes they have responded to John's call to repentance.

43. See J. P. Meier, 'The Debate on the Resurrection of the Dead: An Incident from the Ministry of the Historical Jesus?' *JSNT* 77 (2000), pp. 3–24. Van der Horst, 'Celibacy in Early Judaism' (5), p. 399 and n. 32, notes the link between celibacy and Mk 12.25 and the possibility that the saying in *Gos. Thom.* 22 and *2 Clem.* 12 may go back to Jesus.

44. See Loader, *Sexuality* (2), pp. 210–12.

45. See Loader, *Sexuality* (2) pp. 199–207; M. Fieger, *Das Thomasevangelium: Einleitung, Kommentar und Systematik* (NTAbh, 22; Münster: Aschendorff, 1991), pp. 101, 131; see also R. Uro, 'Is *Thomas* an Encratite Gospel?' in R. Uro (ed.) *Thomas at the Crossroads: Essays on the Gospel of Thomas* (Studies of the New Testament and its World; Edinburgh: T&T Clark, 1998), pp. 140–62 (149–56) and J. D. Crossan, *The Birth of Christianity: Discovering What Happened in the Years Immediately After the Execution of Jesus* (San Francisco: HarperSanFranciso, 1998), pp. 267–69.

metaphorical.[46] I think the more one wants to claim Thomas reflects earlier tradition, the more likely a literal meaning is intended. It appears then to espouse a view of primal innocence, like that of little children (*Gos. Thom.* 22, 37), where sexual differentiation is irrelevant and all are basically in the primal state which on the basis of a certain reading of Genesis 1–2 may have been assumed to be male (cf. *Gos. Thom.* 114) or neither male nor female or both but in any case not sexually engaged. Perhaps as D. R. McDonald has suggested there is a tradition behind Gal. 3.28 which reflects such ideas of oneness,[47] although in Paul the oneness does not imply denial of differences among any of the pairs listed, but only that these do not count as a basis for inclusion or exclusion.[48] Such a statement is potentially much more revolutionary than Paul apparently assumed; it could directly challenge hierarchies between masters and slaves and men and women. It does not lead Paul to espouse celibacy for all, as such a tradition might have done in Corinth, assuming they had known it.

Celibacy is likely to be on the agenda in many parts of the early Church because it was on the agenda of Jesus and John and others of the time. I think a likely structure of thought which informed response to celibacy was eschatological syntax, according to which we engage now through the Spirit in the life to come, while at the same time acknowledging we have not yet arrived. In some circles one might also speak of protological syntax. The distinctive feature in relation to celibacy was that it was seen as a gift or calling to some to espouse already now what would be the norm for all in the age to come.[49]

If, as we suppose, Jesus stands in a tradition which assumed the holiness of the age to come had no place for sexuality and saw his calling to live in celibacy already in this life without requiring it of others, this would put Jesus generally among those espousing a heightened awareness of holiness. But that would stand in stark contrast to the many anecdotes and sayings where Jesus runs into strife for the opposite reason. People

46. As S. Petersen, *'Zerstört die Werke der Weiblichkeit!': Maria Magdalena, Salome und andere Jüngerinnen Jesu in christlich-gnostischen Schriften* (NHS, 48; Leiden: Brill, 1999), pp. 169–78 (171–72); T. Zöckler, *Jesu Lehren im Thomasevangelium* (Manichaean Studies, 47; Leiden: Brill, 1999), p. 237. See also the discussion in M. Franzmann, *Jesus in the Nag Hammadi Writings* (London: T&T Clark, 1996), pp. 196–99.

47. D. R. MacDonald, *There is No Male and Female: The Fate of a Dominical Saying in Paul and Gnosticism* (Philadelphia: Fortress, 1987), pp. 113–26.

48. See Loader, *Sexuality* (2), pp. 193–99 and J. M. Gundry-Volf, 'Christ and Gender: A Study of Difference and Equality in Gal 3,28', in C. Landmesser, H. J. Eckstein, H. Lichtenberger (eds.), *Jesus Christus als Mitte der Schrift: Studien zur Hermeneutik des Evangeliums* (BZNW, 86; Berlin: de Gruyter, 1997), pp. 439–79.

49. On other possible influences towards the choice of celibacy such as abstinence from sexual intercourse in readiness for battle, see Loader, *Sexuality* (2), pp. 215–26.

have spoken of Jesus' 'liberal' interpretation of Torah in relation to sabbath, mixing with tax collectors and sinners, touching lepers and such like. Is it thinkable that Jesus might have been 'liberal' in these instances but not so, for instance, in the broad realm of sexuality? Surely this can easily be the case and many examples can be cited across the centuries right through to our own day.[50] It also depends on how one understands the basis for his approach, which can be understood as reflecting a creation perspective (as in Mk 2.27 and 10.2–9) but should not be reduced to that.[51] In Jesus' case his strict sayings about divorce and remarriage are seen by many as belonging to the bedrock of the tradition.[52]

We should also observe a similar phenomenon with John the Baptist.[53] On the one hand he offers the opportunity to repent liberally to all, thus crossing many traditional barriers. On the other, he (like probably Jesus and certainly Christians after him) provides a rite for cleansing and makes high demands. These are not just ethical demands – baptism is a rite! More importantly we find him espousing a very strict, debatably over strict, legal interpretation of the incest laws in Leviticus 18 to attack Herod Antipas' marriage to Salome (Mk 6.17–29; Mt. 14.3–12; cf. Lk. 3.19–20; see also *Ant.* 18.116–19). She was, after all, only his half-brother's wife. It is fascinating in this context that nothing is said of the fact that she is also his niece (some Essenes, unlike the Pharisees, would have seen this as sin),[54] nor that to make this gain he divorced his first wife, the daughter of Aretas, who would avenge the act in later years.

What has this to do with Jesus? It is probable that Jesus would have shared John's view. It is probable that the goings-on of Antipas were a topic of conversation, at least a good way along the probability scale with which all history must measure itself. I think that such discussions would inevitably also have included negative assessment of the divorce. I think it

---

50. As J. P. Meier, *A Marginal Jew: Rethinking the Historical Jesus*, vol. 3: *Companions and Competitors* (ABRL; New York: Doubleday, 2001), p. 503, notes: 'Perhaps one reason that we have so little from the historical Jesus on sexual topics is that, apart from the two special cases of divorce and celibacy, where he diverged from mainstream Judaism, his views were those of mainstream Judaism.' His issues were largely elsewhere.

51. See my discussion forthcoming in W. Loader, 'Jesus and the Law', in T. Holmén, S. E. Porter (eds.), *The Handbook of the Study of the Historical Jesus* (Leiden: Brill, 2006).

52. K. Niederwimmer, *Askese und Mysterium: Über Ehe, Ehescheidung und Eheverzicht in den Anfängen des christlichen Glaubens* (FRLANT, 113; Göttingen: Vandenhoeck & Ruprecht, 1975), pp. 39–41, argues that they should not be suggests that played off against an alleged Jesus' liberal approach, but rather be seen as belonging to the absolute claims of the kingdom. As Meier, *A Marginal Jew: Companions and Competitors* (50), p. 502, observes, 'this eschatological radicalism can work itself out in different ways and with different results'.

53. On John the Baptist and Antipas, see Loader, *Sexuality* (2), pp. 108–12.

54. They saw it as the equivalent of marriage of nephews by aunts, which is expressly forbidden (Lev. 18.12–13; 20.19); 4Q251 frag. 12, line 7; 11QT 66.15–17; CD 5.8–11.

likely as some have suggested that this may have influenced Jesus' assessment of the issue of divorce and remarriage.[55]

Here is not the place to review again the divorce sayings (Mt. 5.31–32; Lk. 16.18; Mk 10.11–12; Mt. 19.9; 1 Cor. 7.10–11) or the divorce anecdote (Mk 10.2–12; Mt. 19.3–12).[56] Let me make some general points. The anecdote uses Gen. 1.27 and 2.24 in a way which must be seen as affirming marriage, including the coming together of a man and a woman in sexual intercourse, as part of God's will for creation. On the strength of such a stance, whether he knew the anecdote or not, Paul is to be noted for his reluctance to disparage marriage and sexual intercourse. In addition we should note that this is not primarily about reproduction, to which some of the world of the time reduced sex's role. The anecdote also reflects the view that sexual union creates an indissoluble union. Again Paul, probably not knowing this tradition directly, assumes the same effect when arguing against sexual intercourse with a prostitute, strikingly also by citing Gen. 2.24 in 1 Cor. 6.16.

I have speculated that perhaps behind the anecdote is a simple form without the biblical proofs and that Jesus' original response was a confronting throwaway line: 'What God has yoked let no one separate' (Mk. 10.9).[57] As it stands, it functions as a fundamental law for the Christian community. In a way the saying simply extrapolates its own logic. If the joining is permanent, it is against God's will to change that. And certainly to remarry would have to mean committing adultery against that permanent relationship. Paul does know this tradition and applies it creatively in a new situation.

Broadly speaking Jesus appears to belong among those who favoured monogamy and for whom therefore issues of adultery and divorce had become acute. Inspired perhaps by Antipas' adventure, but doubtless by more than that, Jesus takes a very strict line. David Instone-Brewer speculates that Jesus draws on the same tradition of argument for monogamy as does the *Damascus Document* (CD 4.20–5.6).[58] I am not

---

55. F. Crawford Burkitt, *The Gospel History and its Transmission* (Edinburgh: T&T Clark, 2nd edn, 1907), pp. 98–101, cited in R. Banks, *Jesus and the Law in the Synoptic Tradition* (SNTSMS, 28; Cambridge: Cambridge University Press, 1975), p. 158 n. 2; W. F. Luck, *Divorce and Remarriage: Recovering the Biblical View* (San Francisco: Harper & Row, 1987), pp. 88–99, 98, 111–29; Instone-Brewer, *Divorce and Remarriage* (8), pp. 160–61.

56. See my discussion, Loader, *Sexuality* (2), pp. 61–120.

57. W. Loader, *Jesus' Attitude Towards the Law: A Study of the Gospels* (WUNT 2.97; Tübingen: Mohr Siebeck, 1997), pp. 39–55, 518–19; see also Loader, *Sexuality* (2), p. 95.

58. Instone-Brewer, *Divorce and Remarriage* (8), pp. 136–44, 171–75. Originally it included Gen. 7.9 beside Gen. 1.27. See also his detailed discussion in D. Instone-Brewer, 'Jesus' Old Testament Basis for Monogamy', in S. Moyise (ed.), *The Old Testament in the New Testament: Essays in Honour of J. L. North* (JSNTSup, 189; Sheffield: Sheffield Academic Press, 2000), pp. 75–105. See my discussion in Loader, *Sexuality* (2), pp. 105–06.

convinced, although there is a common argument based on the order of creation (fortunately Jesus did not add, like CD: monogamy is proved by the animals going into the ark two by two!). Jesus belongs, like the Essene groups, at the conservative end on such issues, although they clearly accepted divorce (11QT 54.4–5; 66.8–11; CD 13.15–17).[59] He did not. Rabbinic tradition tells us that the Schools of Shammai and Hillel debated the issue,[60] but Jesus goes beyond either. Some see Matthew's versions of the sayings as a modification or even an adaptation to the alleged position of Shammai on Deuteronomy 24. Matthew allows an exception: adultery.[61] The text, however, still sets Jesus' position in contrast to such an interpretation of Deut. 24.1–4 (notice the twofold δέ in Mt. 19.8–9).[62]

On the exception I agree with those scholars who rather see Matthew spelling out what was the common assumption, already reflected in Deut. 24.1–4 and propounded by the *Lex Iulia*: that adultery required divorce.[63] The woman became unclean for the man. There was no room for the reconciliation and new beginning which many later would argue was a more creative approach warranted by the core values of the tradition. Nothing indicates that the strictness derives from concern for the plight of women.[64] I do not see evidence in subsequent tradition for the interesting speculation of D. Instone-Brewer that such sayings also assumed the

---

59. Earlier CD 4.20–5.6 had been widely seen as forbidding divorce, but its focus is polygamy. On this see Instone-Brewer, *Divorce and Remarriage* (8), pp. 65–71.

60. For rabbinic debates, see Instone-Brewer, *Divorce and Remarriage* (8), pp. 110–17.

61. On the vexed question of the meaning of the exception clauses in Mt. 5.32 and 19.9 see Loader, *Sexuality* (2), pp. 66–73.

62. See Loader, *Sexuality* (2), pp. 106–07. So Instone-Brewer, *Divorce and Remarriage* (8), pp. 152–59. This had earlier also been my own view. See Loader, *Jesus' Attitude Towards the Law* (57), p. 225.

63. See Loader, *Sexuality* (2), pp. 70–72. See the Augustan laws pertaining to adultery, *Lex Iulia* and *Lex Papia Poppaea* excerpted in M. R. Lefkowitz, M. B. Fant, *Women's Life in Greece and Rome: A Source Book in Translation* (Baltimore: Johns Hopkins University Press, 1982), pp. 181–89; on Athenian law, see pp. 50–57, esp. p. 57. Instone-Brewer, *Divorce and Remarriage* (8), pp. 95–96, argues that before AD 70 divorce for adultery was not compulsory, because the rite of bitter water applied and it was assumed the adulterous woman would die. See the discussion in K. Berger, *Die Gesetzesauslegung Jesu. Ihr historischer Hintergrund im Judentum und im Alten Testament. Teil I: Markus und Parallelen* (WMANT, 40; Neukirchen-Vluyn: Neukirchener Verlag, 1972), pp. 566–70. Cf. J. P. Meier, 'The Historical Jesus and the Historical Law: Some Problems within the Problem', *CBQ* 65 (2003), pp. 52–79, who dismisses this view too quickly (p. 78 n. 59).

64. So most recently also A.-J. Levine, 'Jesus, Divorce, and Sexuality: a Jewish Critique', in B. F. Le Beau, L. Greenspoon, D. Hamm (eds.), *The Historical Jesus through Catholic and Jewish Eyes* (Harrisburg: Trinity, 2000), pp. 113–29 (115–20). See also Loader, *Sexuality* (2), p. 76; U. Luz, *Das Evangelium nach Matthäus. 1. Teilband: Mt 1–7* (EKKNT, I.1; Zurich: Benziger; Neukirchen-Vluyn: Neukirchener, 2nd edn, 2002), pp. 360, 364; J. A. Fitzmyer, 'The Matthean Divorce Texts and Some New Palestinian Evidence', in *idem, To Advance the*

validity of divorce where the matters of Exod. 21.10–11 had not been properly attended to.[65]

Another aspect of the historical Jesus in relation to sexuality relates to warnings about adultery and about abuse. The saying that for those who cause children to stumble it would better for them sink in the sea with a millstone around their neck (Mk 9.42; Mt. 18.6) now comes in a context of traditions concerned with community life among believers (Mk 9.42–48; Mt. 18.6–9). While not overtly sexual, this aspect of abuse should not be excluded; indeed, I would argue, it is probably the primary focus for those who heard it.[66] Similarly the sayings about excision (Mk 9.43–48; Mt. 18.8–9), which may apply broadly, are also likely to have been understood in a sexual context, as indeed Matthew does in Mt. 5.29–30 and rabbinic tradition does of similar imagery, perhaps reflecting common origins (b.Nid. 13A-B).[67] It is even possible to hear Jesus' encounter with the children in the context of child abuse (Mk 10.13–16), assuming Jesus the teacher is being offered children that he might 'touch' (a word which can have sexual connotations).[68] The disciples' strong reaction would make good sense. I have not found evidence of such a reading in subsequent tradition nor is it easy to imagine it in this way in the context of the historical Jesus, but can we be so sure?

Jesus may have warned about adulterous looking as Mt. 5.28 reports. Warnings about attitude and not just deed and about adulterous looking were not uncommon (Sir. 9.8; Job 31.1; *T. Reub.* 3.10; Susanna 7–8). Mostly they come in contexts where men are being warned about the dangers of women, especially strange women. As Matthew reports it, Jesus does not imply that women are dangerous with the implication that one should not look at them lest one be sexually aroused by their beauty, for instance, and that they should protect men's vulnerability by covering themselves up. Rather men take responsibility whether their attitudes are adulterous or not. The emphasis reflected in Mt. 5.28 and Mk 7.21–23 on attitude, not just deed, places sexuality in the context of a more holistic understanding of human relationships.

Incidentally Mt. 5.28 also reflects an attitude towards women which sees them not as problems. I think this coheres with other anecdotes in the

---

Gospel: New Testament Studies (Grand Rapids: Eerdmans, 2nd edn, 1998), pp. 79–111 (99–101). Mark's version of the saying speaks of wronging a woman (Mk 10.11), but many see that as an addition; the other sayings assume male action and the infringement of male rights.

65. Instone-Brewer, *Divorce and Remarriage* (8), pp. 177–88. Cf. Loader, *Sexuality* (2), pp. 118–20.

66. Loader, *Sexuality* (2), pp. 21–27.

67. W. Deming, 'Mark 9.42–10.12, Matthew 5.27-32, and B Nid 13b: A First Century Discussion of Male Sexuality', *NTS* 36 (1990), pp. 130–41; Collins, *Sexual Ethics*, p. 67.

68. See Loader, *Sexuality* (2), pp. 59–60.

Jesus tradition where Jesus appears very inclusive of women,[69] not inclined to avoid acts of women which might be deemed sexual (such as the anointing), supportive of their presence among his disciples. Such an attitude may reflect the inclusivity which can be characteristic of marginalized groups – at the bottom of the heap all stand on the same ground. It also coheres with the evidence of his solidarity with other marginalized groups in society. It also helps explain the prominence of women in at least the earlier strands of the Christian tradition before it succumbed to what were seen as appropriate values for the good citizen of the household of faith.

In conclusion we have little explicit evidence.[70] I have suggested that some features of the early tradition are explicable on the assumption of attitudes of the historical Jesus which in turn make sense in the light of his precedents. These include generally a strict attitude in relation to matters of sexuality, already evident in John, and especially in Jesus' sayings about marriage and divorce. Assumptions about sexuality and holiness also most likely go back to Jesus, including his understanding of eschatology and of his own calling. They lead to the potential for the denial of sexuality, when Jesus' affirmation of Genesis 1 and 2 is ignored. Nevertheless it was inevitable that some would use heavenly reality as a template for abiding values, and that raised a question over human sexuality. It was also inevitable that those who switched Matthew's 'with a view to' to read 'with the result' that men are sexually aroused combined such tendencies along with broader social values into a demand for the control and subordination of women.

As I have noted elsewhere,[71] the most important statements which Jesus made about sexuality are the ones which do not mention it but teach us to respect and honour difference in others and to seek always what is compassionate and healing for people. For faith, that provides a broader canonical context within which to engage the particularities and peculiarities of the few likely historical statements which we have, and to honour their cultural indebtedness and if possible their intent.

---

69. See Loader, *Sexuality* (2), pp. 55–59.

70. I have passed over more general statements reflecting rejection of sexual immorality such as Mk 7.21–23 and Mt. 15.18–20; Mk 10.19; similarly Mt. 19.18; Lk. 18.11; Mk 8.38; Mt. 12.39; 16.4. The emphasis on attitude not just deed reflected in Mt. 5.28 and Mk 7.21–23 places sexuality in the context of a more holistic understanding of human relationships. See my discussion in Loader, *Sexuality* (2), pp. 38–43, 55–59.

71. Loader, *Sexuality* (2), pp. 231–52, especially p. 251.

How a Woman who Fought Back and Demanded her Rights Became an Importunate Widow: The Transformations of a Parable of Jesus[1]

Annette Merz

The parable of the widow and the judge (Lk. 18.1–8) seems to me an excellent test case for the investigation of the continuities and discontinuities in the transmission of Jesus' teaching. F. Bovon rightly remarks: 'Few passages in the Gospels bear such vivid testimony to the path that an instruction took from the time at which it was first formulated to its final expression.'[2] Scholars take widely divergent views of the extent of the textual basis which may go back to Jesus himself, and of the early Christian interpretations which have clustered around this basis. Very different views are held about what Jesus originally intended to say by means of this parable. The reason for the latter divergence may perhaps lie in something noted by Bovon, namely that investigations into the historical Jesus have paid strikingly little attention to this parable.[3] This is reason enough to make the parable the centre of the present investigation; I am convinced that it is possible to apprehend Jesus as an historical figure only when we pay equal attention to his links to contemporary Judaism and to the way in which early Christianity took up and elaborated traditions which go back to him.

1. *An Evolved Text and Controversial Interpretations: Highlights of Research and Methodological Presuppositions*

I believe that the overwhelming majority of exegetes are right to see Lk. 18.1–8 as an 'evolved' text which displays clear traces of a series of

---

1. Translated from the German original by B. McNeil.

2. F. Bovon, *Das Evangelium nach Lukas. 3. Teilband: Lk 15,1–19,27* (EKKNT, III.3; Neukirchen-Vluyn: Neukirchener, 2001), pp. 187–88.

3. See F. Bovon, 'Apocalyptic Traditions in the Lukan Special Material: Reading Luke 18.1-8', *HTR* 90 (1997), pp. 383–91 (384).

reinterpretations.[4] Widely divergent views are taken of whether and how the various strata of the interpretation can be perceived, and above all of whether the continuing process of 'writing' the parable is in agreement with Jesus' original intention. Without pretending to offer an exhaustive illustration of such disagreements, let us look briefly at a few important questions regarding the exposition of the parable.

While vv. 2–8a are mostly regarded as pre-Lukan, v. 8b[5] and above all v. 1 are almost unanimously ascribed to the evangelist, who wished to give an unambiguous direction to the interpretation of the parable by means of the absolutely clear indication of its theme: πρὸς τὸ δεῖν πάντοτε προσεύχεσθαι αὐτοὺς καὶ μὴ ἐγκακεῖν. Many scholars agree with A. Jülicher that these words of Luke stand in unbroken continuity with the intention of Jesus' original parable.[6] For example, R. Bultmann claims that the parable 'in fact originally' intended 'to exhort the hearers to pray'.[7] This involves a crucial decision which has far-reaching consequences for the evaluation of the tradition of this text as a whole, since – as W. R. Herzog II well puts it – 'if the parable was about prayer and the widow was the petitioner, then the judge had to be a God figure'.[8] In comparison, it is less important at what stage or stages of the tradition scholars locate the comments in vv. 6–8, and which new accents they believe are introduced at individual points. Some have located the

---

4. This consensus is not absolute. On the one hand, we find interpretations that regard the entire text as coming from Luke's hand (e.g. Edwin D. Freed, 'The Parable of the Judge and the Widow (Luke 18.1–8)', *NTS* 33 (1987), pp. 38–60); on the other hand, some scholars regard the entire text (perhaps with the exception of v. 1) as going back to Jesus (e.g. G. Delling, 'Das Gleichnis vom Gottlosen Richter', *ZNW* 53 (1962), pp. 1–25).

5. The addition of a concluding logion in v. 8b, which may go back to a traditional logion about the Son of Man, is mostly ascribed to the evangelist, who thereby brings to a close the larger complex of the eschatological remarks of Jesus, which begins at Lk. 17.20. Interpreters often see in the hesitant question πλὴν ὁ υἱὸς τοῦ ἀνθρώπου ἐλθὼν ἆρα εὑρήσει τὴν πίστιν ἐπὶ τῆς γῆς; a reservation on the evangelist's part vis-à-vis the intensity of eschatological expectation which dominates in vv. 6–8a. This was asserted as long ago as 1910 by A. Jülicher, *Die Gleichnisreden Jesu II* (two parts in one volume; repr., Darmstadt: Wissenschaftliche Buchgesellschaft, 1963), p. 289. G. Schneider, *Parusiegleichnisse im Lukas-Evangelium* (SBS, 74; Stuttgart: KBW Verlag, 1975), pp. 75–78, regards v. 8b as the work of Luke himself.

6. Jülicher, *Gleichnisreden II* (5), pp. 283–84, 288–89. It is striking to note how many scholars find it necessary to emphasize that the continuity *genuinely* exists and that the indication of the theme of the parable is *in fact* accurate; see e.g. A. J. Hultgren, *The Parables of Jesus: A Commentary* (Grand Rapids: Eerdmans, 2002), p. 258: 'But the parable is surely one about prayer.'

7. R. Bultmann, *Die Geschichte der synoptischen Tradition* (FRLANT, 29; Göttingen: Vandenhoeck & Ruprecht, 9th edn, 1979), p. 216. Unlike other scholars, however, Bultmann leaves open the question of what the 'special point' of the original parable was.

8. W. R. Herzog II, *Parables as Subversive Speech: Jesus as Pedagogue of the Oppressed* (Louisville: Westminster John Knox, 1989), p. 220.

beginning of the secondary interpretations at the start of the interpretation of the parable in v. 6;[9] others have perceived the boundary separating the original version and the proto-Lukan interpretation within the interpretation itself,[10] and have attempted to show that vv. 2–8 as a whole form a unit which may go back to Jesus himself.[11] Accordingly, we find several variants of this interpretative model. For example, Jülicher holds that the original parable of Jesus (vv. 2–5), just like the parable of the friend who presents his request at night (Lk. 11.5–8), merely intended to portray 'the certainty that unceasing prayer will finally be heard'.[12] In vv. 6–8a, the oppressed early community applies the figure of the widow and her petition for justice by analogy to its own ceaseless cry for redemption and to its hope for retaliation at the final judgment.[13] Other authors, who believe that at least vv. 6–7a go back to Jesus, see the widow's petition as expressing prayer for the coming of the rule of God or of the last judgment, and they interpret the parable in the framework of Jesus' expectation of the imminent eschaton.[14]

However, all these interpretations prompt the question whether they are inexcusably importing interpretative elements of the possibly secondary framework into the parable itself. Can we truly be certain that this *is* a parable about praying and having one's prayers answered, and that we are

9. Many have followed Jülicher, *Gleichnisreden II* (5), pp. 284–89, and Bultmann, *Geschichte* (7), p. 189: e.g. H. Paulsen, 'Die Witwe und der Richter (Lk. 18,1–8)', *TGl* 74 (1984), pp. 13–39; Bovon, 'Apocalyptic Traditions', pp. 383–91; B. Heininger, *Metaphorik, Erzählstruktur und szenisch-dramatische Gestaltung in den Sondergutgleichnissen bei Lukas* (NTAbh, 24; Münster: Aschendorff, 1991), p. 200.

10. Here I mention only three of the most important interpretative models, which are exemplified in the following reconstructions: (a) Lk. 18.2–6 original, vv. 7–8 secondary: J. A. Fitzmyer, *The Gospel According to Luke X–XXIV* (AB, 28A; Garden City: Doubleday, 1985), p. 1176; J. R. Donahue, *The Gospel in Parable: Metaphor, Narrative and Theology in the Synoptic Gospels* (Philadelphia: Fortress, 1988), p. 181; (b) Lk. 18.2–7a goes back to Jesus, and vv. 7 (last four words)–8a are pre-Lukan: H. Weder, *Die Gleichnisse Jesu als Metaphern: Traditions- und Redaktionsgeschichtliche Analysen und Interpretationen* (FRLANT, 120; Göttingen: Vandenhoeck & Ruprecht, 1978), p. 269; (c) Lk. 18.2–7 are a Jewish parable, vv. 1, 8 are Lukan redaction: W. Ott, *Gebet und Heil: Die Bedeutung der Gebetsparänese in der lukanischen Theologie* (SANT, 12; Munich: Kösel Verlag, 1965), pp. 32–72.

11. Delling, 'Gleichnis' (4), pp. 1–25; K. E. Bailey, *Poet & Peasant* and *Through Peasant Eyes: A Literary-Cultural Approach to the Parables of Luke* (Combined Edition; Grand Rapids: Eerdmans, 1983), pp. 127–41.

12. Jülicher, *Gleichnisreden II* (5), pp. 288–89.

13. Jülicher, *Gleichnisreden II* (5), pp. 284–85.

14. We find a relatively strong divergence on individual points among these interpreters. While Weder (*Gleichnisse* (10), p. 272) holds that the parable is '*an event of the closeness* of the rule of God, since it assures the hearer of the certainty that his prayer for its coming will be heard', J. Jeremias (*Die Gleichnisse Jesu* [Göttingen: Vandenhoeck & Ruprecht, 10th edn, 1984], p. 156) holds that Jesus wanted to comfort the disciples in face of the time of distress and of the concomitant terrors which he has announced.

meant to see an analogy (on the basis of a conclusion *a minore ad maius*) between the judge and God? The obvious incoherences between the core of the parable (vv. 2–5) and the framing verses 1, 6–8[15] have led many to doubt both these claims. If, however, one's analysis begins (like that of most of the authors who will be discussed here) with vv. 2–5 alone, it appears that the large number of competing interpretations indicates the basic problem: that the contextless parable on its own does not force the reader to interpret it in any one particular way.

Several scholars interpret it as a parable of the kingdom of God, which says something not about the certainty of its coming, but about the nature of the *basileia*. The starting point of this interpretation is the successful action of the widow, who induces the judge to yield to her demands: her petition for justice is ultimately heard (ἐκδικήσω αὐτήν, v. 5, takes up ἐκδίκησον με from v. 2). The concluding evaluation by J. R. Donahue is typical of this type of interpretation: 'The hearers are confronted with a new vision of reality, inaugurated by God's reign, where victims will claim their rights and seek justice – often in an unsettling manner.'[16] B. B. Scott sees in the widow 'the outsider' who is 'the bearer for the kingdom. A hearer of the parable discovers the kingdom under the guise not of a just judge but of a pestering widow who exposes her own shamelessness in continually pressing her cause on a dishonorable judge.'[17]

The expositions of W. Bindemann and W. R. Herzog II propose related interpretations. Both scholars explicitly refuse to see in the judge a metaphor for God, and identify the specific theme of the parable as the application of Torah in a manner consonant with God. On points of detail, however, they take a very different line, since Bindemann regards v. 6 as an appeal which belonged to the original parable and sees in the judge the protagonist of the parable, who invites the hearer to identify with him; Herzog, on the other hand, makes his evaluation on the basis of vv. 2–5 alone and sees the widow as the heroine of the parable.

According to Bindemann, this parable was addressed to the scribes who were hostile to Jesus. Their self-understanding was fundamentally different from that of the unjust judge; confronted by the change in the judge's behaviour, they were meant to question their own interpretation of Torah in favour of the privileged. Verse 6 was an invitation to them to change their ways and adopt a legal praxis orientated to the liberation of

15. S. Curkpatrick, 'Dissonance in Luke 18.1-8', *JBL* 121 (2002), pp. 107–21, and *idem*, 'A Parable Frame-Up and Its Audacious Reframing', *NTS* 48 (2003), pp. 22–38, has pointed out these incoherences in a particularly insistent and convincing manner.

16. Donahue, *Gospel* (10), p. 184.

17. B. B. Scott, *Hear Then the Parable: A Commentary on the Parables of Jesus* (Minneapolis: Fortress, 2nd printing, 1990), p. 187.

the weak and the oppressed.[18] I believe that one can make three main critical objections to this exposition. Naturally, the identification of the first persons to be addressed by the parable as enemies of Jesus remains hypothetical. The textual evidence adduced in support of this identification, v. 6 ('hear what the unjust judge says!'), must be suspected of being a part of the secondary interpretation, since it seems to prepare the way for the conclusion *a minore ad maius* which begins in v. 7, and since 'the reference ὁ κύριος cannot possibly be present in an authentic logion of Jesus'.[19] It is also doubtful whether the Pharisees and scribes would have found the act of identification and transference which Bindemann supposes an obvious reaction to the parable. If he is correct to hold that their self-understanding was diametrically opposed to that of the unjust judge, they would scarcely have had sufficient self-knowledge to grasp that their exposition of Torah was at the service of the privileged, and that this parable was challenging them to 'give space to God's righteousness rather than to their own legalism'.[20]

Taken as a whole, the interpretation by Herzog is more plausible. His starting point is an insight, derived from G. Lenski, into how the law functions in agrarian societies. The nominally independent judges, whose only obligation is in regard to the divine law, are *de facto*, as so-called 'retainers', dependent on the ruling elite, and tend therefore to assimilate their legal verdicts to the interests of this elite, thereby bestowing an appearance of legitimacy on structures which are in reality based on naked power. Such judges supply the fiction that the unjust structures are based on impartial law. This is why the situation of the widow in the parable is really hopeless:

> In her appeal to the judge, 'Grant me justice against my opponent', the widow appeals to the Torah as an ideal code of justice. In his failure to respond to her, the judge acts out of the Torah used as a system of expediency designed to protect the wealthy and their interest and to reward him for doing his job. If everything proceeds according to schedule, the judge will do business as usual and strike a deal with the adversary.[21]

---

18. W. Bindemann, 'Ungerechte als Vorbilder? Gottesreich und Gottesrecht in den Gleichnissen vom "ungerechten Verwalter" und "ungerechten Richter"', *TLZ* 120 (1995), pp. 955–70 (958–61, 966–68).

19. Heininger, *Metaphorik* (9), p. 200.

20. Bindemann, 'Ungerechte' (18), p. 961. The plausibility of this interpretation depends entirely on a legalistic perception of the piety of the Pharisees. This does not correspond to the Pharisees' own self-understanding, nor does it give an adequate account of the historical reality.

21. Herzog, *Parables*, p. 228.

Despite this, the widow persists in publicly demanding justice, and succeeds in this one limited case in disturbing so profoundly a system which is based (and continually dependent) on the victims' silence and acceptance of what is done to them, that for once in a way justice wins through. Herzog and some other recent interpreters[22] see the widow not as a model of persistent humble prayer, but as the embodiment of successful action taken on behalf of the divine justice. But here we must point out that the figure of the judge in the parable is not strong enough to symbolize God as the guarantor of justice vis-à-vis the widow, as is presupposed in vv. 7–8a.

This brief overview of highlights in contemporary research indicates some consequences and guidelines for further work.

First, it cannot be presupposed that the assumed pre-Lukan unit Lk. 18.2–8a is a text originally conceived as a whole, nor that the interpretative logia which have been attached to the narrative of the parable appropriately communicate the intention of the parable itself, or are a thematic development of the parable. Methodological considerations make it therefore absolutely necessary to begin the interpretation with the core of the parable (Lk. 18.2–5), without rushing to apply to the parable the interpretative elements in the framing verses. In the evaluation of the parable proper, the following questions must be studied:

Second, is the judge a provocative image for God, in the sense that the conclusion *a minore ad maius* has a basis in the parable itself, and that the interpretation in v. 7a is therefore consistent with the parable? We are often told that 'it was characteristic of the historical Jesus ... to do something almost intolerable, namely to let an unjust judge be a metaphor for God';[23] but is this really true?

Third, is the widow a model of persevering prayer, so that the interpretation of the evangelist in v. 1 is consistent with the parable? Or are those interpreters correct who take their starting point in the contents of the widow's plea (ἐκδίκησόν με ἀπὸ τοῦ ἀντιδίκου μου), her active commitment, and the fact that ultimately, against all expectations, justice is done? This question obliges us to investigate thoroughly the societal reality reflected in the parable, and the culturally conditioned expectations and evaluations which contemporary hearers would necessarily have brought to their understanding of the situation described at the beginning of the parable.

Fourth, the coexistence of strongly divergent interpretations of the parable shows that the point of dispute in this case is not so much the

---

22. W. Cotter, CSJ, 'The Parable of the Feisty Widow and the Threatened Judge (Luke 18.1–8)', *NTS* 51 (2005), pp. 328–43; Curkpatrick, 'Dissonance' (15), pp. 107–21, and *idem*, 'Parable Frame-Up' (15), pp. 22–38; Heininger, *Metaphorik* (9), pp. 205–06.

23. Weder, *Gleichnisse*, p. 272 n. 150.

historicity of Jesus' parable, but rather (a) the question of the meaning (and the extent) of the original parable and, (b) the question whether the early Christian interpretations of the parable went in a completely new direction, or were in continuity with the original intention of the story.

Fifth, our working hypothesis, which this essay will examine, is that at least Lk. 18.2–5 is a parable that goes back to Jesus.[24] We must investigate the most plausible meaning of the parable in the framework of a proclamation by Jesus addressed to Palestinian Jews (*contextual plausibility*), and how it is possible to understand historically the genesis of the tradition as a whole, in its contradictory unity, on the basis of the original parable (*plausibility of effects*).[25] Both these questions assume a relationship of tension between continuity and discontinuity. When we attempt to locate a Jesus tradition plausibly in its historical context, we are looking for the individuality of Jesus in the Jewish context which must be presupposed as the framework within which we are to understand the text; this is why *contextual appropriateness* and *contextual distinctiveness* are complementary subcriteria. Similarly, when we attempt to understand an early Christian unit of tradition as reflecting the impact made by the historical Jesus, two complementary aspects must be borne in mind: (a) Can we argue plausibly on the basis of *source coherence*, i.e. the agreements with related traditions about Jesus, that a unit goes back to Jesus? (b) Sometimes, however, a tradition should be considered authentic precisely because it proves especially awkward in relation to dominant early Christian interpretative tendencies (the so-called *tendential recalcitrance*),[26] and is thus in tension with other traditions or the interpretative

24. Only a few scholars dispute that this parable goes back to Jesus. In addition to Freed. 'Parable' (4), whose attempt to use linguistic characteristics to demonstrate that the entire parable is Lukan is scarcely convincing (since linguistic shaping by the evangelist does not preclude his adoption of tradition), cf. above all E. Linnemann, *Gleichnisse Jesu* (Göttingen: Vandenhoeck & Ruprecht, 3rd edn, 1964), pp. 127–28, 185–86. Her arguments do not hold water, since they are based primarily on the (surely correct) judgment that vv. 6–8 are inauthentic. She argues that since the parable would remain incomprehensible without an application, the entire tradition of this parable must be secondary. This is not in the least convincing; it is possible that Jesus' own interpretation or the insertion in a context which supplies an interpretation may have been lost. Curkpatrick, 'Dissonance' (15), p. 121 (see also p. 108), asserts: 'the parable (vv. 2–5) may have been produced in the same community as the Gospel', but he does not specify any evidence that would make this supposition more plausible than that of the adoption of a parable with an older tradition history (and in the latter case, the origin in Jesus himself is the most obvious starting hypothesis).

25. On these criteria and their subcriteria, cf. G. Theissen, D. Winter, *Die Kriterienfrage in der Jesusforschung: Vom Differenzkriterium zum Plausibilitätskriterium* (NTOA, 34; Göttingen: Vandenhoeck & Ruprecht, 1997), pp. 175–217; English translation: *The Quest for the Plausible Jesus: The Question of Criteria* (trans. M. E. Boring; Louisville: Westminster John Knox, 2002), pp. 172–210.

26. This criterion is sometimes also called 'criterion of embarrassment' or 'preservation against the grain'.

co-text. Ideally, it is possible to combine our observations about source coherence and tendential opposition to form a total picture which is historically plausible.

In the case of Lk. 18.2–5, as my overview of contemporary research has indicated, scholars discuss intensively the question of the continuity between Jesus' parable and early Christian interpretations, and offer extremely different answers. Much less attention has been paid to the evaluation of a question which is at least of equal importance for the evaluation of a tradition about the historical Jesus: how is this parable embedded in Jewish narrative and interpretative traditions; and what special emphasis does Jesus posit within these Jewish traditions? Accordingly, the following investigation will begin with this aspect.

2. *The Parable in the Context of Contemporary Judaism: The Interaction between Narrative Logic, Everyday Experience and the Biblical Interpretative Framework*

If we are to interpret the parable in its historical context, we must pay heed to a number of dimensions which supplied its original hearers with clues to its interpretation. First of all, we have the narrative logic of the parable itself, which develops step by step; we can call this the *co-textual* dimension. The constellation of the persons and their characterization by the narrator awaken in the intended readers expectations which will be either confirmed or disappointed by the subsequent course of the action. The associations and expectations linked to the individual narrative elements depend on two overlapping interpretative contexts: the cultural environment, which structures the everyday experience of the hearers (the *contextual* dimension), and the traditional interpretation of this everyday experience by Scripture, which constitutes the omnipresent interpretative and legitimating background for Jesus and his contemporaries (the *intertextual* dimension). I hope to show in this chapter that an exact analysis of the interplay of co-, con- and intertextual dimensions definitively demonstrates the inadequacy of a number of interpretations of the parable which have been proposed by scholars.

The narrative of the parable has a simple structure: vv. 2–4a describe a conflict between a judge and a widow who for a long time asks him in vain for help. These verses build up a tension, while vv. 4b–5 relate how the problem is resolved. Clearly, this structure of the parable intends to involve the readers in the problem described, and thereby encourage them to imagine for themselves how the parable will end, before they are confronted with the outcome of the case which the narrator of the parable himself has invented. The parable itself therefore seems to demand that our interpretative approach begin by linking the narrative constellation in the first half with the interpretative impulses which may be expected from everyday experience and from Scripture. In a second step, this reconstructed horizon of expectation on the part of the first readers will be confronted with the end of the narrative and with the contextual and intertextual interpretative impulses which are evoked by this end.

2.1. *The Constellation of the Figures and the Development of the Conflict in the Light of Everyday Experience and of the Dominant Biblical Tradition about Widows (vv. 2–4a)*

> In a certain city there was a judge who neither feared God nor had respect for people. In that city there was a widow who kept coming to him[27] and saying, 'Grant me justice[28] against my opponent.' For a while he refused.[29]

This is indisputably a parable with two antagonistic main characters, the judge and the widow. But the customary interpretations have not taken sufficient account of the presence of minor characters, and of the fact that God is a minor character in this parable (he is mentioned in the description of the judge in vv. 2 and 4, and he is implicitly present in the widow's demand for justice).[30] This poses a problem for the usual thesis that the judge is a provocative metaphor for God; but it seems that the proponents of this interpretation do not recognize the problem, still less discuss it. Both the judge and the widow are defined by means of their relationship to other persons who play (or could play) an actual or potential role in the conflict described. In addition to the judge and the widow, the tableau of characters whose action or conviction may be decisive for the outcome of the conflict comprises God, 'people' and the opponent, i.e. the potential adversary of the widow in a lawsuit.

Scholars recognize in principle that this parable has recourse in a large measure to everyday experience, and that knowledge of the biblical

---

27. As is generally recognized, ἤρχετο in v. 3 is an iterative imperfect.

28. ἐκδικεῖν has the double meaning of 'winning justice' (often with the accusative of the person, especially in the papyri which deal with legal matters) and 'taking vengeance' (especially in the LXX); cf. G. Schrenk, 'ἐκδικέω κτλ.', *TWNT* 2, pp. 440–44 (440–42). It is not acceptable to make the meaning in v. 3 dependent on the expression ποιεῖν τὴν ἐκδίκησιν in vv. 7–8, which envisages retribution when God acts at the final judgment. Delling, 'Gleichnis' (4), pp. 8–11, holds that the idea of satisfaction is in the foreground, but none of the texts from the LXX and Josephus which he adduces in evidence belongs to the context of earthly legal cases. This is why we must reverse his ranking on p. 11: naturally, the idea of the re-establishment of justice before a court can be linked with the idea of satisfaction, but the achieving of satisfaction is seldom the primary motivating force of a lawsuit.

29. Lk. 18.2–4a.

30. It is above all in Luke that we find God, or dwellers in the heavenly world as God's representatives, as characters in parables: Lk. 12.20; 15.7, 10, 18, 21; 16.22–31; 18.11, 13.

traditions about widows and their position in Israel is necessary if one is to understand it; but they usually fail to draw the correct inferences from this. Let us then ask what evaluations and interpretations contemporary hearers brought to the conflict described in the parable. What did they think would happen next in the narrative, on the basis of their everyday experience and of the dominant interpretative traditions?

Although Jesus is describing a fictitious case, which need not be true to reality in every detail,[31] his hearers could certainly recognize a familiar situation and fill in the considerable gaps in the picture which he briefly sketches. Since the widow appears on her own, the hearers or readers will have inferred that she was completely alone, without any male relatives to give her help and support,[32] and that she was being wronged. The parable is not interested in giving a more detailed account of the lawsuit; and this shows that we have here a typical situation, something that frequently occurred in everyday life and is presupposed in the biblical tradition almost in a stereotypical manner. In the Old Testament, widows, along with orphans and foreigners, are the classic examples of persons in need of being protected. They are very often afflicted by poverty, and since they do not possess full legal rights, they are continually at risk of being robbed of even the minimal rights they do possess.[33] If the contemporary hearers did imagine a concrete case when they heard the description of the conflict, it would probably have been the situation where a widow is denied her share in the inheritance of her husband by one of those who benefit from his will. In the context of the narrative constellation and above all of the traditional associations with the idea of a 'widow', they must suppose that this is a life-threatening situation for her. Since the opponent disregards the widow's claims, the only way for her to obtain

---

31. Doubts about whether the parable is true to life have been prompted above all by the fact that only one judge seems to be responsible for the case. This is probably due, not so much to the assumed object of the lawsuit, as to an increasing discrepancy between the legal ideal and the number of men who were sufficiently educated to take on the position of a judge de facto. Cf. Herzog, *Parables* (8), pp. 222–24.

32. This is correctly observed *inter alia* by Herzog, *Parables* (8), p. 228. Cotter, 'Parable' (22), pp. 332–35, refers to a Roman literary polemic by Valerius Maximus against women who presented their own case or represented their clients before a court. For relevant rabbinic texts, cf. Bailey, *Peasant Eyes* (11), pp. 134–35.

33. On the social and legal situation of widows in Jewish society in the period of the Old and New Testaments, cf. W. Schottroff, 'Die Armut der Witwen', in W. Schottroff, *Gerechtigkeit lernen: Beiträge zur biblischen Sozialgeschichte* (eds. F. Crüsemann, R. Kessler with L. Schottroff; TBü, 94; Gütersloh: Chr. Kaiser/Gütersloher Verlagshaus, 1999), pp. 134–64; S. Safrai, 'The Temple', in S. Safrai, M. Stern (eds.), *The Jewish People in the First Century* (CRINT, 1.2; Assen: Van Gorcum, 1976), pp. 865–907 (887–91).

her rights is by going to law – but the judge steadily ignores her.[34] Both daily experience and acquaintance with Scripture suggest that this is either because of manifest bribery,[35] or because the judge hopes to profit in some unspecified way from the societal interplay between the propertied elite and the class of retainers who were dependent upon them.[36] In her struggle against this alliance, whose only interest is to retain power and accumulate profits, the powerless and impoverished widow has only one ally: the God of Israel with his Torah, which aims at protecting the rights of widows. In her repeated cry, 'grant me justice against my opponent!', every hearer who had even a rudimentary knowledge of the biblical tradition would recognize the allusion to the biblical law which prohibits the oppression of foreigners, widows and orphans, and the appeal to the judge (who was placed in office in order to maintain this law) to behave in keeping with the demands made by Torah. These demands are formulated with especial clarity in the story of the appointment of judges by King Jehoshaphat in 2 Chron. 19.4–6:

> He appointed judges in the land in all the fortified cities of Judah, city by city, and said to the judges, 'Consider what you are doing, for you judge not on behalf of human beings but on the Lord's behalf; he is with you in giving judgment. Now, let the fear of the Lord be upon you; take care what you do, for there is no perversion of justice with the Lord our God, or partiality, or taking of bribes.'

It is worth pausing to reflect on the character of this and the numerous other biblical texts about the rights of widows, orphans and foreigners, and the obligations of judges and all others who held privileged positions in regard to these persons.[37] The sheer number of these texts shows that they were reacting to widespread abuses. When the judges fail to do their duty, appeal is made to God as 'judge of the widows' (Ps. 68.6, see also

34. Two legal scenarios are possible here: either a verdict has already been pronounced which went against the widow, and she is seeking a revision; or else the judge refuses to let her case be heard in court, thus making it impossible for her to assert her claims. Cotter, 'Parable' (22), pp. 335–36, argues convincingly in favour of the second scenario.

35. The Old Testament mentions with striking frequency the partiality of judges to taking a bribe, and the practice of bribery in legal cases (Exod. 23.6–8; 2 Chron. 19.4–6; Amos 2.6–7; 5.10–13). Corrupt judges are a prominent theme in rabbinic literature too (cf. Bailey, *Peasant Eyes* (11), p. 131).

36. Herzog, *Parables* (8), pp. 224–30, on the basis of Lenski's classic work. The same conclusions are reached by Cotter, 'Parable' (22), pp. 332, 336–38, on the basis of J. Harris, *Law and Empire in Late Antiquity* (Cambridge: Cambridge University Press, 1999), and D. W. Hobson, 'The Impact of Law on Village Life in Roman Egypt', in B. Halpern, D. W. Hobson (eds.), *Law, Politics and Society in the Ancient Mediterranean World* (Sheffield: Sheffield University Press, 1993), pp. 193–219.

37. See *inter alia* Deut. 10.17–19; 14.28–29; 24.17–22; 26.12–13; 27.19; Isa. 1.23; 10.1–2; Ezek. 22.7; Zech. 7.10.

146.9). When the Israelites forget what their experience of the Exodus demands of them, God threatens to intervene and to punish their injustice:

> You shall not wrong or oppress a resident alien, for you were aliens in the land of Egypt. You shall not abuse any widow or orphan. If you do abuse them, when they cry out to me, I will surely heed their cry; my wrath will burn, and I will kill you with the sword, and your wives shall become widows and your children orphans.[38]

God's authority, the appeal to his particular concern for the widows and other underprivileged groups and the threat of divine retribution are actively proclaimed in view of what was clearly a regular failure on the part of those charged with responsibility for enforcing the law. W. Schottroff is right to say that, given the societal reality, these texts 'to a large extent have merely an ideological function':[39] the chronic misery of the widows and orphans reveals the weakness of a legal system based on patriarchal and feudalistic structures in which widows (and women as a whole) had only a limited ability to take legal action. The same weakness can be seen in the fact that in all these texts, widows and orphans, foreigners and poor persons are perceived exclusively as objects of other people's behaviour. They are either *victims* of the powerful and the rich (who act against their interests), or else *objects of care* on the part of the judges and prophets, or of God himself (who acts in support of their interests). When the parable is read against this interpretative background, it initially prompts a perception of reality which leads to despair, since it describes a world in which the ostentatiously godless judges are more clearly in evidence than the God in whose name they are supposed to pronounce judgment. The hearers know from their everyday experience and from Scripture that a widow may indeed have God's law on her side, but that she is helpless if a judge refuses to grant her rights. By means of his characterization of the judge, the narrator of the parable suggests to the hearers that they should feel antipathy towards him; but the description of the widow (read in the context of what the biblical tradition has to say about widows) prompts them to sympathize with her or even, if their own experiences have been similar, to identify with her hopeless situation. In view of the strongly typical character of this parable, we are certainly justified in asking whether a collective perception may also be intended. Traditionally, the widow embodies Israel, especially in situations of national crisis (Isa. 54.4; Lam. 1.1; 5.3–4).[40] The parable can be understood either individually or collectively. It offers an accurate

---

38.   Exod. 22.21–24.

39.   W. Schottroff, 'Armut' (33), p. 153.

40.   Cf. G. Stählin, 'Das Bild der Witwe: Ein Beitrag zur Bildersprache der Bibel und zum Phänomen der Personifikation in der Antike', *JAC* 17 (1974), pp. 5–20 (8–10).

description of the distress suffered by many widows in Israel; but thanks to the typical character of the persons in the story and to its system of reference, the parable can also be read as a general verdict on the crisis in Jewish society and in its theonomous legal system: in the day-to-day business of the courts, God's law is trampled under foot by judges who neither feel reverence for God nor take human considerations into account. The victims of this crisis are those without power and possessions. Their only hope is to appeal to God's law, but they are ignored – both by the judges and by the God to whom they make appeal. In view of this interpretative framework of Jesus' hearers, based on their daily experience and on Scripture, what would be their expectations about the outcome of the conflict which the parable describes? It is important to ask this question, if we are to evaluate correctly the unexpected conclusion which Jesus chooses for his parable. First, we must ask: do they expect a happy or a sad ending? The hearers will be torn between the two possibilities, hoping for a happy ending despite their everyday experience, which saw the only plausible outcome as the defeat of the widow. B. B. Scott has drawn attention to a rabbinic parable which at first sight appears to display exactly this narrative structure:

> There was once a poor woman who dwelt in the neighborhood of a landowner. Her two sons went out to gather gleanings, but the landowner did not let them take any. Their mother kept saying: 'When will my sons come back from the field; perhaps I shall find that they have brought something to eat.' And they kept saying: 'When shall we go back to our mother; perhaps we shall discover that she has found something to eat.' She found that they had nothing and they found that she had nothing to eat. So they laid their heads on their mother's lap and the three of them died in one day.

This, however, is not the last word in the parable. God, the 'judge of the widows', intervenes, in keeping with the biblical tradition, and announces the re-establishment of his legal order:

> Said the Holy One, blessed be He: 'Their very existence you take away from them! By your life! I shall make you, too, pay for it with your very existence!' And so indeed it says, 'Rob not the weak, because he is weak, neither crush the poor in the gate; for the Lord will plead their cause, and despoil of life those that despoil them (Prov. 22.22–23).'[41]

The tragic end of the rabbinic story is thus a shocking element which slows down the narrative. Initially, it agrees with everyday experience, but

---

41. *Fathers according to Rabbi Nathan* 8, cited from J. Goldin, *The Fathers according to Rabbi Nathan* (Yale Judaica Series; New Haven: Yale University Press, 1955), p. 158. This parable is cited by Scott, *Parable* (17), p. 182, to illustrate 'the potentially tragic undertow of the theme'.

not at the price of completely disavowing God as the guarantor of the legal order. There will be a 'happy end', thanks to the punishment of the hard-hearted rich; the narrative can leave open the question whether this happens here on earth or at the last judgment, since its aim is naturally to bring the hearers to a change of heart and to motivate them to practise merciful conduct, in keeping with Torah, in their daily lives. Such conduct brings to a happy ending the story of the widows and orphans, a story which is ancient but ever new.

Let us return to Jesus' parable. The hearers expect that he will achieve a happy ending to his narrative, and there are two main obvious possibilities: either the punishment of the judge by divine retribution (just as God tells the rich fool in another parable that he will die; Lk. 12.20) or else the conversion of the judge to a conduct in keeping with Torah. Both these are morally satisfactory means of bringing the story to a happy conclusion, and the tradition could have led the hearers to expect them; but both would have the disadvantage of not being particularly true to life, and would therefore be out of place in the narrative, since the first part of the parable paints a pitiless picture of a godless reality in flagrant contradiction of the justice which God wants. The question which would have excited the contemporary hearers, in view of the conflict described here between the godless judge and the powerless widow, would therefore have been: Can Jesus succeed in discovering in his parable a genuinely plausible solution to the urgent problem of the widow (who is a figure with whom all those at a disadvantage under the *status quo* can identify)?

2.2. *The Solution to the Conflict in the Light of Everyday Experience and of the Biblical Narrative Tradition about Widows who Secured their Rights (vv. 4b–5)*

In his parable, Jesus the narrator has skilfully sharpened the conflict between a godless custodian of the law and a powerless victim of his legal practices. She appeals to the divine legal ordering which is indeed in force but *de facto* is denied, but her appeal goes unheard. In view of the acute and fundamental quality of this conflict, the solution presented in the soliloquy of the judge may at first sight seem trivial and disappointing. His reflections are egotistical and concern only this one case. The description presented earlier in the author's voice is repeated in v. 4b as a statement made by the judge about himself; this shows that the judge has not changed his attitude in the slightest. And yet he will help the widow get her rights. An astonishing explanation is offered: she is making his life a misery, and he wants to prevent her from coming one day and striking him on the face (v. 5). We shall now examine the dynamics of the narrative in the light of daily experience and of the biblical tradition about widows.

First, we must note that the solution presented in the narrative, namely the inconsistent treatment by the judge of the individual case described in the parable, is true to life. Although some scholars disagree,[42] we must maintain that in an analogous case it could certainly have been in accordance with the correctly calculated interest of the judge to satisfy *one* importunate petitioner. It can certainly lie in the interests of a corrupt legal system to preserve the outward appearances of the law in exceptional instances which attract a special degree of attention; this lends the system an added legitimation.[43] Besides this, it is clearly important for the narrator to emphasize that God and his legal order play no motivating role in the judge's revision of his earlier decision. We cannot assume either a fresh insight or a fear of punishment. The judge is and remains an unrighteous judge, even when he resolves in this individual case to help right prevail. On his side, this is sheer opportunism – the judge is not an advocate of God's legal order. This points the hearer all the more unambiguously to the widow, since it is in her *de facto* (τὸ παρέχειν μοι κόπον) and anticipated conduct (ἵνα μὴ εἰς τέλος ἐρχομένη ὑποπιάζῃ με) that we find the only reason for the judge's change of attitude. As her words show, the widow is motivated by God's legal ordering, and she behaves as if this ordering were not called into question by the conduct of the judge. She does not despair; nor does she have recourse to bribery or other potential means of influencing the judge. Her repeated request – ἐκδίκησόν με ἀπὸ τοῦ ἀντιδίκου μου – is a permanent reminder to the judge of the task which he has received from God. From a formal point of view, she remains in the role of petitioner, but her words do not emphasize the relational aspect. Rather, her words concentrate exclusively on her legal claim, which the judge's office obliges him to grant her.[44] Finally, we must underline the destruction in vv. 4b–5 of the image of the powerful judge and the powerless widow. His words reveal the judge's weakness. He simply lacks the nerve to keep up his godless conduct in this case. She is pestering him and he is afraid that her importunate activities might become even more intense.[45] Because he wants to get rid of her and her

42. For example, W. Harnisch, 'Die Ironie als Stilmittel in Gleichnissen Jesu', *EvT* 32 (1972), pp. 421–36, writes on p. 433 n. 67: 'In reality, a judge of this kind would naturally not have yielded' (cf. also p. 431); Paulsen, 'Witwe' (9), p. 23, agrees.

43. Herzog, *Parables* (8), p. 231.

44. Cotter, 'Parable' (22), pp. 335–36, shows that in legal papyri submissions made by widows to judges are all characterized by polite forms of address and sometimes by an extreme emphasis on the widow's own helplessness. It is at any rate striking that the widow in Luke 18 does not even give the judge the title κύριε, even if one cannot expect a parable to employ language that is formally and legally correct.

45. On the problems of the interpretation of ὑποπιάζω, cf. Cotter, 'Parable' (22), pp. 338–42. The literal meaning, 'to give someone a black eye', certainly seems a possibility, when we bear in mind that this is the worst thing the judge thinks he risks, and that the persistent behaviour of the widow throughout the narrative underscores her combative character.

constant admonitions, he gives in. The text makes it perfectly plain that the widow has successfully understood how to employ a mode of conduct that makes her a visible and highly unpleasant part of the judge's life. The parable does not stop to tell us in detail how she did this, but she must at any rate have arranged meetings and sought out situations in which she could confront the judge. This implies many individual actions which go far beyond the rules of social conduct which were applied to a widow who lived on her own.[46] Many interpretations of the parable ignore this decisive point, which is drawn from an analysis of the dominant culture, and especially of the rules governing the relationship between the sexes and behaviour towards those of higher rank in society.[47] Nothing could be more wrong than to interpret the appearances of the widow with her annoying demands, which refused to be silenced, as the expression of her acceptance of her powerless situation, as the only thing left for her to do, as the absence of all activity. *This* widow does not lie down hopelessly in the dust to die. Nor does she weep in secret, in the hope of inducing God, the 'judge of the widows', to intervene (Ps. 68.6; Sir. 35.14–15). A widow who lived alone was meant to lead a life of great reserve; ideally, she ought to be silent and invisible in public, especially vis-à-vis men who were not her own relatives. Since she had not studied the law, her role was to submit without a protest to the decisions taken by the judge, who had studied the law and enjoyed official authority. But *this* widow continually transgresses all these restrictive codes of conduct. She makes herself permanently visible, and in a culture which was obsessed with honour and shame, this made her *shameless*, as a number of scholars have shown. But this is not all: her quasi-prophetic insistence on her right, which God has guaranteed, is also outrageous and presumptuous in the eyes of the legal elite, since it implies a massive criticism of the verdicts they have issued. Nevertheless, as a 'defenceless woman' she is protected in public against physical violence on the part of the dominant men and their police. She can go much further in the vehemence of her public appearances than a male petitioner – she can even allow herself to launch a physical assault in

---

46. This has often been pointed out. Cf. e.g. Herzog, *Parables* (8), pp. 229–31; L. Schottroff, *Lydias ungeduldige Schwestern: Feministische Sozialgeschichte des frühen Christentums* (Gütersloh: Kaiser/Gütersloher Verlagshaus, 1994), pp. 155–58, 176–79; Cotter, 'Parable' (22), pp. 338–43; Curkpatrick, 'Parable Frame-Up' (15), pp. 29–33.

47. Ignorance of the culturally conditioned regulations of acceptable behaviour sometimes leads to seriously wrong interpretations, e.g. the claim by Weder – the fruit of Protestant dogmatics rather than of an appropriate historical evaluation – that the parable is concerned with the contrast between an attitude which trusts in petition (i.e. the *word*) alone, and the endeavour to get what one wants by means of one's own *works*; the latter attitude is to be rejected. Cf. Weder, *Gleichnisse* (10), pp. 271, 273.

public, as the judge fears.[48] The widow exploits in a cool calculation the freedom of movement which she is permitted by the symbolic ordering of the sexes precisely at the point where it was intended to limit this freedom. Psychologically, it is very easy to understand the unease provoked in the judge by a woman who plays in this way with the traditional rules. When we see her in the original cultural context, the widow whom Jesus portrays is not in the least a model for those sufferers 'who must endure in powerlessness the lack of justice'.[49] On the contrary, she is portrayed as a powerless person who does not accept her role. She is empowered by the knowledge that she has God's law on her side, and she pesters a powerful man who is apparently inviolable and untouchable, until her shameless conduct brings him to his knees. Before we discuss the difficult question of the theological relevance of the parable, we must first evaluate it against the background of the biblical traditions about widows.

In his description of the conflict (vv. 2–4a), Jesus evokes very clearly the traditions about God's especial care for the widows and the poor, and he presupposes both the validity of these traditions and the awareness that precisely this aspect of Torah is trampled underfoot by the violence meted out to widows every day. However, the solution which he relates shows that he does not share the optimism of the biblical authors, who hold that repeated appeals to those in positions of responsibility, and especially to the judges' independence and their particular obligation to take care of the weak, will ensure that the widows get their rights. Jesus' judge remains an incorrigible egotist, a partisan of the mighty, a man who despises both God and other people. Unlike the interpretation in vv. 7–8, the parable shows not the slightest trace of an attempt to defuse the dilemma by an appeal to God's avenging power (whether thought of as acting within history or as eschatological). And the absence of any such appeal must be seen as a conscious decision on the part of Jesus, precisely because the hearers could have expected it, given the Old Testament background sketched above. In the parable, the widow's existential problem is resolved only by the activity of the widow herself. The judge is induced to yield by the tiresome presence of the woman, an activist in her own cause who extends the borders of propriety and of acceptable conduct. The petition which she so tirelessly presents necessarily implies that he has failed to act justly up to now, and this poses a threat to his authority. Quite unlike the widows in the Old Testament tradition whom we have seen, the widow in Jesus' parable is neither a defenceless victim nor a powerless recipient of care by God or by patrons who act in his name, since we are unambiguously told that the judge who acts on her behalf has been

48. Bailey, *Peasant Eyes* (11), p. 135, mentions a modern example from the civil war in Lebanon.
49. Harnisch, 'Ironie' (42), p. 434.

defeated by her. She takes her demand for justice into her own hands, and she knows that God authorizes her to act in this way. Scholars in general have not drawn attention to the fact that the solution chosen by Jesus contradicts the tradition which the beginning of his parable obviously echoes. We must however ask whether this kind of portrait of a widow can be legitimated in biblical terms. When Jesus tells a parable which so clearly deviates from the image of the widow that we find in the biblical majority tradition, could he still feel himself to be in continuity with the Scripture and the traditions of his people? I believe that he could do so, because his parable displays an obvious closeness to a narrative tradition that deviates from the main trend in the Bible. Here, widows play an active role in carrying out the will of God. Two primary narratives must be recalled here, in which we find shocking transgressions of boundaries in the name of God: the protagonist of the first story is Tamar, the protagonist of the second is Judith. In a wider sense, examples of this particular narrative tradition can be found in the book of Ruth, the episode of the wise widow of Tekoa who becomes David's counsellor (2 Samuel 14), and the heroic model provided by the mother of the seven sons in *4 Maccabees*.

First, in its basic narrative constellations the story of the widow Tamar (Genesis 38)[50] shows clear similarities to Lk. 18.2–5. After her husband's death, the widow Tamar is repeatedly cheated of her due (in this case, the Levirate marriage with the hope of giving birth to a son) by those very men who were obliged by law to grant her rights. First, Onan agrees to the Levirate marriage, but he refuses to beget a child with her; and after Onan's death, her father-in-law Judah refuses to give her his youngest son as her husband. Tamar is sent back to her father's house, and since her father clearly takes no steps to enforce her rights, she seems to have lost every possibility of influencing the further course of events. She is a typical powerless widow. In this hopeless situation, however, where no one – not even God – helps her, she works out an extremely risky plan. She disguises herself as a prostitute and has intercourse with her father-in-law, thereby making him a partner in a Levirate marriage without his knowledge. As we know, her plan succeeds. When her pregnancy is discovered, she is able to present the tokens which identify Judah as the father of her child, and thus escapes being burnt alive (the penalty for adulteresses). Judah must publicly admit that she is in the right, not he. All the men involved in this story fail to do what is right, but Tamar's deliberate action enforces the

50.   For a good analysis of the patriarchal coercions against which Tamar must fight to get her rights, cf. F. van Dijk-Hemmes, 'Tamar and the Limits of Patriarchy: Between Rape and Seduction (2 Samuel 13 and Genesis 38)', in M. Bal (ed.), *Anti-Covenant: Counter-Reading Women's Lives in the Hebrew Bible* (JSOTSup, 81; BLS, 22; Sheffield: Almond Press, 1989), pp. 135–56 (146–53).

law of God, and the story leaves no doubt that this end sanctifies every means, even very grave transgressions of the norms of sexual conduct which were laid down for women, in the form of shameless behaviour that actually deserved the death penalty. The two husbands of Tamar displease God, and he 'puts them to death' (Gen. 38.7, 10); but God clearly approves of what Tamar does. In intertestamental and rabbinic Judaism, the story of 'our mother Tamar' (*LAB* 9.5) was extremely popular.[51]

Second, in the book of Ruth we find another young widow who must employ a good deal of cunning and seductive skill in order to attain the goal of a Levirate marriage with Boaz in which she will be provided for: her mother-in-law Naomi supports her in the whole matter (Ruth 2–3). The individual legal details against which Ruth and Naomi fight are unclear and a matter of scholarly dispute, but the plot of the story makes it clear that it is only thanks to the initiative taken by the two widows that the men who bear responsibility find themselves compelled to fulfil their legal obligations (Ruth 4).[52] Then, however, Boaz becomes a model Israelite who acts on behalf of widows (and foreigners). Thus, the book of Ruth shows the cooperation of active widows and their patrons against those who are led by economic considerations to reduce the rights of widows (Ruth 4.5–6).

Third, 2 Samuel 14 relates how a widow appeals dramatically to an authority superior to that of the local legal officers, namely the king, in order to prevent a manipulation of Torah (in this case, the law about those who commit murder and manslaughter; Deut.19.4–5, 11–13) which would deprive the widow of all material support. The woman from Tekoa wins over King David to her side by relating a story which is fictitious, but nevertheless true to life. She constructs a situation where the family of a dead man wish to get possession of his property by having the only male heir, the son of the deceased, executed for fratricide. This would deprive the woman – widow of the deceased man and mother of the two sons – of the one son who was still alive. And since as a woman she was unable to inherit, she would be left completely penniless (2 Sam. 14.6–7, 16). As a woman, she cannot take part in the trial of her son. Instead of waiting passively for the outcome of the court case, the widow takes resolute action and urges the king to intervene.[53]

51. Cf. F. Petit, 'Exploitations non bibliques des thèmes de Tamar et de Genèse 38: Philon d'Alexandrie, textes et traditions juives jusqu'aux Talmudim', in *Alexandrina. Hellénisme, judaïsme et christianisme à Alexandrie: Mélanges offerts au P. Claude Mondésert* (Patrimoines; Paris: Cerf, 1987), pp. 77–115; and P. W. van der Horst, 'Tamar in Pseudo-Philo's *Biblical History*', in A. Brenner (ed.), *A Feminist Companion to Genesis* (FCB, 2; Sheffield: Sheffield Academic Press, 1993), pp. 300–04.

52. Cf. W. Schottroff, 'Armut' (33), pp. 155–60, 164.

53. L. Schottroff, *Schwestern* (46), pp. 155–56 has already pointed out some of the similarities between this narrative and the parable at Lk. 18.2–5.

Fourth, the action of Judith is very complex, and we cannot discuss every facet here. On the narrative level, Judith acts in the interest of her people, unlike these other widows, who are acting in their own interests. At the same time, *as a widow*, Judith embodies the oppressed people who must look to God for help.[54] Her name means 'Jewess' and thus 'surely contains a theological program, since her life is the embodiment and model of true Judaism'.[55] The people of Bethulia and the leaders who bear responsibility have lost their trust in God, in view of the overwhelming power of the Assyrians and of the shortage of water in the besieged city, and they put God to the test by demanding that he help them in the next five days – if nothing happens by then, they will surrender. Judith is horrified by this denial of God, and takes the initiative to save the people. But before she puts into action her plan to seduce Holofernes and murder him in his sleep, she asks God for help in a lengthy prayer, explicitly appealing to her status as a widow, since as such, she has the right to call on his especial protection (ὁ θεὸς ὁ θεὸς ὁ ἐμός, καὶ εἰσάκουσον ἐμου τῆς χήρας, Jdt. 9.4; δὸς ἐν χειρί μου τῆς χήρας ὃ διενοήθην κράτος, Jdt. 9.9).[56] The following verses show that the widow is the paradigm of all those weak persons whose strength is their trust in God. Her victory, which is impossible on human reckoning, demonstrates that ultimately God is behind what she does:

> By guile of my lips strike down slave with master, and master with retainer. Break their pride by a woman's hand. Your strength does not lie in numbers, nor your might in strong men; since you are the God of the humble, the help of the oppressed, the support of the weak, the refuge of the forsaken, the Saviour of the despairing[57] ... And demonstrate to every nation, every tribe, that you are the Lord, God of all power, all might, and that the race of Israel has no protector but you.[58]

This reflection shows that the story of Judith with its narrative plot understands itself as an elaboration of this central Old Testament

54. C. A. Moore, *Judith: A New Translation with Introduction and Commentary* (AB, 40; Garden City: Doubleday, 1985), p. 180, with reference to Isa. 54.4; Lam. 1.1; 5.3–4.

55. M. Hellmann, *Judit – eine Frau im Spannungsfeld von Autonomie und göttlicher Führung* (Europäische Hochschulschriften, XXIII.444; Frankfurt am Main: Peter Lang, 1992), pp. 113–14. Cf. the entire section pp. 113–54 for a detailed description of the various dimensions within which Judith functions as a type of the true Israel.

56. Moore, *Judith* (54), p. 180, observes, with a reference to L. Alonso-Schökel: 'Judith's self-chosen role of continuing as a widow also qualified her to make special appeal to the God who is "the protector of widows" (Ps. 68.5; Sir. 35.15) even to the point of making her widowhood the basis of her prayer (Jdt. 9.4–9).'

57. The fivefold variation on this theme shows its centrality; cf. H. Gross, *Tobit. Judit* (NEchtB, 19; Würzburg: Echter Verlag, 1987), p. 95.

58. Jdt. 9.10–11.14.

principle (cf. also Ps. 147.10–11). The decisive point is that 'this programmatic theological affirmation ... is realized, not by a miraculous intervention by God in history, but by courageous and prudent action in the style of Judith'.[59]

Fifth, we could also refer to the martyrdom of the mother of the seven sons in *4 Maccabees* (14.11–17.6). She encourages her sons to oppose the tyrant, thereby proving her sound judgment and piety, and ultimately proving the superiority and invincibility of the God of Israel. *4 Macc.* 16.5, 12, explicitly emphasize that with this combative attitude she shows a behaviour diametrically opposite to what would be expected of a weak widow: she does *not* join in the lament of resignation in the face of her fate, as might have been expected. The substance of such a lamentation is nevertheless quoted: 'Alas, I who had so many and beautiful children am a widow and alone, with many sorrows. And when I die, I shall have none of my sons to bury me' (*4 Macc.* 16.10–11). Thus, this story too fits the narrative pattern of a widow whose untypical conduct helps realize the will of God.[60]

Despite all the differences in points of detail, these stories of Tamar and Judith, of Ruth, the prudent widow of Tekoa and the mother of the seven sons embody a narrative type in which a widow – traditionally the embodiment of a powerless woman who is dependent on help from others – becomes active and enforces God's will against opposition within Judaism or from external foes. In every instance, this demands that the strict societal norms of a withdrawn life for widows be infringed; it also demands that the woman value her own theological judgment of the conduct appropriate to the situation more highly than the (erroneous) judgment of her adversaries, even where these have a much higher status, power and religious education than she herself. In these stories, God functions as a helper more than as a saviour;[61] nevertheless, the success of the action performed must always be understood as proof of *his* power.

I believe that this narrative tradition can shed a decisive light on Jesus'

---

59. E. Zenger, *Das Buch Judit* (JSHRZ, 1.6; Gütersloh: Gütersloher Verlagshaus, 1981), p. 439. It is interesting to note that the act of rescue, which Judith compares to the vengeance taken by Simeon for the rape of Dinah, is called ἐκδίκησις at Jdt. 8.35 (cf. also 9.2). In the story of Tamar, God's consent is found only implicitly in the story; but Judith understands herself consistently as God's instrument in all that she does. This is exemplified in the formulation ἐπισκέψεται κύριος τὸν Ισραηλ ἐν χειρί μου (Jdt. 8.33).

60. Unlike the other narratives mentioned here, however, Jesus perhaps did not know the story of the widowed mother of seven sons from *4 Maccabees* in view of the date of its composition. But one cannot rule out the possibility that the story was transmitted orally much earlier (see 2 Maccabees 7).

61. On this distinction, which points to an historical transformation in Israel's understanding of God, cf. G. von Rad, *Theologie des Alten Testaments I: Die Theologie der geschichtlichen Überlieferungen Israels* (Kaiser-Traktate NF, 2; Munich: Kaiser, 9th edn, 1987), pp. 64–70; Zenger, *Judit* (59), p. 479; Hellmann, *Judit* (55), pp. 147–49.

parable about the judge and the widow, since there is no reason to doubt that he was familiar with this biblical narrative concept of a widow (or of another weak person)[62] who is victorious over adversaries within or outside Israel who oppose God or the divine commandment. And it is precisely this sequence of events and narrative logic that underlies the parable. In its apparently trivial ending, God's power is displayed: despite every experience that might suggest the contrary, he is 'the God of the humble, the help of the oppressed, the support of the weak, the refuge of the forsaken, the Saviour of the despairing' (Jdt. 9.11). God works – not directly, however, but indirectly, through the widow who confronts the judge and pesters him with her words until he yields. Naturally, this interpretation has important consequences for the exposition of the parable: we must take the judge seriously as an adversary of God and of his justice, and the point of the story is that he is overcome by the widow who trusts that God's justice will prevail and who therefore overcomes all obstacles. This is a story about how God's will is enforced against powers which oppose it (precisely in the societal elite); it also tells us about the role that the individual believer is called to play in this process. It has been objected that an interpretation of the parable as an appeal to the disadvantaged to take action to obtain their rights fails to recognize the analogous character of the narrative, and degrades it in a sense to an exemplary tale.[63] This objection cannot however be made to the variant of this interpretation which I have presented here. Nothing guaranteed in advance that the widow's unceasing cries for justice would be crowned by success; in the same way, nothing guaranteed that the actions of Judith and Tamar would be successful. And it is likely that this strategy would not succeed a second time. Normal human criteria would surely suggest that Judith would be raped by Holofernes, and that the judge in the parable would have sent a band of thugs by night to reduce the widow to silence. The parable is a parable of the utterly sovereign irruption of the kingdom of God, for which, however, the way can and should be prepared through human activity. Jesus does not intend to use this parable to consolidate an attitude of powerless waiting for God. Rather, he wishes to increase the capacity to take a calculated action that will create the conditions which can generate some anticipation of the eschatological realization of salvation.

---

62.   First and foremost, of course, one should recall here the victory of the little David over the giant Goliath (1 Samuel 17).

63.   Harnisch, 'Ironie' (42), pp. 434–35 n. 76, against the interpretation by R. Deschryver, 'La parabole du juge malveillant (Luc 18,1–8)', *RHPR* 48 (1968), pp. 355–66.

2.3. *Interim Summary: Jesus' Parable as a Creative Reworking of Traditional Images of the 'Widow'*

The parable of the judge and widow must be plausibly interpreted in the context of Jesus' public ministry in Judaism. *Contextual appropriateness* certainly exists, thanks to the link to the theme of justice for widows which was traditionally so important in Judaism, and we are entitled to assume that the daily experience of Jesus and of his hearers also made them receptive to this theme. Against the horizon of expectation which is created in this way, there is however also a considerable amount of *contextual distinctiveness*, since (as I have shown) the narrative logic of the parable does not function within the parameters of the dominant patriarchal model where widows are either victims or powerless recipients of the care of others: taking up a Jewish narrative tradition which diverges from the mainstream consensus, the parable relates how a widow herself, full of confidence in her God-given rights, finds a way to enforce this right – and ultimately, to enforce God. Second, it is only when these two trajectories of Jewish tradition coalesce that the parable becomes a convincing image of the *kingdom of God*, thereby taking its own distinctive place in the proclamation of Jesus. It is indeed true that the story – this narrative of a widow who gets on the nerves of a judge to such an extent that he finally reveals his weakness and caves in – could also function in a pagan context as a burlesque with subversive political contents. But in such a context, it could never plausibly unfold its double theological point, namely that God's vision of a just social existence is realized in anticipation and paradigm in the limited event whereby one person on occasion gets her rights; and that this happens when those who are in particular need of this justice become *acting subjects* whose priority is their active involvement on behalf of the justice of God, and who thereby refuse to accept the hindrances posed by societal norms and values.

But may we see this interpretation of the parable as truly appropriate to the historical Jesus, especially when we consider the care taken by the proto-Lukan revision and the evangelist himself to counter precisely this affirmation of the parable by means of the interpretative framework within which they place it? We can answer this question only by drawing on other, related traditions about Jesus and by looking at the tendencies of the revision by the (proto-)Lukan redaction. We can regard this interpretation as plausible only when a sufficient *source coherence* exists, i.e. enough other traditions about Jesus support the essential aspects of the interpretation. In section 3 (below), we shall show that the parable in this reconstructed interpretation makes good sense as an authentic parable of Jesus in the total framework of his proclamation. On the other hand, we must also bear in mind the redactional tendencies in the new interpretation of the parable. It is obvious that if the above reconstruction of the meaning of the parable is correct, the history of its exposition took on a new direction as soon as the commentary in Lk. 18.6–8a was added to it. The widow, who had exemplified successful prophetic intervention for justice in accordance with the demands of Torah, now exemplified one who prays for the realization of salvation in the last judgment and is certain that this prayer will be heard. The judge, who had exemplified the godless leader of the people, a foe of Torah whose opposition had to be overcome, now becomes a fallible human image of the God who wants us to pray to him day and night. The decisive transposition occurs when God changes sides: in the original parable, the widow knows that she has God on her side against the judge, but in the newly interpreted version, the judge in his refusal to grant her petition embodies God – not indeed in his arbitrary behaviour, which displays such contempt for other persons, but surely in his freedom to choose the point in time at which he will grant the widow her rights. Is this development plausible? Can the parable in its reconstructed meaning be interpreted as the rebarbative core of a scandalous authentic tradition of Jesus which was toned down in keeping with dominant early Christian tendencies? In that case, we would have to argue for its historicity in accordance with the criterion of the so-called *resistance to the tendency* (see section 4. below).

3. *The Parable in the Context of Jesus' Teaching*

Let us begin by looking at the source coherence, which must be considered as an autonomous criterion, independently of other criteria of authenticity.[64] Since Lk. 18.2–5 is a parable from the specifically Lukan material, this tradition is not attested more than once in mutually independent sources. Nevertheless, we may ask whether there are substantially comparable motifs and texts in the Jesus tradition. I concentrate here on the following closely linked aspects, which are important for the interpretation of the parable: the widows/poor/marginalized, who are the principal addressees of the reign of God, are also active subjects of the realization of this kingdom (see 3.1. below); the refusal to behave in conformity with expected gender patterns, when one acts to bring about the reign of God, and the accusation that the activists of the reign of God are employing violence (see 3.2. below); and the parable in the context of other textual evidence for the anticipatory realization of salvation through symbolic-political actions / speech-acts (see 3.3. below). We shall always attempt to find evidence from the various streams of tradition and in various forms and genres.

---

64. On this criterion, cf. G. Theissen, A. Merz, 'The Criterion of Coherence in Jesus Research Then and Now: The Delay of the Parousia as a Test Case', to be published in P. de Mey (ed.), *Sourcing the Quest* (Louvain Theological and Pastoral Monographs, 2006).

3.1. The Societally Marginalized Addressees of the Reign of God as Active
Subjects of the Realization of this Kingdom

Jesus' message about the reign of God was good news first and foremost for persons with a low societal status, something that promised them a full participation in God's new world. This is supported by so many texts that it may count as certain, irrespective of the question of the authenticity of individual traditions. Similarly, there is in principle no doubt that this promise entailed a threat to the religious and societal elites, since their conduct contributed to the exploitation of the majority of the population and to the religious marginalization of particular groups. In view of the paradigmatic meaning of widows which was already established in the New Testament, it goes without saying that both the widows and the group who profited from their distress were appropriate vehicles to express this dimension of Jesus' teaching. The warning against the scribes 'who eat up the houses of widows' (Mk 12.40) resembles the description of the situation in Lk. 18.2–4a: both texts are generated by the same perception of the societal and legal situation of widows, and of the incompatibility between this situation and the will of God.[65] Independently of whether or not it is historical, the miracle story at Lk. 7.11–18 confirms that Jesus' compassion for a widow who had lost her only son and provider was admirably suited to illustrate his mission. There can therefore be no doubt that the widow, as the paradigm of an underprivileged person, functions appropriately in the parable as the recipient of the good things promised by Jesus. But what of our proposed interpretation of Lk. 18.2–5 as a parable of the irruption of the kingdom of God which creates justice for all – an irruption which is made possible (though not actually realized!) by the active behaviour of the widow, who refuses to stay within the limits of the role imposed upon her as a victim of injustice?

This interpretation is based on a combination of three aspects of Jesus' proclamation of the kingdom of God which I believe to be indisputably historical. This proclamation is characterized first of all by the union of present and future elements (and the parable makes an affirmation about the dimension which is already accessible in the present). A second typical aspect is that the principal addressees of the good news – those who bear a societal and religious stigma – are included in the group of those who proclaim it. And third, God and these messengers whom he commissions work together in the realization of the kingdom.

---

65. This is true, irrespective of the details of the situation presupposed here, which are difficult to reconstruct; see for details A. Merz, 'Mammon als schärfster Konkurrent Gottes: Jesu Vision vom Reich Gottes und das Geld', in S. J. Lederhilger (ed.), *Gott oder Mammon: Christliche Ethik und die Religion des Geldes* (Linzer philosophisch-theologische Beiträge, 3; Frankfurt: Peter Lang, 2001), pp. 34–90 (78–79).

The inclusion of both future and present elements in Jesus' proclamation of the kingdom of God remains the best explanation of the
juxtaposition of traditions speaking of the future with traditions speaking
of the present. One should hope and pray that the comprehensive
establishing of the reign of God, which would annihilate every form of
rule opposed to God, would take place in the future (Mt. 6.10), but at the
same time, it was possible to experience the presence of the kingdom in the
present time.[66] One particularly impressive example, which could be felt in
people's bodies, was the expulsion of demons (Lk. 11.20 Q). But those
with ears to hear and eyes to see could already perceive in Jesus' preaching
and his didactic conversations, and in the everyday table fellowship and
pooled possessions of the Jesus movement, a seed which – as Jesus
believed – guaranteed the subsequent harvest. We will reflect in more
detail on the role played by the parables in allowing people to perceive the
kingdom of God (see 3.3. below); here, we concentrate on a fact to which
scholars have not always paid sufficient attention, namely that Jesus'
central message of salvation very deliberately made messengers of those
groups to whom the promise was primarily addressed, thereby trans-
forming them from victims to activists. The close circle of Jesus' disciples
included at least one former tax collector, and Mary Magdalene was
probably not the only one to have been healed of demonic possession.
These were members of two stigmatized groups who were in a very
prominent manner the addressees of Jesus' message. Above all, however,
we must take into account the fact that the Jesus movement was a
movement of the lower classes, whose members had the bare minimum
necessary for life and could at any moment slide further down into total,
life-threatening poverty. It is surely not by chance that, alongside the
stories of how Jesus successfully calls fisher and farmer to enter the circle
of his disciples, we have only one story of an unsuccessful vocation – that
of a rich young man (Mk 10.17–22). This is why the clearest example of
the collaboration between God and the members of the Jesus movement
in making the divine rule a present reality is the way they dealt with
material goods.

In keeping with the beatitudes pronounced on the poor and the hungry,
to whom the divine rule is to belong in the future and who are to be filled,
the radical followers of Jesus, poor as beggars and wandering from place
to place, are admonished in the present day not to be concerned about
eating, drinking and clothing – i.e., the satisfaction of the elementary
needs of the poor and of those who are accustomed to hunger and

---

66. On the connection between prayer for eschatological fulfilment and the anticipation
of the kingdom in daily life, see S. Freyne, 'Jesus, Prayer and Politics', in L. Hogan, B.
FitzGerald (eds.), *Between Poetry and Politics: Essays in Honour of Enda McDonagh* (Dublin:
Columba Press, 2003), pp. 67–85.

deprivation (Lk. 12.22–30 Q). Rather, they are to seek the kingdom of God, trusting that God will see to everything else (Lk. 12.31 Q) – although God does not do so directly; their needs are met through support from those to whom the preaching is addressed (Lk. 10.7/Mt. 10.10; Mk 6.8–10; 10.29–30). Jesus' exhortations to lend and to practise mutual support often envisage persons who themselves have only just enough to survive (Lk. 6.30a, 35; cf. 3.11). The new material order of the kingdom of God, which God himself will set up in its fullness, is made visible, in the form of a parable, by the wandering preachers who are demonstratively free of possessions, and by those followers of Jesus who have homes and who support these wanderers in an almost aristocratically carefree generosity.[67] It is surely not by chance that Jesus presents a widow as one of the positive models of the divinely willed way to deal with the unrighteous mammon (Mk 12.41–44). Traditionally, the widow is the classic recipient of alms: here, she is a model of generosity in the use of one's possessions.[68] In an analogous manner, in the parable at Lk. 18.2–5, the widow – traditionally the paradigm of persons whose legal claims can be ignored with impunity – becomes the model of successful action undertaken to re-establish justice. Another example from the parable tradition shows that this transformation of objects of care into models of a conduct that changes the world is not an isolated narrative pattern in Jesus' teaching: the Samaritan is himself a foreigner in the country and therefore the object of special protection by Torah. Every Israelite is obliged to love him as he loves his own self (Lev. 19.34). And he is the only one of the passers-by who helps the traveller who had fallen among thieves, thereby ensuring that the requirement of Torah is met (Lk. 10.30–37).

3.2. *Disregard of Gender Roles and the Accusation of Violence in the Context of the Proclamation of the Rule of God*

In the historical and cultural context in which the parable is told, the widow's conduct must be seen as a failure to conform to her (gender) role: instead of accepting her rejection and remaining at home, putting up with her distress in silence, she confronts the judge. Nor does she beg him for

---

67. On the values revolution underlying Jesus' proclamation of the kingdom, see S. Freyne, *Jesus, a Jewish Galilean: A New Reading of the Jesus-Story* (London: T&T Clark International, 2004), pp. 133–49 and G. Theissen, *Die Jesusbewegung: Sozialgeschichte einer Revolution der Werte* (Gütersloh: Gütersloher Verlagshaus, 2004).

68. Cf. G. Theissen, 'Die Witwe als Wohltäterin: Beobachtungen zum urchristlichen Sozialethos anhand von Mk 12,41–44', in M. Küchler, P. Reinl (eds.), *Randfiguren in der Mitte* (Lucerne: Edition Exodus, 2003), pp. 171–82, and *idem*, '"Geben ist seliger als nehmen" (Apg 20,35): Zur Demokratisierung antiker Wohltätermentalität im Urchristentum', in A. Boluminski (ed.), *Kirche, Recht und Wissenschaft* (Neuwied: Luchterhand, 1994), pp. 197–215.

justice, appealing for example to her weak position as a widow when she
makes her request. She demands her rights, without any gestures of
humility. The judge comments that her behaviour is 'wearing him out',
and he fears that she might even take her recalcitrant conduct to the point
of physical violence. From the perspective of source coherence, we must
ask whether the Jesus tradition contains other examples where the
proclamation of God's rule is accompanied by the infringing of societally
accepted gender roles and is linked to the use of force (or the accusation
that force is being used). Both of these are well attested. Many traditions
reflect the so-called 'non-family ethos' of the Jesus movement.[69] The
radical wandering lifestyle of the close circle of disciples who accompanied
Jesus entailed turning their back on the traditional structures of the
extended family. Jesus demanded that one bid farewell to one's closest
relatives and prefer the new fellowship of the circle of disciples who
devoted themselves to the proclamation of the kingdom of God, rather
than carry out one's traditional role in the family. When Jesus calls his
(male) disciples 'eunuchs for the kingdom of heaven' (Mt. 19.12), this is
probably his reply to insults provoked by this conduct on the part of his
disciples; and with reference to women, he explicitly affirms that it is more
important to do the will of God than to carry out one's role as mother
(Lk. 11.27; cf. Mk 3.34–35). Unfortunately, we know little about the roles
and tasks which the women who accompanied Jesus undertook in the
group of disciples, but the prosopographic data, as analysed by R.
Kraemer, are striking: 'Missing among the women portrayed as Jesus'
close disciples and supporters are married women with husbands and
children ... what the Jewish women in the Jesus movement have in
common appears to lie ... in their relative marginality within ancient
systems of gender that are by no means unique to Judaism.'[70] As they put
themselves at the service of the proclamation of the kingdom of God, both
the women and the men who accompanied Jesus came into conflict with
the traditional gender roles, as the logia explicitly tell us. Thus, the hearers
of the parable will not have found it implausible that the exemplary
character of this widow consists in her undeviating action on behalf of
justice, even if the customary rules of conduct for a woman who lived
alone may have made this scandalous. The same applies to the anticipated
violence on the part of the widow. A relatively large number of traditions
about Jesus associate his conduct and that of his disciples with violence.

---

69. An updated overview and discussion of the thesis of the wandering charismatics
characterized by homelessness, lack of family, possessions and protection, which was widely
accepted but also fiercely disputed, can be found in Theissen, *Jesusbewegung* (67), pp. 55–79.

70. R. S. Kraemer, 'Jewish Women and Christian Origins: Some Caveats', in R. S.
Kraemer, M. R. D'Angelo (eds.), *Women and Christian Origins* (Oxford: Oxford University
Press, 1999), pp. 35–49 (45).

The point at which we can most easily see how violent associations became attached to Jesus is his exorcisms, since the culturally accepted pattern here involved a physical testing of strength between the exorcist and the demon. This is why the metaphor of the 'strong man' depicts an exorcism as a violent burglary (Mk 3.27). Independently of this context, however, we also find logia employing an assault and a military campaign as images for the kingdom of God (*Gospel of Thomas* 98) and the costs of discipleship (Lk. 14.31–33). Several logia speak explicitly of the vehement controversies which broke out between people who were close to one another, thanks to the message of Jesus (Mt. 10.34–36/Lk. 12.51–53; Mk 13.12; *Gospel of Thomas* 16), and this explains why the Jesus movement – despite its historically certain profession of non-violence and love of enemies – could be perceived by outsiders as a group of restless provocateurs. When Jesus calls the disciples 'catchers of men' (Mk 1.16), and he and his followers are called 'men of violence' who 'seize the kingdom of God as their booty'. In the Q logion Mt. 11.12/Lk. 16.16, he is probably (as in the logion about eunuchs) taking up negative labels and giving them a positive twist: 'The supposed men of violence and rebels are the true possessors of the rule of God.'[71] Accordingly, when the judge at Lk. 16.5 believes that the widow is capable of losing all self-restraint and striking him in the face with her fist, this reaction chimes in with the experiences of Jesus' followers: those who committed themselves unreservedly to the kingdom of God and thereby continually trampled upon social conventions were quick to be seen as potentially violent. This widow whose persistence makes the judge fear a physical assault illustrates Jesus' demand that one strive for the rule of God, indeed that one take hold of it 'violently', and she is in perfect accordance with other metaphors and parables which make the same point.

3.3. *The Parable in the Context of the Anticipatory Realization of Salvation by Means of Symbolic-Political Actions and Speech-Acts*
In this section, we shall reflect on the relationship between the chance legal victory of the widow in the parable and Jesus' hope of a comprehensive justice in the kingdom of God. J. R. Donahue and B. B. Scott see the widow's victory as a symbol of the coming kingdom of God, but W. R. Herzog II has objected: 'Both commentators fail to account for the flexibility and adaptability of systematic oppression and may confuse the

---

71. G. Theissen, 'Jünger als Gewalttäter (Mt 11,12f.; Lk. 16,16): Der Stürmerspruch als Selbststigmatisierung einer Minorität', in D. Hellholm, H. Moxnes, T. Karlsen Seim (eds.), *Mighty Minorities? Minorities in Early Christianity, Positions and Strategies* (Festschrift J. Jervell; Oslo: Scandinavian University Press, 1995), pp. 183–200, here quoted from *idem*, *Jesus als historische Gestalt. Beiträge zur Jesusforschung: Zum 60. Geburtstag von Gerd Theissen* (ed. A. Merz; FRLANT, 202; Göttingen: Vandenhoeck & Ruprecht, 2003), p. 162.

exception for a new rule.'[72] According to Herzog's convincing analysis of the legal and socio-historical background, one must consider the plausibly described case of the widow as the exception which confirms the rule; indeed, the cynical calculation of the judge and of like-minded persons would ultimately have seen his reaction as a contribution to the stabilization of the system. The conduct of the widow in the parable offers no patent recipe in the context of a political strategy for a fundamental reform of the legal system; it would be equally absurd to call Jesus' activity as an exorcist a successful strategy to introduce a lasting improvement in the health of the Jewish population in his days. Nevertheless, Jesus intends through both forms of action – the narration of parables about ἡ βασιλεία τοῦ θεοῦ and the expulsion of demons – to make the proximity, indeed the presence of the kingdom of God something people can experience. And this gives these actions a direct political relevance.[73] They are part of a strategy which Jesus often employed, namely to work by means of symbolic-political actions in situations where the power-political situation made directly political actions impossible. This way of looking at Jesus' actions is indebted above all to the analysis of the political dimension of his activity by G. Theissen, who has shown that Jesus' symbolic actions (e.g. the appointment of the Twelve as alternative rulers, the cleansing of the temple, the entry to Jerusalem, and the reference to the coin in the question about paying tax; we should also mention the inclusive table fellowship) are a part of his active involvement on behalf of God's rule, aiming to make groups that are far removed from power into powerful subjects in the debates about how a society formed in accordance with the will of God ought to be.[74] This approach points in the right direction, and I believe that it must be taken further by an investigation of the symbolic-political character of the performative aspects of Jesus' preaching. The proclamation of the kingdom of God is linked to a number of speech-acts through which the charismatic speaker performed mighty deeds of power, for example threats and exclamations of woe, beatitudes and other promises of salvation, prophetic predictions, the forgiveness of sins, prayer and parables. In the present study, I limit myself to two speech-acts which have an anticipatory character that changes reality, namely beatitudes and parables. Jesus' beatitudes are not intended to offer a cheap consolation by speaking of something still to come. Rather, they are 'a speech-act which makes the coming reign of God

72. Herzog, *Parables* (8), p. 231.

73. Many scholars have discussed in detail the political relevance of the exorcisms. Cf. S. Guijarro, 'The Politics of Exorcism: Jesus' Reaction to Negative Labels in the Beelzebul Controversy', *BTB* 29 (1999), pp. 118–29.

74. G. Theissen, 'The Political Dimension of Jesus' Activities', in W. Stegemann, B. Malina, G. Theissen (eds.), *The Social Setting of Jesus and the Gospels* (Minneapolis: Fortress, 2002), pp. 225–50.

an event in the present'.[75] The addressees are told that they enjoy a status which runs contrary to the actual facts of their situation, thus permitting them to see both themselves and the present day in a new light. The parables too are speech-acts which allow the hearers to experience the kingdom of God for one specific moment. They restructure the hearers' perception of the world, enabling them to meet their own reality as changed persons. In the case of the widow, this takes place through the identification of the hearers with the widow's joy at her victory over her adversary, which ensures that she will have enough to live on, and through their shared Schadenfreude at the weak judge, who arrogantly despised both God and other people,[76] but who was brought to his knees by the 'threatening' presence of the widow alone. Why does Jesus see a parable of the kingdom of God in this unique instance of a weak widow who gets her rights? This is because he has learned in very general terms to perceive the irruption of the divine rule in limited, often symbolic, actions whereby human beings overcome evil in all its forms – in exorcisms, in the overcoming of social exclusion by means of table fellowship, and in the proclamation and symbolic enactment of the profoundly anti-imperialistic order of values proper to the *familia Dei*. The legal victory of the widow is therefore not 'the laughable image of eschatological salvation',[77] but a complete anticipation of salvation under the conditions of the old eon, something for the hearers of the parable to enjoy. The rulers of the old eon must be brought to their knees by every conceivable means – including their reduction to laughing-stocks. Such a narrative bears a clearly political message, since it deprives of legitimacy the ruling class and its unjust forms of administering the law. It strips the magic from the myth that the rulers are invincible and the weak are powerless. It strengthens the self-awareness of those in the lower ranks of society and their willingness to act to get their rights and to look for effective forms of resistance, even when these involve infringing accepted codes of behaviour. Naturally, this beginning is no larger than a mustard seed. Jesus awaited the great

---

75. H. Weder, *Die 'Rede der Reden': Eine Auslegung der Bergpredigt heute* (Zurich: Theologischer Verlag, 1985), p. 47, see also U. Luz, *Das Evangelium nach Matthäus. 1. Teilband: Mt 1–7* (EKKNT, I.1; Neukirchen-Vluyn: Neukirchener Verlag, 5th rev. edn, 2002), p. 275.

76. The description of the judge as τὸν θεὸν μὴ φοβούμενος καὶ ἄνθρωπον μὴ ἐντρεπόμενος is another indication that this parable goes back to Jesus. The judge is concisely portrayed as a man who refuses to accept the obligation to observe the double commandment of love, as Bovon, *Lukas 3* (2), p. 190, correctly remarks. G. Theissen, 'Das Doppelgebot der Liebe: Jüdische Ethik bei Jesus', in *idem, Jesus als historische Gestalt. Beiträge zur Jesusforschung: Zum 60. Geburtstag von Gerd Theissen* (ed. A. Merz; FRLANT, 202; Göttingen: Vandenhoeck & Ruprecht, 2003), pp. 57–72, has convincingly shown that the double commandment of love had a central place in the preaching of Jesus (and probably already in the teaching of John the Baptist).

77. Harnisch, 'Ironie' (42), p. 435.

redistribution of property and power, linked with the re-establishing of the legal order and the reversal of the political situation, from God alone – and he expected that this would happen soon. But this began wherever the new order of values which Jesus proclaimed gained a foothold in people's daily lives; and this happened also where subversive parables like that about the widow were told.

We can therefore affirm that a comparison with units from various streams and genres and forms of the tradition which substantially make the same points permits us to offer a coherent interpretation of Jesus' parable, in all the salient points of the reconstructed meaning set out in sections 2.1.–2.3., as part of his proclamation of the present kingdom of God. But if this is true, why does the Gospel of Luke present the parable surrounded by pointers which invite the reader to a completely divergent interpretation of the parable as an exhortation to unwearying prayer? What dominant early Christian interpretative tendencies helped 'defuse' the parable about the widow?

4. *New Interpretations of an Awkward Parable*

If what we have said up to this point is correct, our task is to explain why Jesus' parable was interpreted in early Christianity in the light of precisely that dominant biblical tradition about widows which Jesus himself wanted to question and undermine by means of his parable. The answer is obvious: this occurred because, in the absence of clear pointers to its interpretation, the parable was interpreted (probably already at the proto-Lukan stage) in the light of the Old Testament text which seemed to offer the greatest number of points of contact: Sir. 35.12–23. This text supports the traditional image of the widow in an unalloyed form. It also provided the opportunity to impose a futurist-eschatological interpretation of the parable.

4.1. *The Parable is Reread by Scripture Scholars in the Light of Sirach 35 as Dominant Pre-text*

The original parable of Jesus drew its legitimation from the Old Testament legislation about widows and the prophets' social criticism, but Jesus linked this with the subversive narrative tradition of widows who fought successfully for their rights or for their people. It is however clear that the rereading is guided by a text which belongs to the traditional discourse about widows, namely Sir. 35.12–23.[78] This text contains all the

---

78.   Some authors have already noted that Sir. 35.12–23 supplied the interpretative basis for the pre-Lukan rereading of the parable: H. Riesenfeld, 'Zu μακροθυμεῖν (Lk 18,7)', in J. Blinzler (ed.), *Neutestamentliche Aufsätze* (Festschrift J. Schmid; Regensburg: Pustet, 1963), pp. 214–17; Ott, *Gebet* (10), p. 57; Bindemann, 'Ungerechte' (18), p. 958.

relevant main words in the same sequence as the parable. Like the parable and the interpretation in Lk. 18.2–5, 6–8, it also leads from a discourse about a judge and a widow to a discourse about the eschatological judgment of God in favour of the oppressed who pray to him:

> [9] Give to the Most High as he has given to you, as generously as your means can afford; [10] for the Lord is a good rewarder, he will reward you seven times over. [11] Do not try to bribe him with presents, he will not accept them, do not put your faith in wrongly motivated sacrifices; [12] for the Lord is a judge (κριτής) who is utterly impartial. [13] He never shows partiality to the detriment of the poor, he listens to the plea of the injured party. [14] He does not ignore the orphan's supplication, nor the widow's as she pours out her complaint (οὐ μὴ ὑπερίδῃ ἱκετείαν ὀρφανοῦ καὶ χήραν ἐαν ἐκχέῃ λαλίαν). [15] Do the widow's tears not run down her cheeks, as she accuses the man who is the cause of them (οὐχὶ δάκρυα χήρας ἐπὶ σιαγόνα καταβαίνει καὶ ἡ καταβόησις ἐπὶ τῷ καταγαγόντι αὐτά)? [16] Whoever wholeheartedly serves God will be accepted, his petitions will carry to the clouds. [17] The prayer of the humble (προσευχὴ ταπεινοῦ) pierces the clouds: and until it does, he is not to be consoled, [18] nor will he desist until the Most High takes notice of him, acquits the upright and delivers judgment (κρινεῖ δικαίοις καὶ ποιήσει κρίσιν). [19] And the Lord will not be slow, nor will he be dilatory on their behalf (καὶ ὁ κύριος οὐ μὴ βραδύνῃ οὐδὲ μὴ μακροθυμήσῃ ἐπ' αὐτοῖς), [20] until he has crushed the loins of the merciless and exacted vengeance on the nations (τοῖς ἔθνεσιν ἀνταποδώσει ἐκδίκησιν), [21] until he has eliminated the hordes of the arrogant and broken the sceptres of the wicked, [22] until he has repaid all people as their deeds deserve and human actions as their intentions merit, [23] until he has judged the case of his people (ἕως κρίνῃ τὴν κρίσιν τοῦ λαοῦ αὐτοῦ) and made them rejoice in his mercy.

This text is the source of all the definitions and transpositions of meaning vis-à-vis the original parable. There can be no doubt that this is the code for the allegorical exposition of the parable. On the basis of v. 12, God is identified with the judge; in keeping with vv. 13–15, the widow becomes a helpless figure in relation to her oppressor, but her tears and prayers penetrate to God and move him to act. Nothing in the parable itself suggests an allegorical interpretation of the widow's success in gaining her rights; this remains firmly within the dimension of the present world. The allegory in terms of an eschatological retribution that is still to come is made possible by the semantic breadth of the word ἐκδίκησις, and this is clearly inspired by an interpretation of the parable in the light of Sir. 35.18–23; further evidence is the adoption of the theme of delay (cf. μὴ μακροθυμήσῃ ἐπ' αὐτοῖς with Lk. 18.7b). In Sirach 35, the chain of identification runs from the words and tears of the widow via the prayer of the humble (προσευχὴ ταπεινοῦ) to the judgment in favour of God's people, who are humiliated by the Gentiles (ἕως κρίνῃ τὴν κρίσιν τοῦ λαοῦ αὐτοῦ). The early Christian scripture scholars who discovered that Sirach 35 could be used to interpret Jesus' parable put 'the chosen ones of God, who cry to him day and night' in this position, which is traditionally that of Israel. The incompatibility of the narrative logic with the interpretative logic, which I have shown, makes it clear that all this is a secondary interpretation of the parable; one cannot maintain that Jesus himself constructed his narrative in the light of Sirach 35.[79] The assurance that God's retribution will come soon, and that those who experience oppression in the present world will gain their rights in the eschatological dimension, which we find both in Lk. 18.6–8a and in Sir. 25.12–23, is based on the traditional 'script' about the reality of widows in Israel: where all social laws and recommendations to practise mercy are disregarded and no one gives the oppressed their rights, God will intervene and punish. The parable, however, told a completely different story about a widow who unexpectedly proved not to be powerless, and who gained her rights in one specific instance. And this was a parable of the rule of God which is already coming into force in the present time.

4.2. *The Lukan Development of the Interpretation*

The evangelist probably found vv. 2–8a, the combination of parable and allegorical interpretation on the basis of a rereading by Scripture scholars, as an already existing unit, and he did not detach these elements from each other. He saw no need to do so, for (as we shall see) the parable with its allegorical interpretation admirably fitted other traditions involving Jesus and prayer which he adopted, as well as his own moderately conservative view of women and widows. At most, he may have attempted to tone down a little the imminent expectation of judgment which is expressed in vv. 6–8a by means of the framing verses: in v. 8b, he refers to the danger of the loss of faith, and he expands the admonition to continuous prayer in v. 1 with the warning that one should not let oneself be discouraged.[80] Nevertheless, the total eschatological interpretation is clearly given prominence by the placing of the parable within the eschatological discourse which begins at Lk. 17.20. Furthermore, by placing the parable

79. Bailey, *Peasant Eyes* (11), pp. 127–30, considers Sirach 35 as the literary background to the parable of Jesus. If Jesus had Sirach 35 in mind, which cannot be completely ruled out, we would have to conclude that he deliberately used the text in a subversive way, replacing the idea of future retaliation by God with the idea of present achievement of justice through the powerful action of the widow. The main reason why I don't think this happened is the metaphorical description of God as a rewarder and judge in Sir. 35.10, 12, which is consistent with the application in Lk. 18.6–8a, but not with the original parable, as I pointed out in section 2. above.

80. See e.g. E. Grässer, *Das Problem der Parusieverzögerung in den synoptischen Evangelien und der Apostelgeschichte* (BZNW, 22; Berlin: Töpelmann, 2nd edn, 1965), p. 37.

relatively far on in the Gospel, the evangelist has his readers perceive it in the light of the longer discourse about prayer which he has presented at Lk. 11.1–13. The traditions taken up in that passage include the parable (found only in Luke) of the importunate friend and the sequence of parables, derived from Q, about the father who naturally gives his son the good things for which he asks. Both these units have points of resemblance to the parable of the widow and her demands. In the parable of the importunate friend, as we find it in Luke, the attitude of the one who asks for help is likewise called κόπον παρέχειν and here, too, the man who is asked for help yields because the petitioner is behaving in an exceptionally vexatious and pushy manner (Lk. 11.7–8). No application is offered; no explicit inference is made from the friend who grants the request to God, although such an inference is suggested to the reader retrospectively, by means of v. 13 which concludes the sequence of parables in vv. 11–12 with an inference *a minori ad maius* from the wicked earthly fathers to the heavenly Father. This inference already belonged to the Q sequence of parables (and I believe that there are good arguments for seeing it as going back to Jesus himself), but it is not possible to clarify with certainty the extent to which the parallels to Lk. 18.1–8 in the parable of the importunate friend already existed at the pre-Lukan stage, or whether these were created by Luke or at least given special emphasis in his work of redaction.[81] It is indisputable that all Lukan parables about the hearing of prayer form a coherent group of mutually interpreting texts. To recognize this does not however mean positing an unbroken continuity between the parable and the interpretation. Rather, we can see that the parables and logia in Luke 11 structure the interpretation in advance, so that the disturbing incoherencies between the parable and its framework in Lk. 18.2–8 are diminished. But they don't become invisible. They show that at a secondary stage the parable was forced into the corset of a parable about the hearing of prayer; this was not easy, but the history of its interpretation shows that on the whole the work was successfully accomplished. However, the introduction to the parable shows that it does not belong there, since it is not by chance that the parables about the hearing of prayer (Lk. 11.5–8 and 11.11–13), which probably go back to Jesus, take the form of rhetorical questions: τίς ἐξ ὑμῶν. These are parables which indicate at the very outset that they derive their plausibility from foreseeable sequences of events in daily life. One can foresee that earthly ('wicked') fathers and friends will grant a request, even if they may perhaps delay for a short time; but it is much more natural that God should hear the prayers of his children. This argument may succeed in

---

81. A plausible reconstruction of the tradition history is given by Ott, *Gebet* (10), pp. 25–31, 71–72: Lk. 11.8 is a pre-Lukan addition which interpreted the parable Lk. 11.5–7 in the light of Lk. 18.2–7.

attaining its rhetorical goal of strengthening the certainty that one's prayers will be heard. But the parable of the judge and the widow describes the classic unusual individual case, for neither daily experience nor the biblical tradition leads us to expect that a widow would gain her rights against a judge who is unwilling to help her. On the contrary, the plausibility of the negative inference *a minori ad maius* is very weak, when compared to the positive analogies in Lk. 11.11–13.

I have already pointed out that the new interpretation as a parable about prayer for eschatological retribution also involves a massive transposition of the image of the widow. In the parable, she overcomes the judge by her active conduct, which is motivated by the desire for justice. But the framework destroys these associations by its allegorical inter-pretation of the widow as an image of the chosen ones of God who cry out to him by day and night. This portrait of a woman was felt to be scandalous, and it was toned down even before Luke wrote his Gospel. He carried the process further by his interpretation of the widow's behaviour as the model of πάντοτε προσεύχεσθαι (Lk. 18.1) and by making the widow at 18.2–5 only one of a number of figures who are modelled on the traditional image of the widow. His account of the raising to life of the widow's son (Lk. 7.11–17, a tradition found only in Luke) functions entirely within the patriarchal paradigm – Jesus restores to the widow the man in her life, who is capable of looking after her. He also recalls Elijah, who became the provider for the widow in Zarephath (Lk. 4.25–26). Likewise, all the widows who are mentioned in the Acts of the Apostles seem to be recipients of care on the part of others (Acts 6.1; 9.39, 41).[82] When we look for comparisons to Lk. 18.2–5, however, the most important widow is Anna (Lk. 2.36–38), who after only seven years of married life spent the rest of her long life in the temple, serving God by fasting and prayer day and night. Luke does indeed call her a prophetess, but he gives only an indirect account of her words – whereas Simeon's are quoted directly. This widow stands at the beginning of the Gospel as a

---

82. The tradition about Tabitha in Joppa is particularly striking. The author may have deliberately left unclear her relationship to the widows. The text suggests that the widows mentioned in vv. 39 and 41 are recipients of Tabitha's alms (mentioned in v. 36) and of the 'tunics and other garments' which she made (v. 39). In terms of social history and the history of piety, however, it is much more probable that all the women mentioned here were members of a fellowship in which women worked together and produced goods, and that Tabitha was their spiritual leader. Cf. I. Richter Reimer, 'Die Apostelgeschichte', in L. Schottroff, M.-T. Wacker (eds.), *Kompendium Feministische Bibelauslegung* (Gütersloh: Christian Kaiser/Gütersloher Verlagshaus, 1998), pp. 542–56 (549–50). In that case, the widows would have played an active role in earning the money which was given in alms (v. 36) and (in a manner analogous to the widow at Mk 12.41–44) would not have been recipients of alms, dependent on vertical solidarity. They would themselves have been givers in a system of horizontal solidarity which undermined the Roman patron–client system.

model of lifelong, incessant prayer, and her light shines out anew in Lk. 18.1 (πάντοτε προσεύχεσθαι) and 18.6 (the allegorical interpretation of the widow as God's chosen ones, who cry to him day and night). In the light of this trait, which agrees with the traditional image of widows, the widow in the original parable with her successful fight for justice now leads only a shadowy existence.

5. *The Parable in Continuum: Results of Our Investigation*

This essay has investigated whether the tradition at Lk. 18.1–8 is based on an historical core going back to the historical Jesus. What is the relationship of this Jesus tradition to the Jewish context in which it arose, and to the early Christian interpretations which can be perceived in the Gospel of Luke? The result is an extremely complex mixture of continuity and discontinuity in both perspectives. The parable of Jesus, transmitted without any interpretation, belongs best in the context of the parables of the kingdom of God, which employ subjects from everyday life to express the presence and the spreading of God's rule. The earliest Christian interpretation of the parable to which we have access was the addition of vv. 6–8, and this can be plausibly explained as toning down its politically explosive message of present eschatology by an allegorizing interpretation guided by Scripture. This new interpretation agrees so closely with other (probably authentic) traditions about Jesus and prayer that the later interpreters, from Luke to the present day, have repeatedly held that Lk. 18.2–8a is a twin parable to the story of the importunate friend, and that it goes back to Jesus himself. Here, a stroke of genius created a new continuity in the discontinuity; a second parable was created, and its principal affirmation is certainly in accordance with the historical Jesus. This, however, meant the loss of the scandalous portrait of the widow in the original parable, with its politically subversive message, since the framing passages no longer permitted the reader to perceive the sharply drawn characters and the narrative dynamic which destroyed the hierarchies of everyday life as these had been conceived by Jesus when he told the parable. In the parable, the judge who seems all-powerful, and who inspires fear by his scorn for God and other people, unexpectedly proves to be a pathetic figure, while the widow, whose fate had seemed sealed, triumphs in the end. No higher power intervenes: it is exclusively because of her persistent behaviour – which is of course highly unfeminine – that right prevails, and God's rule is enforced through the activity of the judge although he himself knows no fear of God. The (proto-)Lukan parable, on the other hand, smoothes everything out: nothing is changed in the relationships between the genders, or between God and human beings, and the widow is the model of the oppressed community which prays by day and night to the traditional God, who is imagined as masculine (on the analogy of the judge) and who will grant the petition in his own time. The qualitative antithesis between the present time, in which the chosen ones suffer powerlessly, and the future, in which God will avenge them, is likewise solidified. All this is done in accordance with Jewish and early Christian majority discourses about gender roles, images of God and eschatological salvation. In section 2.2., I have suggested that when Jesus speaks of a widow whose unconventional mode of conduct puts an end to her legal disadvantages, he is taking up a Jewish narrative tradition which diverges from the dominant Old Testament image of widows – here, God's will is realized through boundary-breaking behaviour on the part of widows. It is time to rediscover this trajectory of continuity between Jesus and his Jewish environment and to make this the centre of the exposition of the parable of the widow. This figure in the parable deserves to be mentioned in the same breath as the great widows of the Old Testament: a Judith, a Tamar and a Ruth.

Son of Man as Kingdom Imagery: Jesus between Corporate Symbol and Individual Redeemer Figure

Thomas Kazen

1. *Introduction*

In this chapter, I will suggest an originally collective or corporate understanding of the expression 'Son of Man' as the most plausible explanation for its use by Jesus, as well as for its development and transmutation within the early Christian movement. This is grounded in a conviction that any attempt to 'reconstruct' the historical figure of Jesus must take issues of both continuity and discontinuity into account. The criticisms launched against the classical criterion of dissimilarity during the last phase of historical Jesus research has made this more evident than ever.[1] In any historical investigation we must assume that historical figures were not lone islands, but interacted and communicated within their contemporary contexts. It is only reasonable to regard the historical figure of Jesus as having shared common concepts and convictions with his Jewish contemporaries, while at the same time providing some sort of impetus to the ensuing early Christian development. Without balancing issues of continuity and discontinuity, the historian will not be able to suggest historically plausible explanations.[2]

As I have discussed these general issues in detail elsewhere,[3] it will suffice to emphasize that interpreting Jesus from a 'continuum perspective'

---

1. See T. Holmén, 'Doubts About Double Dissimilarity: Restructuring the Main Criterion of Jesus-of-History Research', in B. Chilton, C. A. Evans (eds.), *Authenticating the Words of Jesus* (NTTS, 28.1; Leiden: Brill, 1999), pp. 47–80; G. Theissen, D. Winter, *Die Kriterienfrage in der Jesusforschung: Vom Differenzkriterium zum Plausibilitätskriterium* (NTOA, 34; Freiburg: Universitätsverlag, 1997).

2. This is the intent of Theissen and Winter's criterion of historical plausibility, which they divide into a criterion of *Kontextplausibilität* and a criterion of *Wirkungsplausibilität*. For an earlier important discussion, introducing the idea of historical constraints, see A. Harvey, *Jesus and the Constraints of History: The Bampton Lectures, 1980* (London: Duckworth, 1982).

3. See T. Kazen, *Jesus and Purity Halakhah: Was Jesus Indifferent to Impurity?* (ConBNT, 38; Stockholm: Almqvist & Wiksell International, 2002), pp. 25–41.

in no way entails a naive view of the 'authenticity' or 'historicity' of Gospel material, nor does it rule out cases of severe discontinuity, misunderstanding or reinterpretation. It is rather a question of admitting necessary links between the Jesus of history and early Christian interpretation of the Jesus tradition, attempting to trace lines of development through textual analyses. In this process, I am reluctant to employ traditional methods for isolating 'authentic' materials, as if theological interest or redactional activity could ever be fully peeled away from a text; in addition, the methods traditionally employed usually excluded ideas of continuity by definition. I prefer rather to treat the Jesus tradition as interpretations of memories of the impact that Jesus made,[4] containing enough historical remains for an overall picture to be construed, which must be continuously modified by interpretations of individual traditions in an open and somewhat circular process.[5]

This was my stance in examining Jesus' attitude to purity *halakhah*.[6] In this chapter, I approach the Jesus tradition in a similar way, with the difference that I do not employ redaction-critical tools to any extent. There is no room for such analyses here, and my limited aim is to examine whether a particular understanding of the expression 'Son of Man' can plausibly explain the gist of the Son of Man sayings belonging to the Jesus tradition, without exaggerating the aspects of discontinuity between Jesus and early Christians, i.e., by employing a continuum perspective. My interpretation does not depend on the 'authenticity' of single sayings, nor do I attempt to outline the details of development. If my suggestions are found reasonable, or hopefully plausible, several questions still remain as to where, when and how the transition from a collective to an individual understanding of the Son of Man took place.

2. *Interpreting the Son of Man*

Jesus' use or non-use of 'Son of Man' as an epithet for himself, and the historical and religious context for interpreting this expression, has been a bone of contention among scholars for more than two centuries. The Greek expression ὁ υἱὸς τοῦ ἀνθρώπου, literally 'the son of the human being', has been understood first as referring to Jesus' humanity as contrasted with his divinity, then as a messianic expression associated with Daniel 7, representing fairly widespread apocalyptic ideas, and recently as

---

4. For a recent discussion, see J. D. G. Dunn, *Jesus Remembered* (Christianity in the Making, 1; Grand Rapids: Eerdmans, 2003), pp. 881–93.

5. Theissen, Winter, *Kriterienfrage* (1), pp. 198–205.

6. See Kazen, *Jesus and Purity* (3).

reflecting a Semitic non-titular idiom by which a man could refer to himself in the third person or to humans in general.[7]

All three lines of interpretation are still alive, at least in some forms. There is no consensus emerging. The idea of a uniform Jewish messianic Son of Man concept in pre-Christian times is being increasingly abandoned, mainly due to the late dating of the Similitudes of *1 Enoch* and a growing awareness of the diversity of early Judaism.[8] G. Vermes' claim, based on rabbinic examples, that the Aramaic *bar nasha* be taken as a circumlocution for 'I' has been refuted by a number of scholars; the generic suggestion ('man' in general, a human being) has fared better.[9] The significance of Daniel 7 for the expression is defended by a majority, although opinions differ as to its eschatological or messianic connotations, and whether Daniel lies behind Jesus' own use or not. Recently, both Walter Wink and Joel Marcus have suggested interpretations, which – albeit in various ways – focus on the relationship between humanity and divinity.[10]

To attempt a research report in this context would be not only foolish, since it would fill all the space available, but also unnecessary, since D. Burkett's survey, *The Son of Man Debate*, contains a comprehensive and analytical history of research.[11] A brief outline of the options will suffice. There are basically three points of debate: authenticity, origin and

7. I will not enter into a discussion about the use of definite articles, and whether this implies a generic or an individual understanding, or a particular background for the expression. While the LXX translates אדם בן or אנש בר with the anarthrous υἱὸς ἀνθρώπου, 'the Son of Man' in the Gospels almost always has definite articles (ὁ υἱὸς τοῦ ἀνθρώπου). I fear this discussion is a dead end, as arguments can be turned either way. Cf. J. A. Fitzmyer, *A Wandering Aramean: Collected Aramaic Essays* (SBLMS, 25; Missoula: Scholars, 1979), pp. 143–60; M. Casey, 'Idiom and Translation: Some Aspects of the Son of Man Problem', *NTS* 41 (1995), pp. 164–82 (170–78); J. Marcus, 'Son of Man as Son of Adam', *RB* 110 (2003), pp. 38–61 (40–47).

8. R. Leivestad, 'Der apokalyptische Menschensohn ein theologisches Phantom', *ASTI* 6 (1968), pp. 49–105; R. N. Longenecker, *The Christology of Early Jewish Christianity* (repr., Grand Rapids: Baker, 1981), pp. 82–85; N. Perrin, *A Modern Pilgrimage in New Testament Christology* (Philadelphia: Fortress, 1974), pp. 23–40 (for example). Most of Perrin's book revolves around the Son of Man question. The bulk of the material dates from the sixties.

9. G. Vermes, *Jesus the Jew: A Historian's Reading of the Gospels* (London: SCM, 5th impr., 1994), pp. 160–91. For refutations and modifications of Vermes' views, cf. M. Casey, *Son of Man: The Interpretation and Influence of Daniel 7* (London: SPCK, 1979), pp. 224–34; Fitzmyer, *Wandering Aramean* (7), pp. 152–53; R. Bauckham, 'The Son of Man: "A Man in My Position" or "Someone"?', *JSNT* 23 (1985), pp. 23–33; J. Christensen, *Menneskesønnen: En bibelteologisk studie* (Bibel og historie, 19; Århus: Åarhus Universitetsforlag, 1996), pp. 43–52.

10. W. Wink, *The Human Being: Jesus and the Enigma of the Son of Man* (Minneapolis: Fortress, 2002); Marcus, 'Son of Adam' (7); *idem*, 'Son of Man as Son of Adam. Part II: Exegesis', *RB* 110 (2003), pp. 370–86.

11. D. Burkett, *The Son of Man Debate: A History and Evaluation* (SNTSMS, 107; Cambridge: Cambridge University Press, 1999).

reference. These three are largely interdependent. If Jesus spoke about the Son of Man, from where did he get the expression and to whom did he refer?

Although few scholars would ascribe *every* Son of Man saying to Jesus, most people today would admit that Jesus did speak in this peculiar way. I agree with those who claim that this is one of the safest facts about the historical Jesus.[12] In no other way could we adequately explain the frequent occurrence of this expression on the lips of Jesus, although it is almost completely absent in the New Testament outside the Gospels.[13]

While the influence of Daniel 7 on the Jesus tradition is beyond all doubt, the question has been whether such influence belongs to a post-Easter context only. Does the expression 'Son of Man' on the lips of the historical Jesus have its origin in Dan. 7.13 or not? This question, however, is not identical with that of a possible heavenly Son of Man concept in early Judaism. The idea, so popular in the last century, of the Son of Man as a current, apocalyptic and messianic figure, has been increasingly abandoned today. I am among those who accept the arguments against relying on the Similitudes of *1 Enoch*, or even less decisive apocryphal or apocalyptic literature, in speculating about a general identification of the Danielic Son of Man with a heavenly redeemer figure in Judaism at the time of Jesus.[14] The main alternative is to look at the Aramaic expression בר אנש or בר (א)נשא, meaning 'man' or 'human being' in general, as a source for Jesus' use.[15] While I think that Vermes' particular idea of this way of speaking as a circumlocution for 'I' has been more or less disproved,[16] Burkett seems too cautious in rejecting altogether a generic interpretation.[17] A generic interpretation ('human being', 'man') fits well with the use of the corresponding expression בן אדם in the Hebrew Bible, which must not be left out of the discussion.[18]

The question of reference is intertwined with those of authenticity and origin, already briefly mentioned, and dependent on the stance one takes

---

12. 'If we cannot be confident that Jesus used the phrase "the son of man" in his speech, and quite regularly, then there is almost no feature of the Jesus tradition of which we can confidently assert that Jesus spoke in this way.' Dunn, *Jesus Remembered* (4), pp. 759–60.

13. See Dunn, *Jesus Remembered* (4), pp. 737–39, 761. Outside the gospels, the Son of Man is found only four times, usually anarthrous: twice in the book of Revelation (1.13; 14.14), in allusion to Daniel; once in Heb. 2.6, where Psalm 8 is quoted; once in Acts 7.56 (with definite articles) where its use is clearly secondary, depending on Lk. 22.69.

14. See Burkett, *Son of Man Debate* (11), pp. 68–81; Casey, *Son of Man* (9), pp. 7–141.

15. See Vermes, *Jesus* (9), pp. 160–91; Casey, *Son of Man* (9), pp. 224–40.

16. See n. 9 above.

17. Burkett, *Son of Man Debate* (11), pp. 82–96.

18. Cf. Num. 23.19; Job 35.8; Pss. 8.5; 80.18; Isa. 56.2; as well as the abundant use of the expression in the book of Ezekiel, for God addressing the prophet.

on those issues. Excluding the idea of a current heavenly Son of Man idea, as well as that of a circumlocution for 'I', the options are as follows: If Jesus' use of 'Son of Man' originated with Daniel 7, he could hardly have referred to a future, heavenly, individual redeemer figure, unless he had developed that idea himself. If it originated in an idiomatic Aramaic expression, it must refer to man in general, rather than being a clear self-reference. To put it another way, if Jesus talked about himself as the Son of Man it might have been related in some way to Daniel 7. If he used 'Son of Man' as an expression not for himself, it would have been in a generic sense, but it *could* still have been related to Daniel 7.

These somewhat disparate observations can be dealt with in a number of ways, as history has shown. Two radical solutions are: either to deny entirely that the expression goes back to the historical Jesus,[19] or to claim that Jesus' own use had nothing whatsoever to do with Daniel 7.[20] In both cases the early Church is made responsible, either for ascribing the expression to Jesus in the first place or for the connection between Jesus' use and Daniel 7. Both alternatives seem extremely implausible to me. The first one seems to be a desperate reversion to a position that so many scholars have been forced to abandon, and it begs for a credible explanation of why this expression is present in the Jesus tradition at all.[21] The second suggestion is most unlikely, in view of Jesus' emphasis on the kingdom of God, and of Daniel as the only Old Testament writing in which the kingdom is in focus.

3. *Daniel and the Kingdom*

The influence of the book of Daniel on the New Testament is considerable; proportionally it is quoted and alluded to as frequently as Isaiah and the Psalms.[22] In a recent study, C. A. Evans has shown how a number of Danielic features can be traced in the kingdom ideology of Jesus. These are:

19. Cf. Burkett, *Son of Man Debate* (11), pp. 123–24. Those denying the 'authenticity' of the expression include W. Bousset, E. Käsemann, P. Vielhauer and N. Perrin; see Burkett, *Son of Man Debate* (11), pp. 50–56.

20. E.g. Casey, *Son of Man* (9), pp. 224–40; B. Lindars, *Jesus Son of Man: A Fresh Examination of the Son of Man Sayings in the Gospels in the Light of Recent Research* (London: SPCK, 1983), pp. 158–89. The formerly influential position that Jesus referred to an apocalyptic figure other than himself is less viable today when the existence of a contemporaneous concept of an individual redeemer figure is seriously questioned; cf. H. E. Tödt, *Das Menschensohn in der synoptischen Überlieferung* (Gütersloh: Mohn, 1959); F. Hahn, *Christologische Hoheitstitel* (Göttingen: Vandenhoeck & Ruprecht, 1963).

21. See above, and n. 12.

22. C. A. Evans, 'Daniel in the New Testament: Visions of God's Kingdom', in J. J. Collins, P. W. Flint (eds.), *The Book of Daniel: Composition and Reception*, vol. 2 (VTSup,

(1) the emphatic qualification that the awaited kingdom is God's
kingdom; (2) the language of imminence; (3) the kingdom as 'mystery';
(4) the stone that crushes; (5) the saying about what is 'not made with
hands'; (6) promises to the disciples; and (7) the 'abomination of
desolation'.[23]

Conspicuous details are for example Luke's additional saying about the
cornerstone ('everyone who falls upon this stone will be broken to pieces;
but the one upon whom it falls will be crushed'), or Mark's saying about a
temple not made with hands (ἀχειροποίητος), which could reflect the
little stone in Daniel 2. The Lukan saying assuring the 'little flock' that the
Father will give them the kingdom could be taken as an allusion to Dan.
2.37 and 7.14. And the Q saying promising that the twelve will sit on
thrones, judging the tribes of Israel (Mt. 19.28/Lk. 22.28–30), clearly
seems to refer to Dan. 7.9–10, 22.[24]

It is difficult to claim that *all* these features were originally found with
the historical Jesus. The Daniel tradition continued to influence the
developing New Testament traditions.[25] But it would be very implausible
to posit a Jesus for whom the message of the kingdom was central, yet
who was totally uninfluenced by the ideas and images of the book of
Daniel. The prominence of Daniel in various branches of early Judaism
makes it the evident background for Jesus' focus on the kingdom of
God.[26] The importance of this book in Qumran is attested by the number
of manuscripts found, as well as by allusions and the use of Danielic
ideas.[27] In Hellenistic Judaism, variant readings and additions testify to its
continuing importance. Apocalyptic texts reuse Danielic ideas and motifs.

83.2; Leiden: Brill, 2001), pp. 490–527 (490). Cf. J. D. G. Dunn, 'The Danielic Son of Man in
the New Testament', in J. J. Collins, P. W. Flint (eds.), *The Book of Daniel: Composition and
Reception*, vol. 2 (VTSup, 83.2; Leiden: Brill, 2001), pp. 528–49.

23. Evans, 'Daniel' (22), p. 510.

24. Evans, 'Daniel' (22), pp. 514–19. Evans is here building upon an earlier discussion of
such features by D. Wenham, 'The Kingdom of God and Daniel', *ExpTim* 98 (1987), pp.
132–34. The plural 'thrones' was often interpreted as the saints taking part in God's
judgment *in favour* of them, i.e. a judgment vindicating the faithful. Cf. Casey, *Son of Man*
(9), pp. 41–42.

25. Cf. L. Hartman, *Prophecy Interpreted: The Formation of Some Jewish Apocalyptic
Texts and of the Eschatological Discourse Mark 13 Par.* (ConBNT, 1; Lund: CWK Gleerup,
1966), pp. 145–252.

26. While it is true that the precise expression 'kingdom of God' does not occur in
Daniel, the coming kingdom belonging to, or ushered in by God, is a central concept.

27. Cf. P. W. Flint, 'The Daniel Tradition at Qumran', in J. J. Collins, P. W. Flint (eds.),
The Book of Daniel: Composition and Reception, vol. 2 (VTSup, 83.2; Leiden: Brill, 2001), pp.
329–67. The presence of eight copies of Daniel is regarded as 'surprising in view of the small
size of the book' (p. 365).

In the *Targumim*, Daniel's scheme of four kingdoms keeps appearing as an interpretive key for a number of quite different texts.[28] Although the idea of God's kingdom has roots in the Psalms and in wisdom literature, Daniel played an important role for the understanding of this concept at the end of the Second Temple period. If Jesus did not himself associate the kingdom with traditions from Daniel, a plausible alternative must be found. It might almost be easier to deny Jesus any focus on the kingdom whatsoever; but this would be a desperate move indeed.

If the historical Jesus is allowed Danielic associations together with his message of the kingdom of God, he cannot be conceived of as ignorant concerning Daniel's human-like figure. A number of scholars have referred to the original interpretation of this figure. As we have already mentioned, there are good reasons to doubt a general understanding of the Danielic Son of Man as an individual, messianic redeemer figure at the time of Jesus. Such an interpretation is indeed found in apocalyptic and rabbinic literature, as well as with some of the early fathers, but these texts are not early enough to serve as anything but evidence for the subsequent development of such ideas, among Christians as well as Jews. The individualization of the Son of Man figure seems to go together with the reinterpretation of Daniel's kingdom schema to make it refer to Babylon, Media-Persia, Greece and Rome, respectively. This reflects what Casey calls the 'Western tradition'. Over against this reinterpretation, we have the evidence of the 'Syrian tradition', which preserves an earlier interpretive approach, in which the successive kingdoms are understood as Babylon, Media, Persia and Macedonia, followed by the Son of Man representing the Kingdom of God or the faithful saints.[29]

It is generally agreed that the Son of Man figure in Daniel is a symbol, on the same level as the four beasts preceding it. They are all described as 'like' (כְּ) a beast or a man. Just as the beasts symbolize four successive kingdoms, the one like a son of man symbolizes an eternal kingdom, given to the saints of God (cf. Dan. 7.18, 22, 27). The fact that the Son of Man comes with the clouds of heaven and not from the sea does not invalidate the symbolic character of the figure; why should a symbol of the eternal kingdom come out of those waters of evil and chaos?[30]

It should be noted that the imagery is somewhat fluid. The beasts are said to represent kings, but also kingdoms (Dan. 7.17, 23). We find the same ambiguity with the statue in Daniel 2, which represents the same basic pattern. There the various metals symbolize successive kingdoms, but kingdoms can be represented by their kings; thus Nebuchadnezzar is

---

28. Cf. U. Glessmer, 'Die "Vier Reiche" aus Daniel in der targumischen Literatur', in Collins, Flint *The Book of Daniel*, pp. 468–89.

29. Casey, *Son of Man* (9), pp. 51–98.

30. Although this is actually the case with the 'Man from the sea' in *4 Ezra* 13.

said to be the golden head (Dan. 2.37–38, cf. v. 44). The little stone in Daniel 2 is functionally equivalent to the Son of Man in Daniel 7. The little stone symbolizes a kingdom raised by God (Dan. 2.44), so this ought to be the case with the Son of Man as well. A judgment scene is inserted, however, and it seems as if the kingdom is *given* to the Son of Man (Dan. 7.14), i.e., this figure represents the saints that receive the kingdom as a result of the court action (Dan. 7.18, 26–27).[31] If the ambiguity of the symbols in both chapters is taken into account there is no discrepancy in this; the fifth non-monstrous being symbolizes a divinely established kingdom as well as its representatives.[32]

This means that the Son of Man is not originally pictured as an individual redeemer figure, but as a symbol of the eternal kingdom and its representatives. The difference, however, is that while individual kings are implied or at times defined in the four preceding kingdoms, the corresponding counterparts in God's kingdom are the saints. No messianic leader or royal figure is implied. The Son of Man is in all respects a collective symbol.[33]

Since the Son of Man in Daniel 7 was not originally interpreted as an individual redeemer figure, this has led several scholars to suggest that the book of Daniel did not provide the background for Jesus' use of the expression. There is another possibility, however. If there is evidence for an original collective interpretation of the Son of Man, leaving traces even in early Christian contexts, why could this not form the background to Jesus' own use of the image? Whatever path one chooses, it is possible to embrace Fitzmyer's statement that 'there is no other or more plausible starting-point for the titular use of the phrase for Jesus in the NT than Dan. 7.13, even though the phrase is not used in a titular sense there'.[34] This means, however, that the Son of Man sayings might be consistently interpreted as kingdom imagery.

---

31. Cf. C. F. D. Moule, '"The Son of Man": Some of the Facts', *NTS* 41 (1995), pp. 277–79.

32. Thus I cannot go along with C. Caragounis' identification of the Son of Man in Daniel as a heavenly individual in *The Son of Man: Vision and Interpretation* (WUNT, 38; Tübingen: Mohr Siebeck, 1986), pp. 61–81.

33. Cf. M. Müller, *Der Ausdruck "Menschensohn" in den Evangelien: Voraussetzungen und Bedeutung* (Acta Theologica Danica, 17; Leiden: Brill, 1984), pp. 14–24.

34. Fitzmyer, *Wandering Aramean* (7), p. 155.

4. *Son of Man as Kingdom Imagery*

Since P. Vielhauer stated: 'Da Jesus die Gottesherrschaft verkündigt hat, hat er nicht den Menschensohn verkündigt',[35] the idea of the kingdom and Son of Man being mutually exclusive concepts has been widely accepted. This is based on the observation that the two concepts do not occur together except in obviously redactional material, and thus seem to represent two strands of tradition.[36] Vielhauer's conclusion, that the kingdom is original with Jesus while his identification as Son of Man begins with the early Church, is a possible conclusion, but not a necessary one. Casey's claim to solve 'Vielhauer's dilemma' by denying the authenticity of all sayings about the coming of the Son of Man, and accepting as genuine only those with a generic sense according to an Aramaic idiom, is not really a solution, but only a slight modification.[37]

In spite of denying a Danielic background, Casey's stance does make room for authentic sayings referring to Jesus' death and vindication, 'because these were the circumstances in which the [Aramaic] idiom was used'.[38] We are still left, however, with a situation where an undeniable influence of Daniel on other aspects of Jesus' kingdom teaching is not allowed any possible impact on his ideas of suffering and exaltation. The impact of the Danielic Son of Man is confined to an early Christian interim period, leaving its firm traces in the Jesus traditions, but hardly at all in subsequent Christological development.

Another line of interpretation, associating the Son of Man sayings with Jesus' kingdom proclamation, has been suggested more or less explicitly by a number of English-speaking scholars. These readings have usually acknowledged the collective character of the Son of Man symbol in Daniel and presuppose a more or less original interpretation of this figure as representing the saints of the Most High. However, the implications of this have not always been spelled out clearly.

35. 'Since Jesus proclaimed the Kingdom of God, he did not proclaim the Son of Man', P. Vielhauer, *Aufsätze zum Neuen Testament* (Munich: Chr. Kaiser Verlag, 1965), p. 114; cf. pp. 55–91. The pages refer to material first published in 1963 and 1957 respectively.

36. In traditional Q research, the Son of Man is usually regarded as belonging to a late stratum, but this is being increasingly questioned. For dissenting views, see A. Järvinen, 'The Son of Man and his Followers' in D. Rhoads, K. Syreeni (eds.), *Characterization in the Gospels: Reconceiving Narrative Criticism* (JSNTSup, 184: Sheffield: Sheffield Academic Press, 1999), pp. 180–222; J. Schröter, 'The Son of Man as Representative of God's Kingdom: On the Interpretation of Jesus in Mark and Q', in M. Labahn, A. Schmidt (eds.), *Jesus, Mark and Q: The Teachings of Jesus and Its Earliest Records* (JSNTSup, 214; Sheffield: Sheffield Academic Press, 2001), pp. 34–68.

37. Casey, 'Idiom' (7), pp. 180–81. Cf. the modification of Vielhauer by E. Schweizer, saving present Son of Man sayings by understanding the expression as a circumlocution, in 'Der Menschensohn (Zur eschatologischen Erwartung Jesu)', *ZNW* 50 (1959), pp. 185–209.

38. Casey, 'Idiom' (7), p. 181.

Although he was not the first,[39] T. W. Manson drew attention to this line of interpretation in *The Teachings of Jesus*.[40] According to Manson, Jesus took the Son of Man idea, and with it its primary meaning, from Daniel 7. This ideal figure is an embodiment of the remnant idea and 'stands for the manifestation of the Kingdom of God on earth in a people wholly devoted to their heavenly King'.[41] Jesus' 'mission is to create the Son of Man, the Kingdom of the saints of the Most High, to realise in Israel the ideal contained in the term'.[42] Thus he expects his disciples to suffer together with him, sharing the sacrifice and destiny of the Son of Man, understood as a collective concept.[43] Jesus' demands for the kingdom are parallel to his demands for discipleship; his attempt to create the Son of Man in Israel is part of his proclamation of the kingdom. However, when no one follows him to the end, he has to travel the last part of the road alone, and thus at the cross he alone is the Son of Man, incarnating God's kingdom.[44]

While Manson's grand narrative ending is more speculative than historical, depending in part on his chronological reading of Mark,[45] and in part on Mark's Christological passion narrative, this line of interpretation makes it possible to accept both suffering and coming Son of Man sayings as originating with Jesus, in allusion to Daniel 7. Manson indicated two sayings (Mk 2.10, 28) where an original בר נשא, in the sense of 'human being', had been misunderstood, but he later withdrew from this position.[46] At a time before the findings at Qumran raised serious doubts as to the relevance of the Enochian Similitudes for the discussion, Manson suggested that *1 Enoch* does not support pre-existence, but rather an idea of pre-mundane election both of the Son of Man and of all the righteous elect ones. We thus find an oscillation between the individual and the corporate, a 'remarkable parallelism between the "Elect one" and the "Elect ones"'.[47] Other examples of this conception of 'corporate

39. Note the interpretations of Simon Episcopius (d. 1643), Sytse Hoekstra (1866), J. Estlin Carpenter (1890), Albert Réville (1897), William Sanday (1908) and Nils Messel (1922). References and years in Burkett, *Son of Man Debate* (11), pp. 35–36.

40. T. W. Manson, *The Teaching of Jesus: Studies of Its Form and Content* (Cambridge: Cambridge University Press, 1931), pp. 211–36.

41. Manson, *Teaching* (40), p. 227.

42. Manson, *Teaching* (40), p. 227.

43. Manson, *Teaching* (40), pp. 231–32. Manson finds a later follow-up of this in Paul's idea of being 'in' Christ (pp. 232–34).

44. Manson, *Teaching* (40), p. 235.

45. This weakness is noted by L. Gaston, *No Stone on Another: Studies in the Significance of the Fall of Jerusalem in the Synoptic Gospels* (NovTSup, 23; Leiden: Brill, 1970), p. 394.

46. Manson, *Teaching* (40), p. 214; *idem*, *Studies in the Gospels and Epistles* (ed. M. Black; Manchester: Manchester University Press, 1962), p. 143.

47. Manson, *Studies* (46), p. 140. The article referred to ('The Son of Man in Daniel, Enoch and the Gospels') was written in 1949.

personality' are found in a number of Jewish and Christian texts.[48] Thus, in the sayings of Jesus we should be prepared, according to Manson, to find that the Son of Man

> may stand for a community comparable to 'the people of the saints of the Most High' in Dan. vii., and that sometimes this community may be thought of as an aggregate of individual disciples, at others as a single corporate entity. Again we should be prepared to find that this corporate entity is embodied *par excellence* in Jesus himself in such a way that his followers, who together with him constitute the Son of Man as a group, may be thought of as extensions of his personality, or, as St. Paul puts it later on, limbs of his body.[49]

Manson suggests that all authentic instances of the expression in the Synoptics should be interpreted accordingly.

This line of interpretation was continued to some extent by C. H. Dodd, and by C. F. D. Moule, for whom the Son of Man in Daniel symbolizes 'the martyr-group of loyal Jews coming through persecution and vindicated by God'.[50] Moule agrees with Manson that 'Jesus interpreted his mission in terms of a corporate activity', and gives examples of parallel expectations of, or responsibilities of, Jesus/the Son of Man and the disciples.[51] This is done in the context of a chapter on 'The Corporate Christ', where a collective Son of Man concept is understood as forming the background to Paul's corporate ideas of being 'in' Christ.[52]

The clearest exposition of a collective or corporate interpretation is, however, found with Lloyd Gaston. The discussion is hidden within his large volume on the fall of Jerusalem in the synoptic Gospels.[53] Gaston, too, dismisses the idea of a pre-Christian apocalyptic Son of Man figure, seeing the symbol in Daniel 7 as representing an understanding of Israel, according to a suffering–exaltation pattern.[54] While Vielhauer was right about Jesus speaking of his mission and not of himself, the fact that 'the

---

48. Manson mentions Ps. 89.4; Isa. 41.8f.; Heb. 7.1–10; Eph. 1.4; *Gen. R.* 44, 27a (Manson, *Studies* [46], p. 141).

49. Manson, *Studies* (46), p. 143.

50. C. F. D. Moule, *The Phenomenon of the New Testament: An Inquiry into the Implications of Certain Features of the New Testament* (SBT, 2.1; London: SCM, 1967), p. 34. See also *idem, Essays in New Testament Interpretation* (Cambridge: Cambridge University Press, 1982), pp. 75–90.

51. Moule, *Phenomenon* (50), p. 35.

52. Moule, *Phenomenon* (50), pp. 21–42, especially pp. 38–39.

53. Gaston, *No Stone* (45), pp. 370–409; see also the subsequent section on the kingdom as promise and crisis (pp. 409–28).

54. Gaston, *No Stone* (45), pp. 381–82. Gaston sees the Danielic Son of Man as an interpretation of Isaiah's suffering servant along similar lines (symbolic representations of the suffering remnant people), thus picking up a thread from Dodd and Moule among others. He emphasizes, however, that this is not a question of merging two apocalyptic figures, since

kingdom' and 'Son of Man' normally do not occur together in synoptic
sayings can be explained by the two concepts being used synonymously.[55]
Gaston repeats Manson's identification of the Son of Man as a symbol for
the kingdom even more clearly, but criticizes his idea of a development in
which the Son of Man becomes an individual, as well as his ideas of
'corporate personality' and 'oscillation' of meaning. Instead Gaston
claims that Jesus used the expression for the community while the Gospel
authors came to use it for Jesus,[56] and he gives examples of how the
followers of Jesus elsewhere are ascribed similar powers or characteristics
as are associated with the Son of Man in Daniel 7.[57] In conclusion,

> for Jesus the term Son of Man was a collective concept, referring to the
> community he had come to call into existence, the eschatological Israel,
> which would pass through suffering to vindication. Only in this way can
> the derivation of the phrase from Dan 7 be understood. Only in this way
> can the development of the concept in the later church be understood, in
> which the term became restricted to Jesus and finally to his parousia,
> but many traces of the earlier conception remained.[58]

'Son of Man' is thus almost synonymous with 'kingdom of God'; 'the Son
of Man does not *have* a kingdom, he *is* the kingdom'.[59]

    In spite of asserting or at least suggesting that 'Son of Man' is
synonymous with 'kingdom', proponents of a corporate or collective
interpretation have tended to focus on people: the saints, the elect, the
suffering and faithful remnant, ideal Israel, followers, disciples. This is
quite in line, however, with the ambiguity of the Danielic symbols
themselves; as symbols of kingdoms they also represent leaders and
peoples. As we have seen above, the Son of Man in Daniel 7 represents a
kingdom of faithful Israelites. This is not how the majority in the early
Church interpreted Jesus' Son of Man sayings; they regarded *him* as the
Son of Man. However, if we want to suggest that the historical Jesus
understood and used the expression 'Son of Man' in a collective sense, we
should be able to trace a number of parallels in the Jesus tradition
between sayings about the Son of Man, the kingdom and the disciples.[60]

---

there were no such figures (pp. 379–82). While there are interesting parallels between the
Isaian servant and the Danielic Son of Man figures as both originally symbolizing the faithful
people of Israel, there is no room to discuss this in the present context.

    55. Gaston, *No Stone* (45), pp. 392–93.

    56. Gaston, *No Stone* (45), pp. 394–95.

    57. They will suffer and be exalted, given authority, given the kingdom, sit on thrones
and judge, travel on the clouds, etc.; Gaston, *No Stone* (45), pp. 405–08.

    58. Gaston, *No Stone* (45), p. 408.

    59. Gaston, *No Stone* (45), p. 409 (italics added).

    60. Analogies between the fate of the Son of Man and his followers were noted by G.
Theissen in *Sociology of Early Palestinian Christianity* (trans. J. Bowden; Philadelphia:
Fortress, 1978), pp. 24–30. Theissen's analysis is made from a sociological perspective

5. *The Authority of the Son of Man*

Two Son of Man sayings are often mentioned as clear examples of how an originally generic בר נשא has been misunderstood. They are both Markan, with synoptic parallels.

> ... in order that you shall know that the Son of Man has authority (ἐξουσίαν ἔχει) to forgive sins on earth ... (Mk 2.10)

> The Sabbath was made for man (διὰ τὸν ἄνθρωπον) and not man for the Sabbath; thus the Son of Man is Lord also of the Sabbath (Mk 2.27–28)

We have already mentioned that Manson changed his mind about these sayings. The first saying about authority to forgive sins has obvious correspondences to various sayings concerning the disciples. They are given authority, like the Son of Man in Daniel, and sent out on a mission of preaching and healing (Mk 6.7–13 pars.), which at least later is understood as including the forgiveness of sins (Lk. 24.47). The disciples' authority to forgive sins is presupposed in the special Matthaean material on binding and loosing (Mt. 18.15–18; cf. Jn 20.23). It is true that the Matthaean version of Mk 2.10 could be taken as revealing an original generic interpretation, because of the subsequent comment that the crowds 'praised God who had given such authority to human beings' (Mt. 9.8). This authority, however, does not seem to be given to each and every human being, as a generic interpretation would require. It belongs to the representatives of the kingdom: Jesus and his followers. And it must be understood in connection with the kingdom; Jesus' call to the kingdom concerns particularly sinners (Mk 2.17).[61]

The second saying about lordship is also a question of authority. The first half of the saying invites a generic interpretation of 'the Son of Man'. Perhaps this is the reason why it is omitted not only by Matthew, but also by Luke, since they identify the Son of Man with Jesus. However, this explanation is also possible with a collective interpretation. The point of the Markan version of the corn-plucking incident is that the needs of the disciples carry more weight than a strict interpretation of Sabbath laws. As they, together with Jesus, proclaim and enact the kingdom, their urgent errand at times overrules legal concerns. An example of this could

---

(analysis of roles, social role-taking). From a literary point of view, this connection has been pointed out by Järvinen, 'Son of Man' (36), pp. 189–90, discussing characterization in Q. While I certainly agree with Järvinen that the (limited) characterization of Jesus has the effect of contemporizing the situation of Jesus for the readers, making it possible to step inside the text, I would not regard the connection between Jesus and the disciples as *created* by the narrator of Q. It is present throughout the Gospel tradition (thus already Manson, *Teaching* [40], pp. 201–11, 231–32) and must be regarded as an historical one.

61. Paul's attitude in this respect seems to contradict Jesus; cf. 1 Cor. 6.9.

be the instruction to the disciples proclaiming the coming kingdom, to eat whatever is set before them (Lk. 10.8; *Gos. Thom.* 14).[62] Elsewhere, Jesus' disciples are criticized for not accommodating to legal practices, too,[63] and this could likewise be interpreted in a kingdom perspective.[64]

While it is not possible to prove an original collective meaning from this comparison, I find it likely in the first case (Mk 2.10) and quite possible in the second (Mk 2.28). To Jesus, the authority and priority ascribed to the Son of Man concerned the kingdom and its adherents, i.e., those to whom the kingdom was given, not least himself and his disciples. This included others, however, who were not normally reckoned among the faithful remnant.

6. *The Son of Man Among Sinners and the Homeless*

In Q, we find two sayings about the Son of Man, with no correspondence in Mark, reflecting in various ways the conditions of Jesus' mission.[65]

> The Son of Man has come eating and drinking, and you (Lk.)/they (Mt.) say: look what a glutton and drunkard, a friend of tax collectors and sinners (Lk. 7.34/Mt. 11.19).

> The foxes have holes and the birds have nests, but the Son of Man has nowhere to rest his head (Lk. 9.58/Mt. 8.20).

The first saying reflects a common accusation against Jesus, and compares him with John the Baptizer. In Q, this saying comes at the end of a section which begins with John questioning Jesus' mission. Jesus answers the objections by alluding to Isaiah 61, a text that was associated with the messianic kingdom at this time, as is clear from Qumran.[66] In Q this is

---

62.   Cf. J. Svartvik, *Mark and Mission: Mk 7.1-23 in its Narrative and Historical Contexts* (ConBNT, 32; Stockholm: Almqvist & Wiksell International, 2000), pp. 153–55. The reconstruction by Crossan is too speculative; J. D. Crossan, *The Historical Jesus: The Life of a Mediterranean Jewish Peasant* (New York: HarperSanFransisco, 1991), pp. 332–48. Note the similar formulation of Paul in 1 Cor. 10.27.

63.   Mk 2.18 pars.; Mk 7.1–2 pars.; Lk. 5.30 (in the Matthaean and Markan parallels the accusation is turned against Jesus himself).

64.   Especially the saying about the bridegroom (Mk 2. 18–20 pars.).

65.   Among Q scholars, the Son of Man has usually been thought to belong to a later stratum (Q^2) emphasizing judgment, in distinction to an earlier stratum intent on wisdom teaching (for a convenient summary, see J. S. Kloppenborg, *The Formation of Q: Trajectories in Ancient Wisdom Collections* (SAC; Philadelphia: Fortress, 1987), pp. 317–28. Apart from general scepticism towards detailed stratification of a hypothetical document by some scholars, this particular division has been seriously questioned by Järvinen, 'Son of Man' (36), arguing from the function of Son of Man sayings in Q as interpretive links between deuteronomistic material and wisdom language.

66.   See 4Q521 Frag. 2, 2.1–14; Cf. Kazen, *Jesus and Purity* (3), pp. 246–48.

followed by Jesus confirming the role of John, but simultaneously giving priority to the least in the kingdom (ὁ δὲ μικρότερος ἐν τῇ βασιλείᾳ τοῦ θεοῦ).[67]

The accusation of being a friend of sinners and tax collectors is standard in the synoptic Gospels, and according to Luke it was raised not only against Jesus but also against his disciples.[68] It reflects the historical fact that Jesus extended his kingdom proclamation and fellowship to such groups of people, and that improper eating by Jesus and his disciples was an issue.[69] This could partly be explained as above, by the kingdom having higher priority than legal, or in this case perhaps, moral concerns, but there is also the real question of how the 'saints' are to be defined. The Jesus tradition bears witness in various ways to another type of order, where the poor are praised and the children are blessed, in both cases because the kingdom of God belongs to them.[70] Indeed, according to Matthew tax collectors and whores will enter it before the pious (Mt. 21.31). This is expressed with perhaps typical Lukan moralizing, in the Lukan saying concluding the story of Zacchaeus: 'the Son of Man has come to seek and save the lost' (Lk. 19.10).

The second saying is quite different, belonging to a context dealing with discipleship. In Luke, the man asking to become a disciple of Jesus is followed by two other examples. The first two are found in Matthew too, and were thus joined already in Q. In our text, Jesus' answer refers to the homelessness of the Son of Man. In the following example, Jesus challenges the man who first wants to bury his father to go and proclaim the kingdom of God. Here we actually have a Son of Man saying and a kingdom saying combined. Of course, they are the result of redaction at *some* stage; the men were not historically lining up for job interviews. The point is that the expressions are found in parallel situations: Son of Man means homelessness; kingdom means renouncing family relationships. They are both about the same thing, or expressing similar concerns.

None of these sayings make much sense when interpreted generically, as referring to human beings in general. A collective interpretation, however, corresponds well with what we otherwise consider historically plausible about the group of people identifying with, proclaiming and enacting the kingdom of God: Jesus and his followers. Their hardships, implied in the

---

67. The characterization of John and his relationship to Jesus is ambiguous in Q; on the one hand he parallels Jesus and is viewed as the starting point for the kingdom (cf. below on Mt. 11.12/Lk. 16.16); on the other he seems to be portrayed as a forerunner of and inferior to those belonging to the kingdom. The discrepancies are perhaps best understood as reflecting the need of early Christians to distance themselves from the Baptizer's movement. Cf. Järvinen, 'Son of Man' (36), pp. 191–93.

68. Lk. 5.30.

69. Cf. the corn-plucking incident, discussed above, as well as the issue in Mark 7.

70. E.g. Mt. 5.3–12/Lk. 6.20–23; Mk 9.36–37 pars.; Mk 10.13–16 pars.

Q-sayings, are reinforced and spelled out in the 'suffering Son of Man' sayings.

7. *The Suffering of the Son of Man*

It is not possible in the present context to discuss every Son of Man saying, which refers to suffering. Manson noted that such sayings were not found in Q (which fits the absence of a passion story) or in special Matthaean material (which might be explained by the emphasis on the parousia).[71] Matthew has, however, taken over suffering Son of Man sayings from Mark, and he associates suffering with the Son of Man even where the expression is an obvious redaction.[72] Luke has treated these sayings similarly.

The most prominent sayings in this category are the three so-called predictions of the suffering Son of Man (Mk 8.31; 9.31; 10.33 pars.). In the first of these, Matthew omits the expression altogether, making Jesus talk about himself only. The individual identification between the Son of Man and Jesus is thus assumed or declared by the Gospel author. The key words are 'suffer' (πολλὰ παθεῖν), 'rejected' (ἀποδοκιμασθῆναι; not in Matthew) and 'killed' (ἀποκτανθῆναι).[73] In the second and third sayings, the triad is 'hand over/betray' (παραδιδόναι), 'condemn to death/kill' and 'raise'. There are considerable variations, however, especially in the way the two latter elements are expressed.

The terminology of 'handing over/betraying' the Son of Man is conspicuous, and recurs in the tradition of the last supper (Mk. 14.18–21 pars.) as well as at the very betrayal itself in Gethsemane (Mk 14.41; Mt. 26.45; cf. Lk. 22.48). While all these sayings show signs of being shaped *ex eventu*, we must ask whether the idea of the Son of Man being 'handed over' has a previous history. The first saying uses different language, but speaks of suffering, rejection and death. While at first sight, this is far from Daniel's image of the Son of Man receiving power and glory, the context is that of the saints first having been subject to persecution and suffering at the hands of Antiochos, symbolized by the little horn of the fourth beast. Note the vocabulary of the LXX (o') Dan. 7.25:

---

71.   Manson, *Teaching* (40), pp. 213–27. The evidence for suffering Son of Man sayings in Luke is weak. The examples are probably best understood as Lukan redaction, with a possible exception for Lk. 22.48.

72.   Cf. Mt. 26.2. Although the Son of Man is not said to suffer in Mt. 10.23, the disciples' suffering is associated with the Son of Man. This material might very well be labelled 'M' (against Manson, *Teaching* [40], pp. 221–22).

73.   Note the similarity with Lk. 17.25, supporting the idea that the first suffering Son of Man saying represents a different tradition from the second and third.

καὶ παραδοθήσεται πάντα εἰς τὰς χεῖρας αὐτοῦ ἕως καιροῦ καὶ καιρῶν καὶ ἕως ἡμίσους καιροῦ.

and compare this with Mk 9.31:

ὁ υἱὸς τοῦ ἀνθρώπου παραδίδοται εἰς χεῖρας ἀνθρώπων, καὶ . . . μετὰ τρεῖς ἡμέρας ἀναστήσεται.

Those scholars who doubt that the idea of a suffering Son of Man could originate with Daniel, resorting to a generic explanation, may need to consider the evidence once more.[74] If this figure was taken as faithful Israel, the kingdom of saints, vindicated after persecution and suffering, it might even have been possible to understand the suffering of the Son of Man as a scriptural idea. This could explain the difficult saying in Mk 9.11–13:

Καὶ ἐπηρώτων αὐτὸν λέγοντες· ὅτι λέγουσιν οἱ γραμματεῖς ὅτι Ἠλίαν δεῖ ἐλθεῖν πρῶτον; ὁ δὲ ἔφη αὐτοῖς· Ἠλίας μὲν ἐλθὼν πρῶτον ἀποκαθιστάνει πάντα· καὶ πῶς γέγραπται ἐπὶ τὸν υἱὸν τοῦ ἀνθρώπου ἵνα πολλὰ πάθῃ καὶ ἐξουδενηθῇ; ἀλλὰ λέγω ὑμῖν ὅτι καὶ Ἠλίας ἐλήλυθεν, καὶ ἐποίησαν αὐτῷ ὅσα ἤθελον, καθὼς γέγραπται ἐπ' αὐτόν.

While Matthew reworks this material to speak about the Baptizer as Elijah and Jesus as the Son of Man, the first preceding the second and providing a pattern for Jesus' suffering, Mark seems to reflect a more original understanding. Interpreting 'Son of Man' as a collective concept, the Markan text is not confused, but clear. The reference to Scripture for the eschatological coming of Elijah[75] is met by another reference to Scripture concerning the suffering of the Son of Man. The obvious candidate for a passage is not a hypothetical combination of proof texts together with unproven eschatological ideas, but the corporate understanding of the Son of Man in Daniel 7 as the saints, who receive the kingdom after having suffered much. Expectations of eschatological suffering would have been triggered by such expressions as καὶ ἔσται καιρὸς θλίψεως (Dan. 12.1) in a context dealing with the fate of the people and the possibility of resurrection.[76] In Mark, the idea is not of two figures, one succeeding the other, but of the scriptural idea of Elijah restoring the people in view of God's coming, interpreted through the likewise scriptural idea of the kingdom and its adherents, including the Baptizer, being subject to suffering and contempt. The point is that Jesus and his disciples must not expect to avoid a similar fate to the Baptizer, since such suffering is a necessary prelude to the restoration of the

74. Cf. among others Casey and Lindars; see n. 20 above.
75. Mal. 4.5–6; Sir. 48.10.
76. Cf. Jesus' eschatological discourse, Mk 13.19.

kingdom or the vindication of the Son of Man. Whether the identification of the Baptizer with Elijah is first made by Mark, or possibly by Jesus himself, is not of crucial importance. In any case it seems as if Jesus saw the fate of the Baptizer as part of a suffering Son of Man paradigm.[77]

This fits with numerous sayings warning disciples that suffering, contempt and violent death will be theirs too, and frequently referring to the kingdom or to the Son of Man.[78] The kingdom, with its adherents, is subject to violence from those who oppose it. From this perspective, the Q saying about violence to the kingdom can be seen as parallel to Markan sayings about the suffering of the Son of Man:

ἀπὸ δὲ τῶν ἡμερῶν Ἰωάννου τοῦ βαπτιστοῦ ἕως ἄρτι ἡ βασιλεία τῶν οὐρανῶν βιάζεται καὶ βιασταὶ ἁρπάζουσιν αὐτήν. (Mt. 11.12)

ὁ νόμος καὶ οἱ προφῆται μέχρι Ἰωάννου· ἀπὸ τότε ἡ βασιλεία τοῦ θεοῦ εὐαγγελίζεται καὶ πᾶς εἰς αὐτὴν βιάζεται. (Lk. 16.16)

Whether the βιάσται are interpreted as spiritual powers or human adversaries,[79] the point is clear, according to J. P. Meier, that the kingdom, 'understood in this saying as the palpable, immanent manifestation of God's kingly rule in Israel's history, and more particularly in the ministry of Jesus, is suffering violent opposition'.[80] Violence is being exercised against the kingdom, against its representatives, against the Son of Man, against the saints that are now understood as referred to by this

---

77. Cf. Gaston, *No Stone* (45), pp. 402–03.

78. Mt. 5.10–11; 10.23; Mk 13.9–13, 19 pars.; Lk. 6.22 (Q; in Matthew's version, 5.11, 'Son of Man' is replaced by 'me'. In Lk. 6.22, 'Son of Man' could just as well be replaced by 'kingdom'). Compare this with early Christian expectations of suffering and persecution: Rom. 8.17; 1 Thess. 3.4; 2 Thess. 1.5; Acts 9.16; Jn 15.20.

79. Cf. among others, A. Fridrichsen, 'Jesu kamp mot de urene ånder', *STK* 5 (1929), pp. 299–314 (306); A. N. Wilder, *Eschatology and Ethics in the Teaching of Jesus* (New York: Harper & Brothers, rev. edn, 1950), p. 58; W. G. Kümmel, *Verheißung und Erfüllung: Untersuchungen zur eschatologischen Verkündigung Jesu* (ATANT, 6: Zurich: Zwingli-Verlag, 1953), p. 116; Kazen, *Jesus and Purity* (3), pp. 331–32.

80. J. P. Meier, *A Marginal Jew: Rethinking the Historical Jesus*, vol. 2 *Mentor, Message, and Miracles* (ABRL; New York: Doubleday, 1994), p. 403. The differences in nuance, or even the possibilities of quite contradicting interpretations of the two versions of the *Stürmerspruch*, are well known. Cf. U. Luz, *Das Evangelium nach Matthäus. vol. 2: Mt 8–17* (EKKNT, I.2; Neukirchen-Vluyn: Neukirchener, 1990), pp. 176–80. In Matthew, the most plausible interpretation is that the kingdom is suffering violence. In Luke, a positive interpretation might suit the Lukan idea of periods in salvation history, but a more natural interpretation is that of people forcing themselves into the kingdom. The Matthaean variant is to be preferred as more original, apart from the substitution of 'kingdom of heaven' for 'kingdom of God'; cf. W. D. Davies, D. C. Allison, *A Critical and Exegetical Commentary on The Gospel according to Saint Matthew*, vol. 2: *Commentary on Matthew VIII–XVIII* (ICC; Edinburgh: T&T Clark, 1991), pp. 253–54. Without the preposition εἰς, the plain meaning of the Lukan variant, too, would be that people are causing the kingdom violence.

imagery: Jesus and his followers. The Baptizer serves as a sort of hinge and a precedent for the way of the kingdom/the Son of Man.[81] The final fate expected for the kingdom is, however, that of the Son of Man in Daniel 7: vindication, authority and glory.

8. *The Son of Man Exalted and Returning*

When we turn to future Son of Man sayings, parallels with sayings about the coming kingdom are obvious. This may be explained by the influence of early Christian eschatology, resulting in an identification of Jesus with the Son of Man understood as an individual. A prime example of this process is found in Mt. 16.27, where Mark's 'kingdom of God coming with power' is developed into 'the Son of Man coming with his kingdom'.

Postponing for a moment the coming Son of Man, we may look at his vindication or exaltation, in accordance with Daniel 7. The Danielic figure does come, but as many have observed, not to earth, but with the clouds to the Ancient of Days.[82] The exaltation of the saints was interpreted as their vindication, and at times as their taking part in divine judgment, taking their places on thrones together with God.[83] The Son of Man is described as sitting at the right hand of God, in Mk 14.62 pars. While no claims can be made for this saying reflecting the historical court action against Jesus, it is more likely to represent his own understanding than those sayings which speak about his 'return' to earth. In Matthew we can see how this image of the Son of Man on his throne, exercising judgment, is further developed, but now in the explicit context of an eschatological return of Jesus as individual redeemer.[84] Interpreted collectively, however, this image represents the saints of the kingdom, Jesus and his followers in particular, as taking part in divine judgment as the kingdom takes shape. This idea is found elsewhere, without the Son of Man being mentioned: Mt. 20.21; Lk. 22.30; cf. 1 Cor. 6.2. It is thus likely that the vindication of

---

81. The question of which side or age Luke considers the Baptizer as belonging to cannot be answered on lexical grounds. See F. Bovon, *Das Evangelium nach Lukas. vol. 3: Lk 15,1–19,27* (EKKNT, III.3; Neukirchen-Vluyn: Neukirchener, 2001), p. 99. For the present purpose, the point is that it is possible to argue that Jesus (and his early followers) included the Baptizer in a collective understanding of the suffering Son of Man. The perspective is similar to Mk 9.11–13: 'Vor allem aber gilt: Johannes, Jesus und die Jünger erleiden die gleiche Gewalt, wenn das Himmelreich anbricht'. Luz, *Matthäus 2* (80), p. 180.

82. Possibly, the imagery of 1 Thess. 4.17, where the saints are carried with the clouds to meet the Lord, could be taken as remains of a collective interpretation.

83. For a comparison with some intertestamental material, see C. Grappe, 'Le logion des douze trônes: Eclairages intertestamentaires', in M. Philonenko (ed.), *Le Trône de Dieu* (WUNT, 69; Tübingen: Mohr Siebeck, 1993), pp. 204–12.

84. Mt. 16.27; 19.28; 25.31.

the Son of Man in the Jesus tradition was originally understood in line with Daniel 7 and applied to Jesus and his followers collectively.[85]

This may well be the case with Mk 13.24–27 pars., too. Here the image of sitting, implying thrones and judgment, is missing, seemingly leaving the emphasis on the coming. The idea of *return* is, however, not spelled out. As L. Hartman demonstrated in *Prophecy Interpreted*, the eschatological discourse is best read as a midrash on Daniel, the core of which probably goes back to Jesus.[86] Thus the coming is set in Daniel's apocalyptic context. It is not a coming to the throne of God, however, and the imagery is fused with prophetic imagery belonging to the day of the Lord. In addition, the Son of Man performs the divine task of gathering the scattered elect.[87] Matthew reinforces the apocalyptic imagery (sign of the Son of Man, tribes will grieve, great trumpet), and Luke postpones the 'event' to an indefinite future (after the time of the Gentiles), blending the apocalyptic imagery with allusion to the Psalms.[88] All three versions, however (with some slight reservations for Luke), belong to early Christian contexts where Jesus was expected to return. We can understand some of the mechanisms behind this expectation: the kingdom that Jesus proclaimed did not materialize during his lifetime; his sudden and premature death necessitated revisions of previous hopes; belief in his resurrection and experiences of his continued presence made it possible for his vision to mutate and continue to inspire faith and action. Various Old Testament and early Jewish eschatological and apocalyptic conceptions contributed to this process of reconfiguration.

There is no room here to further pursue this process. It means, however, that we must ask whether an original midrash was focused not on *returning*, but rather on the same issues as Mk 14.62 pars. Although the image of *sitting* is missing, the various allusions mentioned do suggest judgment, which is Matthew's interpretation, evidenced by the number of judgment parables added at the end of the discourse. In an underlying midrash, this would not necessarily imply an end-of-the-world perspective. It should be noted that the eschatological imagery is utilized freely by Gospel authors: Matthew in connection with the death and resurrection of Jesus, Luke in applying prophecies of cosmic upheaval to the day of Pentecost.[89] This language is ambiguous. It is uncertain to what extent it was intended to be understood literally.

85. Cf. J. Dupont, 'Le logion des douze trônes (Mt 19,28; Lc 22,28–30)', *Bib* 45 (1964), pp. 355–92.

86. Hartman, *Prophecy Interpreted* (25), pp. 145–252, especially pp. 172–74, 247–48.

87. Hartman, *Prophecy Interpreted* (25), pp. 156–57.

88. For Luke, cf. Hartman, *Prophecy Interpreted* (25), pp. 226–35; T. Kazen, 'Standing Helpless at the Roar and Surging of the Sea: Reading Biblical Texts in the Shadow of the Wave'; *ST* 60 (2006); pp. 21–41.

89. Mt. 27.51–53; 28.2–3; Acts 2.16–21.

Jesus may have spoken of the coming Son of Man in a collective or corporate sense, too. This would then have been Danielic kingdom imagery, suggesting the imminent coming of God's reign and the vindication of Jesus himself and his followers as proponents of this kingdom, with their even playing a role in divine judgment.[90] The coming of the Son of Man would then be a parallel to the coming of the kingdom. Sayings such as Mk 8.38 pars.; Mt. 10.23; 16.27 or Lk. 12.40/Mt. 24.44 may be interpreted this way.[91] The coming of the kingdom was central to Jesus' message and activity,[92] and the kingdom is described as coming with power, just like the Son of Man (Mk 9.1; 13.26). This is not a future expectation only, but the power of the kingdom is recognized in the healings and exorcisms of Jesus, and associated with the powers of the Son of Man, not only to heal, but also to forgive. The imagery of the coming Son of Man may, in Jesus' context, be understood as the full vindication of the kingdom, which is gradually becoming visible in the message and mission of Jesus and his followers. The idea of the early Church that Jesus would return to earth in person as an individual redeemer – the Son of Man – has later shaped some of these sayings, and is at times read into sayings where it is not explicitly formulated.[93] There are enough old remnants in the traditions, however, for us to see that Jesus may have spoken of the coming Son of Man in a somewhat different sense.

9. *From Corporate Symbol to Individual Redeemer Figure*

The discussion of Son of Man sayings has been far from comprehensive. A number of sayings have not been dealt with, such as the question of blasphemy against the Son of Man (Mt. 12.32/Lk. 12.10) or the Son of Man being ashamed (Mk 8.38 pars.).[94] Most important of the sayings not

90. Cf. A. Yarbro Collins, 'The Apocalyptic Son of Man Sayings', in B. A. Pearson (ed.), *The Future of Early Christianity: Essays in Honor of Helmut Koester* (Minneapolis: Fortress, 1991), pp. 220–28. Yarbro Collins argues (against Perrin) that the Danielic Son of Man language in Mk 13.26 was Jesus' own way of expressing the future dimension of the kingdom. She suggests, however, that Jesus might have been the first to interpret Dan. 7.13 as the coming of an eschatological individual redeemer figure (p. 228).

91. Cf. Lk. 17.30; 18.8. In Mk 8.38 this interpretation is obvious on a redactional level, as the coming Son of Man and the saying in Mk 9.1 about God's kingdom coming with power are juxtaposed. A process of mutual influence between these two imageries seems to be going on, as they are being reinterpreted by early Christians.

92. Mk 1.15; 9.1; Mt. 10.7; 12.28; Lk. 10.9, 11; 11.20; 17.20.

93. Cf. Gaston, *No Stone* (45), pp. 403–08; Dunn, *Jesus Remembered* (4), pp.747–58. Dunn suggests that the idea of Jesus' *return* to earth was the result of a 'post-Easter merging of the Son of Man coming motif with the return motif of the crisis parables' (Dunn, *Jesus Remembered* [4], p. 761).

94. In the first case, the Markan version (Mk 3.28–29) suggests that an original generic 'sons of men' has been somehow corrupted. In the second case, a generic understanding is

discussed is Mk 10.45 (repeated by Mt. 20.28), reversing the Danielic idea of all people serving the Son of Man, i.e., the kingdom (Dan. 7.14, 27) to a different vision: the Son of Man serving the many.[95] We have tried to show, however, that a collective or corporate understanding of the expression ὁ υἱὸς τοῦ ἀνθρώπου in the synoptic Gospels makes it possible to understand both Jesus' own usage and the early Christian identification of him, individually, as the Son of Man. While it is quite possible that certain Son of Man sayings do originate with a generic use of the Aramaic בר נשא, this idea – as a blanket explanation for the origin of the expression in the Jesus tradition – does not make it easy to explain the transition from Jesus to the early Church. A Danielic, corporate understanding of the Son of Man symbol depends on a basic generic use of the Aramaic expression and respects the original interpretation of the figure in Daniel 7. Taking 'Son of Man' as a collective reference to God's coming kingdom, its saints, representatives or adherents, fits with the influence of Daniel not only on the Jesus tradition, but also on Jesus' own focus on the kingdom. We have seen that Son of Man sayings of various types can profitably be interpreted from this perspective, and that there are numerous parallels between what is claimed for the Son of Man and what is said of the kingdom or required of the disciples.

Since Jesus and his followers are included in the Son of Man concept, there was some ground for the subsequent transition of this expression to become an individual title for the Christian redeemer. Jesus and his movement had a crucial role in the embodiment of the kingdom in their own eyes, even before Easter. As Jesus died, and reinterpretation of the kingdom vision was made necessary, his own part did not diminish, but rather increased, as the ensuing Christological development – some would say explosion – shows. As the proclaimer became the object of proclamation, the Son of Man as kingdom imagery became identified with Jesus as individual. The Jesus tradition was accordingly modified over time, to reflect the present understanding of Jesus' message. In spite of this, a more original corporate understanding can be traced in a number of texts, as we have seen. This interpretation of the Son of Man *includes* Jesus, however, and thus makes the transmutation both possible and comprehensible. While it is reasonable to assume that the early Church came up with some entirely new and original ideas, it would be unwise to postulate such a line of development in an area as central as this one, when a much simpler solution is available.

---

quite impossible, but a collective interpretation makes sense: those who are ashamed or deny (Mt. 10.33) the message of Jesus will themselves be put to shame or denied at the vindication of the kingdom.

95. Cf. Dunn, *Jesus Remembered* (4), pp. 814–15.

JESUS AND THE 'SERVANT' COMMUNITY IN ZION:
CONTINUITY IN CONTEXT

Sean Freyne

The proposal by G. Theissen and A. Merz of a criterion of contextual plausibility is intended as a counter to the criterion of dissimilarity as this has been practised in recent discussions of the historical Jesus. The application of this latter criterion had divorced Jesus from his Jewish matrix, thereby presenting us with an a-historical, non-localized figure whose life had little or no impact on the movement that arose in his name. The formulation by Theissen and Merz acknowledges the diversity of the Jewish context within which Jesus' ministry took place and allows for Jesus' own distinctive contribution within that setting.[1] There is still plenty of room for debate, therefore, as to the most appropriate context – social, geographical and religious – within which to situate the Jesus movement and to evaluate his own distinctive contribution within that setting. In this chapter I would like to explain the underlying argument of my recent book, *Jesus, a Jewish Galilean*,[2] while also expanding its applicability to a discussion of the links between Jesus and the Early Christian movement as represented by the Jerusalem church.

I shall develop the following four theses:

1. The primary context for Jesus and his movement is that which has come to be described as 'Jewish Restoration Eschatology', a concept that was by no means univocal for all who shared hopes of restoration.
2. This shared horizon was contested among different groups and movements on the basis of geographical, social and religious differences.
3. Jerusalem is the symbolic centre of the Restoration Eschatology of the Second Temple period, even when there was severe criticism of its present role. Contrary to some recent claims that as a Galilaean Jesus was opposed to Jerusalem, the Jesus movement saw itself in

1. G. Theissen, A. Merz, *The Historical Jesus: A Comprehensive Guide* (trans. J. Bowden; London: SCM Press, 1996), pp. 114–18.
2. S. Freyne, *Jesus, a Jewish Galilean: A New Reading of the Jesus-Story* (London: T&T Clark International, 2004).

continuity with a minority version of the prevailing Zion tradition, as this was first articulated in the latter part of the book of Isaiah (Isa. 55–66), and carried forward subsequently by others such as the *maśkilîm* who appear in the book of Daniel. These literary expressions are indicators of extra-textual realities of conflict – social and religious – between the group that espoused the particular values associated with the servant figure and those who controlled the dominant ethos within the temple community of the post-exilic period.

4. The importance of Jerusalem's symbolic role within the restoration hopes of the Second Temple explains the presence of a community there. headed by James, 'the brother of the Lord', shortly after the crucifixion. The Jerusalem community, both in terms of its lifestyle and its theology, continued to play this symbolically legitimating role for the early Christian movement despite the success of the Pauline mission.

I will expand on each of these proposals, concentrating in particular on the last two since these are central to any discussion of Jesus in continuity.

1. *Restoration Eschatology*

Both terms are quite important in the context of understanding the Jesus movement. 'Restoration' on its own need not imply a final solution, but merely a return to the *status quo ante*. For some at least the return from the Babylonian exile meant no more than re-establishing the institutions that had been lost in exile – temple, priesthood and cult in particular – an exercise in *realpolitik* within the Persian empire. Adding an eschatological factor to the mix introduces the further element of myth-making, or idealization of the past with a view to the present and the future. When this kind of eschatological thinking adopts an apocalyptic or millennial turn, as it did at various moments of crisis during the Second Temple period, there is the added note of urgency. This arises from a deep sense of dissatisfaction with the present and a desire to express the restoration in the most universal and comprehensive manner possible, calling for a new creation that is national, cosmic, social and personal.

All these dimensions of restoration are expressed in the literature of the Second Temple period including the final redaction of the Law and the Prophets, which must be included in any estimation of that varied corpus of writings.[3] Various trends can be discerned, even within the same work, all of which are expressive of competing viewpoints, as we shall see. The spectrum of opinion on what is to be done is a broad one – everything

3. See J. M. Scott (ed.), *Restoration: Old Testament, Jewish and Christian Perspectives* (Leiden: Brill, 2001).

from militant activism to apocalyptic quietism, and in such an atmosphere of expectation and hope it is important to highlight the myth-making capacity of Jewish theological thinking. The final version of the Pentateuch locates the story of Israel's election and occupation of the Promised Land within the cosmic and universal horizons of the figures of Adam and Abraham as described in the book of Genesis, thereby indicating that Israel could never be satisfied with mere restoration of what had been lost through exile. Likewise, the book of Isaiah and other prophetic books show that in exile Israel had explored deeper levels of the meaning and purpose of her election. In the light of these insights history becomes prophecy, a typology for the present and the future, whose hidden meanings are to be explored, rewritten and reinterpreted in the often confusing, but always creative, variations of the literature of the Second Temple period.

We must allow Jesus of Nazareth, no mere peasant in any conventional sense, but a disciple of John the Baptizer, to participate personally (and not just posthumously, through his disciples) in this activity of creative interpretation of the restoration traditions of his own people. Otherwise his *persona* is forever lost, denied by modern critical scholarship of the opportunity to express itself through the rich heritage of the tradition as this is to be found in the Gospel portraits. Such a suggestion does not in any way represent a return to a pre-critical stance with regard to the Gospels, but rather begins with the very legitimate presupposition that behind the chorus of witnesses *to* Jesus there is a distinctive 'voice' and 'vision' *of* Jesus that on solid historical grounds can still be heard and experienced. Indeed it is this presupposition which also makes it possible and legitimate to explore the real continuity between Jesus and the movement that arose in his name.

2. *The Contested Horizon of Restoration Hopes*

In a Jewish context restoration meant return, and return implied allotted place. The stories of conquest and settlement in the books of Joshua and Judges suggest an incomplete process. The land 'not-conquered' (Josh. 13.1–6) and the failure of the tribes to occupy fully their allotted territories (Judges 1) meant that the actual boundaries of Israel never attained their ideal dimensions and hence Israel had not established itself properly in the land of Canaan. While there are some variations with regard to what those ideal boundaries were, at their most expansive they corresponded to the journey of Abraham (Gen. 13.13–17), which on an east/west axis covered the Great Sea to the Euphrates, and in a north/south direction extended from the Wadi of Egypt to the Taurus mountains (Ezek. 47.17;

Num. 13.31; 34.7–9; 1 Kgs 4.21; 2 Chron. 9.26).[4] In the eschatological realization of the promise whereby Israel would become her true self, tribal and land boundaries would at last coalesce. Successive generations of Jews viewed the process of achieving this goal differently: the Maccabees, for example, considered military conquest, whereas the rabbis concentrated their efforts on defining the boundaries with regard to the purity regulations for those 'who came up from Babylon'.[5] While their respective concerns show that the issue of the greater Israel was alive in the first century, Jesus did not share either perspective. His journeys of healing and proclaiming the kingdom of God as described by Mark seem to have some awareness of this 'greater Israel' in view, since they take him well outside the borders of political Galilee of his own day. Either we attribute these 'fictitious' journeys to Mark and his theological agenda, as many scholars do, even when they differ as to their significance, or we adopt the long perspective that the narratives of the Hebrew Bible provide and enquire as to the possible significance for Jesus himself of such movement within the context of a restoration perspective.[6]

Closely related to this ideology of the ideal land was that of the centrality of Jerusalem, based on the traditions to do with the Davidic kingship, but developed independently in terms of Zion, once the institution of the monarchy had failed. The 'mythopoiesis of Zion', to use Joseph Blenkinsopp's expression, intensified in the exilic and post-exilic periods. Zion's significance is cosmic and universal in Isaiah and in the Psalms of Zion, but this concentration on Jerusalem as the 'centre of the middle of the earth', as *Jubilees* expresses it (*Jub.* 8.19), did not exclude or ignore the more limited, but equally important boundaries of the ideal land. Zebulon and Naphtali can expect light also, together with 'the way of the sea' and $g^e l\hat{\imath}l$ $hagg\hat{o}yim$. The servant who is destined to bring salvation to the end of the earth has also the task of restoring the tribes of Jacob (Isa. 8.23; 49.6).[7]

The Jesus movement would appear to have shared both of these aspects of restoration, the particular and the universal. The symbolic significance of the Twelve suggests the importance of a reconstituted Israel as the first stage of universal restoration. However, while the number Twelve was clearly important, it is significant that for Jesus the idea does not have a territorial dimension as described in some versions of restoration, for

---

4. S. Freyne, 'The Geography of Restoration: Galilee–Jerusalem Relations in Early Jewish and Early Christian Experience', *NTS* 47 (2001), pp. 289–311 (293–95); M. Bockmuehl, 'Antioch and James the Just', in B. Chilton, C. A. Evans (eds.), *James the Just and Christian Origins* (NovTSup, 98; Leiden: Brill, 1999), pp. 155–98 (169–79).

5. R. Frankel *et al.*, *Settlement Dynamics and Regional Diversity in Ancient Upper Galilee: IAA Reports 14* (Jerusalem: Israel Exploration Authority, 2001), pp. 110–14.

6. T. Schmeller, 'Jesus in Umland Galiläas', *BZ* 38 (1994), pp. 44–66.

7. Freyne, *Jesus, a Jewish Galilean* (2), pp. 94–95.

instance Ezekiel. Rather, it is what the collective group represents that is essential, namely that the restoration of Israel has been set in train. Jesus and his group would not engage in any militant reclamation of the ideal land, or even the tribal territories – the agenda of militant nationalists since the Maccabean times as expressed by the third of the brothers, Simon (1 Macc. 15.33). Such a course of action was still very actual in Roman Galilee, as emerged later in the first century, but the Jesus movement had other ideas of restoration that would be more conciliatory towards 'the nations round about' even if it is unclear as to how Jesus viewed their ultimate inclusion at the eschatological banquet with the Patriarchs (Mt. 8.11; Lk. 13.28).

This image of shared food is employed in his response to the Syro-Phoenician woman also, suggesting that Jesus' own focus was firmly on Israel first, yet it was a focus that was neither ethno-phobic nor exclusivist. The 'lost sheep of the house of Israel' may well be Matthew's designation for those to whom both Jesus and the Twelve believed themselves to have been sent in the context of his later polemic with 'the synagogue across the street' (Mt. 10.6; 15.24). Yet Matthew was not the originator of such a vision; Isaiah had already formulated it with regard to the servant's role. Any attentive reader/hearer of Isaiah could not have been unaware of this hope of restoration, especially if they were located in 'Galilee of the nations'. Many of those 'lost sheep' were to be found in the greater Israel within which Jesus journeyed, as both literary and archaeological evidence indicates. Ethnic identity, human need and ideological claims, then as now, had created a tense situation of, often, violent conflict in these 'occupied territories'. Jesus certainly did not espouse their reoccupation. A programme of 'loving your enemies' and 'doing good to those who hate you' had highly political as well as practical implications for Jews in Roman Galilee, and was far removed from the Hasmonaean ideology of enforced circumcision or leaving the territory (*Ant.* 13.318–19). Later Jewish history shows that the Jesus way, living peacefully, Abraham-like, with other ethnic groups in the land, was more realistic, but also more in tune with the universalist ideals of the inherited tradition, than the Mosaic pattern of conquest and expulsion that the Maccabees and their spiritual heirs had adopted.

3. *The Jesus Movement and the Servants of Yahweh of Isaiah*

The claim of my third thesis brings us to Isaiah but also to Jerusalem. Contrary to those scholars who suggest religious, cultural and even ethnic opposition between Galilee and Jerusalem, it is my contention that the dominant *ethos* of first-century Galilee was Jewish (or Judaean, if you wish) in the sense that the majority of the region's inhabitants had close religious and emotional (as anthropologist C. Geertz would describe it) ties with the Jerusalem temple and its symbolic world-view. This claim, based again on both archaeological and literary evidence, does not preclude tensions arising from regional differences (even those of accent), urban–rural relations and the like. These tensions most certainly did not involve a Jewish restoration prophet from Galilee, possibly with southern lineage, and certainly with exposure to southern dissident groups, ignoring the symbolic centre of his people. There was a long-standing tradition in Israel – from Amos and Jeremiah to the various 'sign prophets' of whom Josephus speaks – of country prophets challenging the centre. Jesus of Nazareth is only one example of this prophetic critique of concern for cultic observance that is devoid of ethical responsibility.[8] The neglect of the evidence of the Fourth Gospel, in particular with regard to Jesus' relations with Jerusalem, ever since Schleiermacher and Strauss, has made us moderns too reliant on the 'Galilaean Jesus' of the Synoptics, to the point of distorting the range of his religious as well as his social concerns. Even the so-called Q lament for Jerusalem (Mt. 23.37; Lk. 13.34) with its clear import of Jesus' repeated concern for the holy city and its people, has been lost sight of in some modern discussions.

The suggestion already made, that the twofold mission of the Isaian servant provided a coherent and plausible framework for Jesus' sense of his own mission, immediately raises the question as to whether Zion's role in the restoration, which the servant is expected to accomplish, might not have been significant in the development of Jesus' vision also. We should not be deterred by the fact that Jesus does not appeal directly to the Zion myth. To some extent the name had already been commandeered by others, it would seem, who espoused the more militant approach to Jewish restoration. Isaiah, the prophet *of* and *for* Jerusalem *par excellence*, challenges the whole militaristic outlook on Jewish restoration: 'For all the boots of trampling warriors and the garments rolled in blood shall be burned as fuel for the fire' (Isa. 9.5; cf. Isa. 2.4). Yet some of his formulations of Zion's restoration do have a triumphalistic air. The theme of the repatriation of the exiles being accomplished by the leaders of foreign nations, who would function as servants and bag-carriers, is a recurring one in all sections of the book (Isa. 11.12; 14.2–3; 45.13; 49.22–23; 60.4–7), thus easily giving rise to a mentality of reverse superiority vis-à-vis foreign nations, especially in contexts of oppression. While this is the dominant view of Zion's restoration, it is not the only one represented in the book. In the final section (Isaiah 56–66), which is reliably dated to the Persian period when the book as a whole was redacted in its present form, another, competing, voice appears in the text. This is the voice of those

---

8. G. Theissen, 'Die Tempelweissagung Jesu: Prophetie in Spannungsfeld zwischen Tempel und Land', *TZ* 32 (1976), pp. 144–58.

who designate themselves 'the servants of Yahweh' (Isa. 65.13–14; 66.14) or 'those who tremble at his (Yahweh's) word' (Isa. 66.2, 5), and who clearly see themselves as sharing a lineage with the Servant figure described in the middle section of the book (Isaiah 40–55). It is this group and the values they espouse that provide the closest analogue to the Jesus movement, I maintain, especially when their textual profile is seen against the backdrop of the Persian-period politics within the restored community.[9]

Discussion of the significance of the Servant figure for understanding Jesus has in the past concentrated mainly on the idea of a suffering servant whose death was deemed redemptive for the sins of the many. Drawing attention to the paucity of explicit reference to the text of Isaiah 53 in the New Testament, Bruce Chilton, for example, following Morna Hooker, concludes that 'the evidence is too slender to support the contention that Jesus or even his followers saw the servant spoken of in Isaiah as a detailed model of his ministry'.[10] Yet Chilton goes on to point out that the Targum on Isaiah can use the term 'servant' to designate the messiah, and that the interpretation of Isaiah 53 points to an understanding of the Isaian figure 'as a messianic servant commissioned by God whose ministry involves at least the risk of death'. Chilton is therefore prepared to accept that such an understanding could well have influenced early Christian followers of Jesus who believed him to be the messiah and who sought to make sense of his death. Indeed he suggests leaving the issue open as to whether or not Jesus might have seen himself in this light as he faced his death.

There are indeed points of correspondence between the Targum and the Gospels' account of Jesus, particularly the idea of building a restored temple and a teaching role for the messiah (Tg. Isa. 53.5).[11] The obvious reworking of the original in the Targum to address new situations is highly significant in terms of the ongoing reception of the figure of the servant in later Judaism, especially in view of the difficulty in pinning

---

9. I am indebted to the invaluable and lucidly written commentary of J. Blenkinsopp (*Isaiah 1–39: A New Translation with Introduction and Commentary* [AB, 19; New York: Doubleday, 2000]; *Isaiah 40–55: A New Translation with Introduction and Commentary* [AB, 19A; New York: Doubleday, 2002]; *Isaiah 56–66: A New Translation with Introduction and Commentary* [AB, 19B; New York: Doubleday, 2003]) for my understanding of the book of Isaiah and for many insights on individual aspects of the text. Cf. also *idem*, 'A Jewish Sect in the Persian Period', *CBQ* 52 (1990), pp. 5–20.

10. B. Chilton, *A Galilean Rabbi and his Bible: Jesus' Use of the Interpreted Scripture of his Time* (Wilmington: Michael Glazier, 1984), pp. 199–200.

11. B. Chilton, *The Isaiah Targum: Introduction, Translation, Apparatus and Notes* (The Aramaic Bible, 11; Edinburgh: T&T Clark, 1987), pp. xvii, 103–05. Cf. also R. Syren, *The Blessings in the Targums: A Study on the Targumic Interpretation of Genesis 49 and Deuteronomy 33* (Acta Academiae Aboensis, 64; Åbo: Åbo Akademi University Press, 1986), pp. 101–15.

down 'clear and substantial traces of its influence in the remaining literature' with the exception of Daniel as we shall see.[12] The difficulty with seeing the Targum of Isaiah 53 as itself providing the background for Jesus' own self-understanding would seem to be that it envisages the servant-messiah having a negative attitude towards the Gentiles in a manner that is more reminiscent of the Psalms of Solomon (Tg. Isa. 53.8–9; *Pss. Sol.* 17.21–25; cf. also Tg. Isa. 10.27c; 16.5). In this regard the original Isaiah would appear, occasionally at least, as in Isa. 49.6, to have had a more inclusive perspective on the Gentiles than does the Targum. A broader approach to the enigmatic figure of the servant, one that would not only concentrate on Isaiah 53, but would take account of the developing biography of the servant as this emerges from a reading of Isaiah 40–55 as a whole, might prove to be more satisfactory, therefore.

Within this broader context of the 'book of the Consolation of Israel' a distinction can be made between the use of *ebed* as a collective term for Israel (Jacob) in Isaiah 40–48 and as a personal reference to an individual prophetic figure in Isaiah 49–55. According to Blenkinsopp, we must allow for considerable reinterpretation and internal commentary within these chapters, as the hopes associated with Cyrus as the Lord's shepherd and anointed (Isa. 44.28; 45.1) seem not to have been fully realized.[13] Thus, in the later chapters the universal mission devolves on an individual prophetic figure whose developing profile over against the larger group begins to emerge more clearly, especially in regard to his rejection, death and eventual vindication by God (Isa. 49.6; 50.4–9; 52.13–53.12). Each of these three 'servant songs' are thematically and often verbally interconnected in terms of the presentation of the servant, the reassurance of ultimate success despite present rejection and suffering, and a transition from humiliation to exaltation.[14]

As has already been noted, this mission had a twofold dimension: 'to restore the tribes of Jacob', so that 'my salvation may reach the ends of the earth'. Yet as the story of the servant unfolds, the first task becomes the priority, since it is only when it has been achieved that Israel can truly function as Yahweh's servant to the nations. In the climactic final passage the voice is not, as in the previous songs, that of Yahweh or the servant, but rather a 'we' who are astounded by the reversal of fortune that the servant, of whom they were previously so ashamed, now enjoys. This 'conversion' has led the narrator(s) to understand the deeper purpose of the servant's suffering and their own failures with regard to the divine plan. Through the life and suffering of the servant the sins of the many have been atoned and the sheep who had strayed have been re-gathered.

12.   Blenkinsopp, *Isaiah 40–55* (9), p. 82.

13.   Blenkinsopp, *Isaiah 40–55* (9), pp. 76–80.

14.   Blenkinsopp, *Isaiah 40–55* (9), pp. 349–57.

And there is yet more to follow, since the servant's reward, despite suffering a cruel death, is the promise of 'seeing a long life' and having progeny (*zera'*) – clearly a biblically charged reference to followers who will successfully carry on his mission.

If this is an accurate reading of the servant's biography, the final song points to the fact that this enigmatic figure did in fact have followers after his death, and the narratorial 'we' of the final song identify themselves as belonging to this group. This would seem to be borne out by the emergence of those who designate themselves as servants of the Lord in the closing chapters of the book (Isaiah 65–66), who, as mentioned already, appear as a persecuted minority, over against those who control the temple and pride themselves as recipients of divine favour, but who do not match this with their behaviour. On the other hand the servants of the Lord are the ones whom Yahweh will favour, something that is expressed forcefully at Isa. 65.13–14:

> My servants will eat, but you will go hungry;
> My servants will drink, but you will go thirsty;
> My servants will rejoice, but you will be put to shame;
> My servants will exult with gladness, but you will cry out for sadness.

These servants are later described as those 'who tremble at God's word' because they are 'humble and contrite of heart' (Isa. 66.2). They are reassured that even though they have been hated by their own people and rejected in the name of God, it is those who mock them that shall be put to shame (Isa. 66.5). Their profile is similar to that of the servant of Isaiah 53: patient acceptance of rejection by their own people and ultimate vindication by God in highly eschatological terms that include both a new creation and a miraculous birth by mother Zion (Isa. 65.17; 66.8).[15]

The similarities of religious sentiment and the social circumstance represented by this group suggest a close analogy between them and dissident Jewish groups of the first century, including the Jesus group, whose charter, as expressed in the beatitudes, seems to be structurally and thematically closely related to that of the servants of the Lord, just cited. Their piety, consisting of confident trust in Yahweh despite their apparent social humiliation in the present, is akin to that of the *ᵃnāwîm*, as this finds expression in many psalms. They stand over against the dominant group, who in Isaiah clearly control the temple and access to its worship, while at the same time engaging in some form of syncretistic practice (Isa. 65.1–7). These represent the triumphant Zion mentality that is implicitly critiqued by the interruption of the celebratory tones of the returnees at two crucial points in the narrative: first, through the introduction of the

---

15. Freyne, *Jesus, a Jewish Galilean* (2), pp. 105–08.

'Suffering Servant' song (Isaiah 53; cf. Isa. 52.1–12; 54.1–10), and later, by the reference to the prophet anointed by God to bring good news to the poor and proclaim the year of the Lord's favour (Isa. 61.1–7; cf. Isa. 60.1–22; 62). As Blenkinsopp points out, the language and style of commissioning of this latter figure also recall the servant passages of the earlier part of Isaiah (cf. for example Isa. 42.1; 52.7), thereby suggesting continuity of the servant's mission to a later period in terms of an individual prophet who is the champion of the ostracized group of servants. In this instance the situation envisaged is one of social oppression, not dissimilar to the social conditions in Judaea of Roman times: it is for the poor that the prophet has good news, and the announcement of the Jubilee is intended to redress the social inequalities that have arisen within the post-exilic community in the Persian period (cf. Isa. 49.8; Neh. 5.1–11; *Ant.* 20.181, 206–07).[16]

Luke's picture of Jesus reading from the prophet Isaiah in the Nazareth synagogue (Lk. 4.18–19) may be drawn to suit his own theological agenda, but it was surely also expressing something that was obvious to other first-century observers, namely, that Jesus' understanding of his mission had been shaped by his reading of Isaiah, as indeed the response to John the Baptist in Q (Mt. 11.2–4; Lk. 7.23–24) makes clear. The fact that other groups from the first century with similar attitudes towards the current temple and its personnel were also appropriating the same Isaian passages to formulate their messianic hopes (4Q521) would seem to add considerably to the plausibility of such a claim. There can be variant receptions of the one text in life as well as in literature.

Despite the close thematic and even verbal parallels with the Gospels (for example the beatitudes), the major difficulty in seeing the group of servants of the Lord as profiled in Isaiah as the most suitable analogue for the Jesus movement is the fact that we cannot trace its history through the intervening centuries with any certainty. However, it seems clear that the figure of the servant did provide inspiration for the *maśkilîm* of Daniel in the midst of the crisis of the second century BC. Verbal and thematic links are acknowledged between the description of this group as they emerge in the final vision of Daniel and Isaiah 53: their very name *maśkîlê 'ām* and their function of teaching wisdom to the many (*rabbîm*; Dan. 11.32–33) recall the servant's introduction: *hinnēh yaśkîl 'abdî* (Isa. 52.13), and both the servant and the *maśkilîm* are believed to vindicate the many (*rabbîm*) by their lives and their death (Isa. 53.11; Dan. 12.3).[17]

---

16. Blenkinsopp, *Isaiah 56–66* (9), pp. 221–27.

17. Blenkinsopp, *Isaiah 40–55* (9), pp. 81–92, especially p. 85; cf. also M. Hengel, D. P. Bailey, 'The Effective History of Isaiah 53 in the Pre-Christian Period', in B. Janowski, P. Stuhlmacher (eds.), *The Suffering Servant: Isaiah 53 in Jewish and Christian Sources* (Grand Rapids: Eerdmans, 2004), pp. 75–146.

The book of Daniel only hints at the social circumstances of this group. Presumably their piety is similar to that of Daniel, who is introduced as 'proficient (*maśkîl*) in all righteousness' (Dan. 1.4, 17). This means that they were devout in their Jewish observance (prayer and dietary laws), refusing to assimilate to Hellenistic culture and trusting in Yahweh's protection rather than in military response to the crisis that the 'reform' of Antiochus IV had initiated. In this regard their lifestyle was to be seen as offering an alternative view of what the response should be to the religious and national threat of imperial power. From this perspective it is interesting to note that Egyptian Jews had also appropriated the servant figure as a model of the death of the wise ones whom God will vindicate because of their faithfulness in face of persecution, and whose death has retrospectively, like the narrator of Isaiah 53, become an embarrassment for their co-religionists (Wis. 2.12–24). Of particular interest is the mention in Daniel of the fact that the *maśkilîm* received only a 'little help' from their co-religionists and many who joined them were insincere (Dan. 11.34). For this particular period (i.e., mid second-century BC) this is most likely a reference to the leaders of the Maccabaean freedom fighters and/or the Hasidim, a group of whom we hear very little, but who seem to have supported the militaristic response to the crisis (1 Macc. 2.42; 7.12–13; 2 Macc. 14.6).[18]

Once again we are encountering hints of division (possibly even sectarianism) within the restored community of the Second Temple period and the fault line is that of how best to remain faithful to Yahweh's promise in times of national and religious crisis. The same issues continued to be present in the Roman period, as is well known. Reading the Gospels one could easily have the impression that the prevailing political situation had little or no impact on the Jesus movement, especially in its Galilaean phase. However, greater attention to the social and political realities of the region has helped to sharpen the focus on the political as well as the religious implications of the stance which Jesus himself adopted, and the 'wisdom' that he imparted to his followers. The fact that this has many echoes of the strand of Jewish response which we have been tracing provides, I believe, the proper context within which to explore Jesus' continuity with his own tradition, even when it is difficult to pinpoint all the stages and manifestations of the 'minority' point of view which was developed.

18. J. J. Collins, *Daniel: A Commentary on the Book of Daniel* (Hermeneia; Minneapolis: Fortress, 1995), pp. 62–69.

4. *Early Christian Identity and the Hopes of Zion*

An adequate development of my fourth and final thesis would demand a separate paper, but I propose to outline briefly the lines of the argument for continuity between Jesus and early Christianity based on my previous discussion. One of the enigmas of the Early Palestinian Jesus movement is the emergence in Jerusalem shortly after his death of a group in his name, that was centred on James the brother of the Lord, but who was not one of the Twelve. Unfortunately, we do not have any early literature from this group with the possible exception of the Epistle of James, and even in the case of this work the dating, if not the milieu, is debatable. All our other early witnesses are either Pauline or Paulinist, with the exception of Josephus, each with their own particular slant on James and the role of his group within the new movement. There may well be important information in later writings (Hegesippus, Eusebius and the various apocryphal works attributed to James), but for purposes of this essay it is sufficient to explore the possible significance of this branch of the Jesus movement in the immediate post-Easter situation in the light of the profile that has been proposed for the historical Jesus and his movement during his own lifetime. Given the nature of the sources, it is all the more impressive, surely, that James is attributed such an important and influential role within the new movement at that early stage, especially since he does not seem to have been an actual member of Jesus' retinue of permanent followers before Easter.[19]

Why would a group of Jesus-followers assemble in Jerusalem so soon after the violent death of their leader, a death in which the Jewish priestly aristocracy and the Roman authorities had, in all probability, colluded? Such a daring, even provocative, act would not appear to make much sense, unless some other factors were at play. It is here that the idea of continuity with Jesus and his vision would seem to offer an obvious, if largely unexplored, key to the problem. If it can be plausibly shown that the James group shared the restoration eschatology espoused by Jesus, their presence in Jerusalem in the immediate aftermath of his death becomes much more understandable. Furthermore, if it could be established that the James group both in their lifestyle and values resembled the servants of Zion in Isaiah, their active presence in the holy city would constitute confirmation of the claim about the importance of Jerusalem for Jesus also, as argued above. Thus, the apparent divergences between Jesus and James, as one of 'the brothers of the Lord' (Mk 3.22; Jn

---

19. Cf. J. Painter, 'Who was James? Footprints as a Means of Identification', in B. Chilton, J. Neusner (eds.), *The Brother of Jesus: James the Just and his Mission* (Louisville: John Knox Press, 2001), for a detailed discussion of the sources both canonical and extra-canonical for James.

7.1–7) on the one hand, and between Paul and James on the other (Gal. 1.19; 2.6), that are often pushed to the extreme of opposition, even conflict, could be explained more readily as a difference of emphasis on the role of Gentiles within a shared horizon of meaning with regard to the realization of Israel's restoration hopes.[20]

The centrality of Jerusalem for restoration hopes has already been discussed with regard to Jesus' repeated expression of concern for its failure to listen to the prophetic word. The temple as the place where Yahweh was present to Israel was the symbolic centre, but its holiness extended to the whole city (Ezek. 45.1–8). Mount Zion, with all the symbolic resonance that the name evoked, situated on the south-western spur, was particularly important for the early Christians, but also for the Essenes, it would seem on the basis of literary and archaeological evidence, thus setting up the intriguing possibility of close contacts at least between the two dissident groups.[21] In view of Jesus' 'attack' on the temple it is surprising to hear from Luke that the apostles continued to worship in the temple, and James in particular is presented in later tradition as both a Nazirite (Num. 4.1–5) and a priest, who was allowed to enter the holy place, to pray, but there is no mention of his offering sacrifice (Hegesippus in Eusebius, *Hist. Eccl.* 2.23, 3–18).

Despite these later reports, there is evidence that the early community began to think of itself as in some sense replacing the temple as the focal point of the restoration to come. The architectural metaphor of 'pillar apostles' which Paul uses for James, Peter and John (Gal. 2.9) points in this direction, and there is clear evidence (1QS 8.5–9; 1QH 6.25–28) that the Qumran Essenes also transferred the temple imagery to the community. Isaiah had prepared the way for these developments, since despite the euphoria of the return to Zion that finds expression in the final section of that book, there is evidence of a serious criticism of the temple also. Thus, the prophetic oracle of Isa. 56.1–7 envisages foreigners and eunuchs who cling to Yahweh offering sacrifice there, in clear breach of the temple regulations, and significantly, the temple is described as a 'house of *prayer* for all peoples', thus, it would seem, implicitly criticizing the sacrificial system. Later still, Yahweh declares that as the creator God he has no need of a temple – heaven is his throne and the earth his footstool, and an ominous voice from the temple proclaims judgment on those who have persecuted and ostracized his servants (Isa. 66.1, 6; cf. *War* 6.301).

20. B. Chilton, 'James in Relation to Peter, Paul and the Remembrance of Jesus', in Chilton and Neusner, *The Brother of Jesus*, pp. 138–59 (142–46).

21. B. Pixner, D. Chen, S. Margolit, 'The "Gate of the Essenes" Re-excavated', *ZDPV* 105 (1989), pp. 85–95; R. Riesner, 'Jesus, the Primitive Community and the Essene Quarter in Jerusalem', in J. H. Charlesworth (ed.), *Jesus and the Dead Sea Scrolls* (ABRL; New York: Doubleday, 1993), pp. 198–234.

Against this background of the relativizing of the actual temple and the continued significance of Zion, Ben Meyer perceptively spells out the symbolic import of the early Jesus group in Jerusalem:

> As God's dwelling place, the community is the first fruits of messianic salvation; and, as the first fruits sanctify the whole harvest to come, this community on Zion sanctifies all Israel on the point of entry into its heritage. Not the community in place of Zion, but on Zion. Between Zion and the community there was a bond of reciprocal dependence: it was the community that made Zion the Zion of fulfilment, and it was Zion that established the accord between the Scriptures and the community, between the terms of prophecy and fulfilment.[22]

Such a self-understanding of the James group needs to be explored further as to the manner in which it continued to play out its key role in the unfolding mission of the Pauline churches. In the light of the Isaian background the nations were expected to come streaming to Zion in search of Torah, even as it was called on to cause wisdom to go forth from its midst (Isa. 2.2–4). There is a clear assumption that Torah and wisdom were intimately linked together, something that the second-century BC scribe, Ben Sirach, spelled more fully (Sir. 24). The implication was obvious – that as Israel fulfilled its proper destiny, the nations would acknowledge in the Torah the light that they were longing for (Isa. 42.4; 49.6; 51.4). Thus, as the restored community of Zion, the vocation of the Jerusalem Jesus community was clear – to bring the light of Torah to the nations, not by abandoning the distinction between Israel and the nations, but by replacing the dividing wall of hostility by one of mutual respect.

This explains the mission of James to the Antioch church – not to insist on circumcision of Gentiles as some of the 'false brethren' were demanding, but to ensure that Peter and those of the circumcision, i.e., Diaspora Jews, were observing their side of the agreement that had been arrived at in Jerusalem previously (Gal. 2.8–14), namely, to live out their Torah-centred calling in the midst of the Gentiles. In this regard the Epistle of James, significantly addressed to 'the twelve tribes of the dispersion' (Jas. 1.1), can be read as a manifesto for such Jewish Jesus-followers, combining a Torah-centred approach which extols 'the perfect law of freedom' (Jas 1.25) that can also be described as the 'royal law' (*basilikos nomos*; Jas 2.8), presumably because it is based on Jesus' preaching of the kingdom. Consequently, the author can cite freely from the sayings of Jesus as these are known mainly from Q (a total of 54 clear allusions on the basis of a recent detailed study). All these function as intensifications of central aspects of the Torah, as this was being preached

---

22. B. F. Meyer, *The Early Christians: Their World Mission and Self-Discovery* (Wilmington: Michael Glazier, 1986), p. 57.

and lived by the 'radical itinerants' who stand behind the Q collection, thus replicating the lifestyle of Jesus.[23] The use of this collection by the author of the Epistle of James, may, as J. Kloppenborg has argued, have occurred in more settled community circumstances, yet the example of the contrasting reception of the rich and the poor man within the community shows how much the memory of Jesus' espousal of the blessedness of the poor was important for the author and his readers (Jas 2.1–6).[24]

One final aspect of convergence between the Isaian servant group, the Jesus-followers and the James group can be noted in passing, namely, that of social location and lifestyle. The servants of the Lord group had suffered social and, presumably also, economic ostracization at the hands of the aristocratic elite who controlled the temple and its revenues, leading to the promise of a prophet who would proclaim good news for the poor. The Jesus group had espoused voluntary poverty based on total trust in Yahweh's care and protection. Both groups were deemed 'blessed'. The James group was also economically compromised, as the request to the Antioch community makes clear (Gal. 2.10).[25] Subsequently, Paul insists on economic support for 'the poor' or 'the poor among the saints' in Jerusalem when writing to the Gentile churches (Rom. 15.26–28; 1 Cor. 16.2–4; 2 Cor. 8–9; Acts 11.30; 24.17). He sees this as an obligation on these churches because Jerusalem has shared its spiritual wealth with them (Rom. 15.27). Thus, the offering of material assistance was for Paul a symbolic act of recognition of the centrality of Jerusalem within the divine plan. This acknowledgment is nowhere more in evidence than in Paul's desperate efforts to understand why in fact the restoration of Israel as a whole has not taken place, in view of the success of the Gentile mission (Rom. 11). As he contemplates 'the depths of the riches and wisdom and knowledge of God', his greatest consolation and hope is that 'the remnant chosen by grace' who can be described either as the dough that sanctifies what is offered as first fruits, or as the root that sanctifies the branches (Rom. 11.5, 16), will eventually bring about the complete restoration of Israel.

23.   R. Bauckham, 'James and Jesus', in Chilton and Neusner, *The Brother of Jesus*, pp. 100–35 (123–31).

24.   J. S. Kloppenborg, 'The Reception of the Jesus Tradition in James', in J. Schlosser (ed.), *The Catholic Epistles and the Tradition* (BETL, 176; Leuven: Leuven University Press, 2004), pp. 93–141.

25.   D. Hutchinson Edgar, *Has God Not Chosen the Poor? The Social Setting of the Epistle of James* (JSNTSup, 206; Sheffield: Sheffield Academic Press, 2001), pp. 95–106.

5. *Conclusion*

In this chapter I have attempted to argue for continuity between a minority Jewish movement that finds a clear expression in Isaiah and the Jesus movement, both in its pre- and post-Easter phases. Not everybody will agree with the working hypothesis of the paper, especially the attempt to extrapolate from textual references to extra-textual realities, particularly when the evidence is often suggestive rather than probative. There is also the problem of ascribing to Jesus a much greater knowledge of and creativity in regard to his own tradition than would be normal for those who have come to see the Jesus movement as primarily a peasant one, with all the innuendos of backwardness and isolationism that that term implies. I must confess that my effort is in part a reaction to what I regard as distorting aspects of recent scholarship about Jesus, not least the option for a purely social understanding of his life and ministry at the expense of any consideration of religious motivation, one that neglects the power of symbols in shaping historical processes, in short approaches that are model-driven rather than historically sensitive to the issues, the contexts and the evidence. I have deliberately subtitled my book *A New Reading of the Jesus Story* to indicate that it makes no more claims than that it is an essay – in every sense of that word – which hopefully might provoke others to explore the contexts and the continuities more exhaustively and constructively.

JESUS AND THE PRIESTS OF ISRAEL

Edwin K. Broadhead

The historical Jesus stands in a continuum which stretches from the faith of Israel to the faith of the early Church. While the criterion of discontinuity has been helpful in isolating traits, sayings and deeds unique to Jesus, this approach also carries the danger of separating Jesus from his culture and context. A more helpful approach is to investigate the larger framework within which Jesus lived and died.

I also wish to propose a second continuum of analysis: possibility, plausibility, probability. Quite a number of elements are possible, but not plausible; most helpful are those traits which are not only plausible, but probable. The goal of these criteria is a plausible portrait of Jesus framed within the continuum of Judaism and Christianity as they emerged within a Graeco-Roman context.

This analysis investigates a particular piece of that continuum – Jesus and the leadership of Israel. While the attempt has been made to understand Jesus in relation to various groups – Essenes, Pharisees, Zealots – for the most part critical scholarship has found these connections to be dubious or of limited value. A more fruitful avenue may lie in the relationship between Jesus and the priestly leadership of Israel.

My research and analysis will support five major conclusions.

1. From a historical perspective, the priesthood of Israel was never a monolithic development, and it was never an exclusive institution.
2. In the time of Jesus there were Jewish temples outside Jerusalem, and there were important differences between Jerusalem and the Galilee.
3. The aftermath of the first Jewish War (AD 66–72) required a new understanding of the priesthood. This process of redefinition can be seen in Philo, in Josephus, in rabbinical literature and in the New Testament.
4. A clear line of development is evident in the New Testament and in other early Christian writings. This development moves from competition to conflict to supersession.

5. Jesus stands fully within this line of development, but there are distinctive elements in his relationship to the priests of Israel.

1. *A Survey of the Priesthood of Israel*

Because there were no Hebrew temples in the patriarchal period, there was no distinct priestly class. The origins of Israel's priesthood are to be found in the Yahwism implemented by Moses, and Aaron is presented as the first of the priests. The true realization of the priesthood belongs to the era of the conquest and settlement of Canaan. The tribe of Levi is designated with consistency as the home of the priesthood. While Aaron is associated with this tribe, the Hebrew Bible also exhibits tension between the house of Aaron and the tribe of Levi.[1] At its earliest stages, the primary priestly work is mantic – the delivery of oracles. Though sacrifice could be offered by any head of a family, the cult centres became places of sacrifice, then of instruction in the law.[2]

While various Levitical families attended the temples scattered throughout Israel, the Aaronic priesthood falls to Eli, who is seen as his descendant. Eli attends to the ark of the covenant at the temple of Shiloh, which gained priority among the tribes of Israel.[3]

With the advent of the monarchy significant changes occurred. Several priestly families benefited from their connection to the monarch and served as court priests. More significantly, the family of Eli was surpassed by the family of Zadok, which controlled the central temple in Jerusalem. David brought the ark to Jerusalem and created two high priests: Abiathar from Shiloh and Zadok, whose origins are ambiguous.[4] Solomon banished Abiathar and recognized Zadok as high priest (1 Kgs 12.31). In the reforms of Josiah the temples, altars and high places outside Jerusalem were destroyed and the priests of Judah were brought to Jerusalem.[5] At this point there appears to be tension between the Levites from the countryside and the Jerusalem Zadokites. In the time of the exile, the prophet Ezekiel calls for a renewal of the priestly function; in doing so he criticizes the Levites who are not a part of the Zadokites (Ezek. 44.10–15; 48.11). Furthermore, the priests gain exclusive control over the cultic activity in Israel.[6]

In the post-exilic reforms of Ezra, only those considered true descendants of Aaron serve in the priesthood, though Levites assist them in this

1. C. Roth *et al.*, 'Priests and Priesthood', *EncJud* 13 (1971), pp. 1069–91 (1082).
2. G. Schrenk, 'ἱερεύς, ἀρχιερεύς', *TDNT* 3, pp. 257–83 (260–61).
3. Roth *et al.*, 'Priests and Priesthood' (1), p. 1083.
4. M. Rehm, 'Levites and Priests', *ABD* 4, pp. 297–311 (305–09).
5. Roth *et al.*, 'Priests and Priesthood' (1), p. 1084.
6. Schrenk, 'ἱερεύς' (2), p. 261.

role.[7] Scribes now serve alongside priests to transmit and to interpret the Law.[8]

In the Hellenistic era the priests became an administrative class with high social status. The priestly office was passed from father to son, and a priest served until his death – a practice ended by Antiochus Epiphanes. The Hasmonaean high priest became the leader and king of an independent nation.[9]

When the Jewish nation came under Roman control, Herod ended the lifetime appointments and chose the high priest from various families. With the death of Herod and the removal of Archelaus, Roman governors began to appoint the high priest. When the power of appointment was restored to the Herodian dynasty, priests were appointed from wealthy, influential families who formed a Sadducaean oligarchy.[10] The Talmud (b.Yom. 18a; b.Yeb. 61a) says the high priests bought the office and were changed each year. This priestly oligarchy was considered a protected class of collaborators.

There were priests from outside the Sadducaean oligarchy, and tensions mounted around the social divide and the urban/rural contrast. At the time of the First Jewish War (AD 66–72), the Zealots expelled the Sadducees, killing a number of them, and chose a high priest from among the ordinary priests. Phinehas ben Samuel – a stonemason and a relative by marriage of Hillel – was the last Jewish high priest.[11]

This survey makes it clear that the Hebrew priesthood legitimized itself through claims to Levitical, Aaronic and Zadokite descent. It is also clear that competing claims and shifting political connections are determinative in the history of Israel's priesthood and that no consistent line of development exists.

2. *The Jewish Priesthood in the Time of Jesus*

In the time of Jesus the office of high priest was a limited appointment subject to the whims of the Herodians or to the transactions of the Sadducaean oligarchy. As such, the leading priests would be largely viewed as wealthy collaborators. In the eyes of the people, their status could hardly compare with the ideals of Aaron and Eli and Zadok. The Sadducaean priests would also pale in comparison with the patriots from the Hasmonaean period.

Alongside this changed image of the ruling priests, there were probably

---

7. Roth *et al.*, 'Priests and Priesthood' (1), p. 1085.
8. Schrenk, 'ἱερεύς' (2), p. 261.
9. Roth *et al.*, 'Priests and Priesthood' (1), p. 1087.
10. Roth *et al.*, 'Priests and Priesthood' (1), p. 1087.
11. Roth *et al.*, 'Priests and Priesthood' (1), p. 1088.

differences between the priests of Jerusalem and those of the rural villages. This contrast would involve not only wealth and social standing, but it would also invoke the tension between an urban and rural ethos. Some elements of this surface in the revolt against Rome, when the Sadducaean high priest is replaced by Jewish Zealots.

Recent scholarship has identified six areas in which Galilaean and Judaean Judaism might differ. The following claims are made:

1. Galilaeans are more drawn to the teaching of Shammai (c. 50 BC–c. AD 30). This would agree with the Jerusalem aristocrats, but it would differ from the common people of Judaea.
2. Galilaeans showed less interest in and affinity for Torah scholarship than did Judaean Jews.
3. Jews of Galilee were less faithful in the observance of Torah prescriptions.
4. Galilee was inhabited by an uncommon number of Jewish charismatic figures such as Hanina ben Dosa, Abba Hilkiah and Jesus of Nazareth.
5. The degree of Hellenization differs between Galilee and Judaea. For some scholars, Galilee is more Hellenistic; for others, it is less Hellenistic.
6. Galilee is a hotbed of political revolt.

Martin Goodman assesses these claims of distinction, and he reaches the following conclusion:

> It seems certain that in at least a few respects the cultural and religious customs of the Galilaeans differed from those of the Judaeans, but the theological significance, if any, of such divergences cannot now be ascertained. If a distinctive Galilaean Judaism existed in the first century CE, as is quite possible, its nature is likely to remain unknown.[12]

When these six areas are applied specifically to the question of the priesthood, the results are similarly mixed. First, recent scholarly attention to the Galilee has found no archaeological evidence of priests living in the Galilee.[13] If there were priests in the Galilee, affinity for

---

12. M. Goodman, 'Galilean Judaism and Judaean Judaism', in W. Horbury, W. D. Davies, J. Sturdy (eds.), *The Cambridge History of Judaism*, vol. 3: *The Early Roman Period* (Cambridge: Cambridge University Press, 1999), pp. 596–617.

13. See especially the work of S. Freyne (*Galilee from Alexander the Great to Hadrian, 323 BCE to 135 CE* [Notre Dame: Notre Dame University Press, 1980]; *Galilee, Jesus and the Gospels: Literary Approaches and Historical Investigations* [Minneapolis: Fortress, 1988]; *Jesus, a Jewish Galilean: A New Reading of the Jesus Story* [London: T&T Clark International, 2004]; 'The Geography of Restoration: Galilee–Jerusalem Relations in Early Jewish and Christian Experience', *NTS* 47 [2001], pp. 289–311) and of J. Kloppenborg (J. S. Kloppenborg, S. G. Wilson [eds.], *Voluntary Associations in the Graeco-Roman World* [London: Routledge, 1996]).

Shammai and a lack of Torah scholarship would not sharply distinguish Galilaean priests from their counterparts in Jerusalem. The question of the level of Torah observance might differentiate priests from Pharisees, but little distinction between Galilaean and Judaean priests would be evident. Likewise, the presence of charismatics, of Hellenization and of political revolt does not draw sharp lines between priests in Galilee and Judaea.

On the other hand, G. Schrenk suggests a clear distinction between priests and Levites in the time of Jesus. Ordinary priests pursued a secular calling in their own home towns, and their temple duties were limited to two weeks per year and to the three major festivals. Each of 24 classes or watches served a week at a time.[14] This arrangement is evident in Luke's description of Zacharias (Lk. 1.5–23), who serves in the watch of Abijah, and in Josephus' description of 'priests and Levites' (*Ant.* 7.78, 363; 8.169; 10.62). Luke further distinguishes between priests and Levites in the Samaritan parable (Lk. 10.30–37). Josephus often distinguishes ordinary priests from the chief priests with terms such as οἱ πολλοί, πάντες, ἄλλοι, λοιποί, ἱερεῖς.[15]

While such a distinction may be based on genealogical claims, a real difference would lie in the proximity to the temple and its urban, aristocratic leadership. If there were commuting priests from rural Galilee, they might have a distinct dialect, and they might stand apart from both the common priests of Judaea and the high priests of the Jerusalem temple.

A related tension may be present in the distinction between temple and synagogue. The temple was a pre-exilic institution centred around cultic piety. In contrast, the synagogue emerged outside Judaea in the post-exilic era as a house of prayer, as a place of study, and as a community centre. The synagogue differs from the temple in terms of place, cult and personnel.[16]

In addition to these internal distinctions, there were historical alternatives to the Jerusalem temple and its priesthood. Samaritans followed a different Judaism at their temple on the slopes of Mount Gerazim. A distinct temple tradition developed at Leontopolis in Egypt. This temple claimed a Zadokite priesthood and existed from the middle of the second century BC until the time of the first Jewish revolt.[17] Jewish temples

---

14. Schrenk, 'ἱερεύς' (2), p. 262.

15. Schrenk, 'ἱερεύς' (2), p. 263. Examples are found in *Ant.* 3.158, 172, 277.

16. S. J. D. Cohen, 'The Temple and the Synagogue', in W. Horbury, W. D. Davies, J. Sturdy (eds.), *The Cambridge History of Judaism*, vol. 3: *The Early Roman Period* (Cambridge: Cambridge University Press, 1999), pp. 298–325

17. L. I. Levine, 'The Hellenistic-Roman Diaspora CE 70–CE 235: The Archeological Evidence', in W. Horbury, W. D. Davies, J. Sturdy (eds.), *The Cambridge History of Judaism*, vol. 3: *The Early Roman Period* (Cambridge: Cambridge University Press, 1999), pp. 991–1024 (995–98).

existed at Elephantine, where sacrifice was being offered,[18] and possibly at Araq el-Amir. The Essenes at Qumran rejected the Jerusalem leadership and developed a different calendar and a different priesthood with the expectation of an eschatological reversal of temple leadership.

Thus, the priestly leadership of Israel in the time of Jesus was never monolithic, and it was never exclusive. Significant variations, based on culture, geography and theology, existed within the wider orbit of the Jerusalem temple. Beyond this, other temples and other traditions were attended by other Jews.

3. *Transformations of the Priesthood*

The aftermath of the first Jewish War (AD 66–72) required a new perspective on the priesthood. This transformation can be seen in Josephus, in Philo, in rabbinical materials and among various Christian groups.

In the aftermath of the first Jewish War, Josephus describes the era of Judaism that has just closed. In doing so, he intends to honour his own role in these events, and he is engaged in apologetics aimed at Roman approval. Thus, Josephus describes the Sadducees as an inferior group:

> the Sadducees have the confidence of the wealthy alone but no following among the populace, while the Pharisees have the support of the masses.[19] ... There are but few men to whom this doctrine has been made known, but these men are of the highest standing. They accomplish practically nothing, however. For whenever they assume some office, though they submit unwillingly and perforce, yet submit they do to the formulas of the Pharisees, since otherwise the masses would not tolerate them.[20] ... the Sadducees are, even among themselves, rather boorish in their behaviour, and in their intercourse with their peers are as rude as to aliens.[21]

Philo speaks of the priest as a symbol of the *logos* or of reason. The ideal priest for Philo is marked by the characteristics of the Stoic sage, who is free from entanglement with the senses and passions.[22]

A similar polemic is found among the rabbis. As Stemberger notes, 'The Rabbinic sources on the Sadducees certainly offer a one-sided picture.

18.   J. Gwyn Griffiths, 'The Legacy of Egypt in Judaism', in W. Horbury, W. D. Davies, J. Sturdy (eds.), *The Cambridge History of Judaism*, vol. 3: *The Early Roman Period* (Cambridge: Cambridge University Press, 1999), pp. 1025–51 (1028–29).

19.   *Ant.* 13.298.

20.   *Ant.* 18.17.

21.   *War* 2.166.

22.   Schrenk, 'ἱερεύς' (2), pp. 259–60.

Their accounts necessarily add to the fame of the Pharisees and downgrade the Sadducees.'[23]

4. *Portraits of Israel's Priests in Early Christianity*

A similar process of apologetics and identity formation is at work among the various Christian groups emerging in the aftermath of the first Jewish War. The explanation of Jesus' connection to the heritage of Israel is a key part of the identity formation of early Christianity and its attempt to position itself over against its heritage and its competition. A clear line of development is evident. In the initial stages Jewish followers of Jesus interpret their own heritage. Later stages sponsor a theory of replacement.

4.1. *The Gospel of Mark and the Priests of Israel*
Foundational for the attempt to frame Christian identity is the Markan description of Jesus' relationship to the priests of Israel.

Anti-Temple Rhetoric. The temple at Jerusalem plays a limited role in the Gospel of Mark. The linguistic term (ἱερόν) is employed nine times, and only in relation to one focused unit (Mark 11–13) and in one reflection upon that unit (Mk 14.49). Thus, Jesus' engagement of the temple space is a limited one, and it is wholly negative. A different term (ναός) is used in Mk 14.58 and in 15.38. In the first trial, witnesses claim to have heard Jesus say that 'I will destroy this temple made with hands and after three days I will build another not made with hands' (Mk 14.58). At the moment of Jesus' death, the curtain marking off the holy place of the temple is torn (Mk 15.38), thus destroying and making public the holy of holies.

The simple term for priest (ἱερεύς) has very limited use in the Gospel of Mark, appearing only twice (Mk 1.44; 2.26), one of which refers to the Old Testament (Mk 2.26). Almost all priests in the Gospel of Mark are chief priests (ἀρχιερεύς). This term appears some 22 times and is scattered throughout the story.

Significantly, some priests appear to operate not in Jerusalem in the vicinity of the temple, but in proximity to the villages of Galilee. In Mk 1.44 Jesus commands the healed leper to go and show himself to the priest. The normal association, however, is with Jerusalem and the temple environs.

The only substantive use of sacrifice (ὁλοκαύτωμα) is found in Mk 12.33, and here a critique is offered: 'and to love the neighbour as yourself is greater than all the whole burnt offerings and sacrifices'. The verb form (ἔθυον) is used as a temporal marker in Mk 14.12.

23.   G. Stemberger, 'The Sadducees – their History and Doctrines', in W. Horbury, W. D. Davies, J. Sturdy (eds.), *The Cambridge History of Judaism*, vol. 3: *The Early Roman Period* (Cambridge: Cambridge University Press, 1999), pp. 428–43 (439).

This linguistic field provides a base for the characterization of priests and priestly activity in the Gospel of Mark. Priests are mentioned in two of the three passion predictions (Mk 8.31; 9.31; 10.32–34): Jesus will be rejected by the chief priests (Mk 8.31), and he will be betrayed into their hands (Mk 10.33). Priests question Jesus in the temple (Mk 11.27). After observing his activity and hearing his instruction in the temple, they seek a way to kill Jesus (Mk 11.18; 14.1, the implied subject of 12.12). Jesus' arrest is arranged and carried out by the priests (Mk 14.10, 43, 47). They are in charge of his first trial (Mk 14.53 [twice], 54, 55, 60, 61), and they pronounce the verdict against him (Mk 14.63). It is they who hand Jesus over to Pilate (Mk 15.1, 10) and argue the case against him there (Mk 15.3, 11). At the cross, Jesus is reviled by priests: 'Others he saved, himself he is not able to save. Let the Christ, the King of Israel come down now from the cross, so that we might see and believe' (Mk 15.31–32).

Thus, the Gospel of Mark constructs a narrative image of priests as opponents of Jesus who are partially responsible for his death. The issue between Jesus and the priests is Jesus' condemnation of the temple practice (Mk 11.15–18), his parable against the keepers of the vineyard (Mk 12.1–12), and his claim to be the Christ, the Son of God, the Son of Man (Mk 14.55–65). Whether or not there is any historical reality to this portrait, the Gospel of Mark characterizes the priests as the defenders of the temple and its orthodoxy, and thus as the opponents of Jesus. This description of the priests is more than a character sketch; it plays a key role in the plotting of the Gospel of Mark.

This characterization of the Markan priests is roughly congruent with Old Testament images of Israel's priests. The Markan priests are not only the custodians of holiness, but more so the keepers of Israel's heritage, the guardians of its sacred places, and the defenders of God's name. Seen from this position, Jesus represents a clear threat to their status and to their place.

Thus, the discourse sketched around the Markan priests is wholly negative, disruptive and destructive. This, however, is only one line of the Markan priestly discourse.

Counterpoint: Another Priest. The priest title (ἱερεύς, ἀρχιερεύς) is never applied to Jesus in the Gospel of Mark, and the Melchizedek speculation is never employed. Despite this, the Gospel of Mark generates an unusual priestly image around the character of Jesus. This priestly image, though briefly developed, has been woven into the larger tapestry of the Gospel of Mark and contributes to its wider Christological portrait.[24]

---

24. A more developed form of this argument may be found in E. Broadhead, *Naming Jesus: Titular Christology in the Gospel of Mark* (JSNTSup, 175; Sheffield: Sheffield Academic Press, 1999), pp. 63–74. See also E. Broadhead, 'Christology as Polemic and Apologetic: The Priestly Portrait of Jesus in the Gospel of Mark', *JSNT* 47 (1992), pp. 21–34.

This priestly image of Jesus is developed through four closely related passages: Mk 1.39–45; 2.1–13; 2.23–28; 3.1–7a. The concentration of these stories within the same unit (Mk 1.1–3.7a) provides a decisive narrative impact. In addition, the priestly portrait is also found in Mk 7.1–23. In these five scenes Jesus does what a priest should be doing: he declares a leper clean, he offers God's forgiveness, he interprets Sabbath and food laws, he labours on the Sabbath. These priestly Christological images are limited in scope and should be considered a minor theme of the narrative. At the same time, these priestly images are not isolated from the larger plot and characterization of the Gospel of Mark.

First, the priestly Christological images are developed in correspondence with the religious controversy theme. Second, because of this correlation with the controversy theme the priestly Christology is linked to the larger plot development – particularly to the passion. The result is clear: the conflict with the temple and the religious authorities provides the context of Jesus' death. Because priestly images play a vital role in the formative stages of this controversy (Mk 1.1–3.7a), the priestly Christology flows ultimately into the larger stream of passion Christology. Beyond its significance as a Christological image and its role in the larger plan of the Gospel, the priestly image probably served an important role in the life of the Church which lived by this Gospel.

Counterpoint: Another Place. What is the sociological situation, the setting in life for such a literary construction? Can the rhetorical strategy at work in the Gospel of Mark tell us anything about the people for whom it works?

I would suggest this priestly rhetoric has its home in a community of faith in a post-70 setting. The overthrow of 'this mountain' and the larger critique of the temple speaks to the continued life of a community which has witnessed the fall of Jerusalem and the destruction of the temple. From the perspective of the aftermath of this tragedy, the events of the first Jewish War are seen as the final death throes of a city and a temple that have long stood under the judgment of God.

From the positive side, the Markan rhetoric provides a way forward. The temple, which had become a den of thieves, has been replaced by houses of prayer (Mk 11.22–24). Forgiveness, once the commodity of the priests, is available to all who ask with a willingness to forgive (Mk 11.25–26). This community of faith is located in the Galilee, because that is where Jesus sent them long before the final fall of the temple (Mk 14.26–28; 16.7). This community may still be Jewish in its outlook, for it is unwilling to abandon the pillars of its heritage. The concepts of temple, priest, Sabbath, food laws, forgiveness, holiness have not been abandoned, but have been reappropriated within the community of Jesus' followers. Loosed from its bonds to Jerusalem and the fallen temple, all things are possible for this community of faith. Even in their sufferings, they have a model and a leader in Jesus, who gave his life for the many (Mk 10.45). The one who endured suffering and execution is also the Son of Man (Mk 8.21; 10.32–34; 10.45); at the end of these trials he will gather his elect from the ends of the earth (Mk 13.26–27).

Through the unique priestly discourse articulated within the Gospel of Mark, and through a host of other literary strategies, the story of Jesus is proclaimed for a new place and a new age.

4.2. *The Gospel of Matthew and the Priests of Israel*

The Matthaean presentation of the engagement between Jesus and the priests of Israel draws heavily upon the Markan portrait.[25] Like the Gospel of Mark, Matthew is concerned primarily about ruling priests, and he does so almost exclusively in connection with the final days of Jesus. The five remaining instances represent typical Matthaean concerns.[26]

Thus, the Gospel of Matthew has taken over the linguistic presentation of the priests from the Gospel of Mark. The Markan anti-temple agenda has been absorbed in the Gospel of Matthew, but not developed. In a similar way, the structural components of the Markan priestly Christology are employed.[27] The primary Matthaean agenda, however, is aimed not at the priests, but at the Pharisees. Most scholars see in the Gospel of Matthew and in its Christology an extended argument that the true heritage of Israel lives on not with the Pharisaic leaders of the synagogue, but with the messiah Jesus and with his followers in the Church. Almost all scholars agree that this debate, which is set in the time of Jesus, is used to address the situation of the Matthaean community.

4.3. *The Gospel of Luke and the Priests of Israel*

The Gospel of Luke employs ἱερεύς only five times. Two of these are drawn from Markan usage (Lk. 5.14 = Mk 1.44; Lk. 6.4 = Mk 2.26). Lukan usage is found in the designation of Zacharias as a priest (Lk. 1.5), in the parable of the Samaritan (Lk. 10.31), and in the healing of the ten

---

25.   The Gospel of Matthew uses ἱερεύς only three times (Mt. 8.4; 12.4; 12.5). The first two uses are drawn from the Gospel of Mark, and the third (Mt. 12.5) may be a Matthaean epexegetical expansion upon a Markan story. The Gospel of Matthew uses ἀρχιερεύς some 25 times. Only one usage (Mt. 2.4) is not connected to Jerusalem and to the passion of Jesus. Of the 25 uses of ἀρχιερεύς in the Gospel of Matthew, some 20 are drawn from the Gospel of Mark.

26.   In the birth story Herod enquires about the birth of the messiah (Mt. 2.4). The story of Judas' remorse (Mt. 27.3–10) is a Matthaean construction and makes reference to the chief priests (Mt. 27.1, 3, 6). The placing of the tomb guards (Mt. 27.62) and their subsequent report (Mt. 28.11) are a Matthaean account.

27.   Mk 1.39–45 = Mt. 8.2–4; Mk 2.1–13 = Mt. 9.2–8; Mk 2.23–28 = Mt. 12.1–8; Mk 3.1–7a = Mt. 12.9–14; Mk 7.14–23 = Mt. 15.17–20.

lepers (Lk. 17.14). The Gospel of Luke uses ἀρχιερεύς some 15 times, but only once outside the context of Jerusalem and the death of Jesus (in Lk. 3.2 as a temporal marker). Eight of the 15 instances are adapted from the Gospel of Mark (Lk. 9.22; 19.47; 20.1; 22.2; 22.4; 22.50; 22.54; 22.66). In two further instances Luke has replaced a Markan pronoun with explicit reference to the ruling priests (Lk. 20.19; 22.52), and Lk. 23.4 is an explication of Mk 15.10. Distinct Lukan usage of ἀρχιερεύς is found only in the scene before Herod (Lk. 23.10, 13) and in the remembrance at Emmaus (Lk. 24.20).

A distinct Lukan perspective is to be found in five places. First, the story of Zacharias, Elizabeth and Mary (Lk. 1.5–80) creates a genealogical connection of John and Jesus to the priesthood of Israel. Second, the Samaritan parable (Lk. 10.30–37) carefully distinguishes the priests from the Levite and shows both of them to be morally inferior to the Samaritan passer-by. Third, the healing of the ten lepers (Lk. 17.11–19) recognizes the validity of priestly duties (unlike Mk 1.44). One leper, however, gives obeisance to Jesus priority over cultic obligations. While all are cleansed, this leper alone experiences salvation (Lk. 17.19). Luke creates the interpretive frame for this story through his explicit commentary: 'And he was a Samaritan' (Lk. 17.16). Fourth, Luke uses the scene before Herod to insist that blame for Jesus' death falls not on the Roman officials, nor even on the Jewish client king, but squarely upon the ruling priests of Israel (Lk. 23.1–25). Finally, in the remembrance at Emmaus the role of the chief priests in Jesus' death is confirmed: 'our chief priests and leaders handed him over to be condemned to death and crucified him' (Lk. 24.20).

Luke has embraced the Markan theology that the leaders of Israel and the cultic centre at Jerusalem have failed God and the people. Luke also retains the remnant of Mark's priestly Christology. Luke, however, moves the conflict to a new level with his attempt to acquit the Roman officials and with his suggestion that even the despised Samaritans stand closer to God's will and the way of Jesus than do the priests of Israel. In the Gospel of Luke the first hints of supersession emerge.

4.4. *Acts*

In the book of Acts, the term ἱερεύς is used three times (Acts 4.1; 6.7; 14.13), one of which refers to the priests of Zeus (Acts 14.13). As they gathered around Jesus, so the priests gather around the imprisoned Peter and John (Acts 4.1). In Acts 6.7 Luke reports the conversion of a host of priests.

Luke uses ἀρχιερεύς some 22 times in Acts. While the Gospel of Luke embraces and expands the Markan treatment of Jesus and the priests, Acts presents a post-Easter perspective throughout. The ruling priests are central to Luke's presentation of the arrest of the followers of Jesus: Peter and John (Acts 4.6, 23; 5.17, 21, 24, 27); Stephen (Acts 7.1); Jerusalem disciples (Acts 26.10); the Damascus disciples (Acts 9.1, 14, 21; 22.5; 26.12); Paul (Acts 22.30; 23.2, 4, 5, 14; 24.1; 25.2, 15).

In Acts two key themes are developed around the priests. First, the same people who brought Jesus to death are now active in the persecution and execution of his followers. In particular, the trials of Paul parallel those of Jesus. Second, the priesthood of Israel is being suppressed. Many priests are converting to the way of Jesus (Acts 6.7), and Luke suggests that Paul no longer recognizes the status of the high priest (Acts 23.5). The condemnation of Israel's priests and the hints of supersession which emerged in the Gospel of Luke are brought to fruition in Luke's account of emerging Christianity.

4.5. *Sayings Traditions*
The Sayings Traditions Q and the Gospel of Thomas contain no mention of priests or of Sadducees. This absence stands in conjunction with the scarce mention of Jerusalem[28] and with the absence of focus on the death of Jesus. Both texts, however, offer criticism of the Pharisees (*Gos. Thom.* 39, 102; Q 11.39, 42, 43, 44).

4.6. *The Fourth Gospel*
The Fourth Gospel speaks once of 'priests and Levites' (Jn 1.19), but 21 times of chief priests. These references consistently pose the ruling priests of Israel as opponents of Jesus who are responsible for his death. Five references are used to indict the Pharisees by association (Jn 7.32, 45; 11.47, 57; 18.3).

4.7. *The Revelation*
In the Revelation there are no chief priests and no temple (Rev. 21.22). The synagogue at Philadelphia is said to belong to Satan (Rev. 3.9). Ironically, in a land with no temple, those who believe in Jesus are now priests (Rev. 1.6; 5.10; 20.6) who share in the new kingdom. In the vision of the coming age the chief priests and the temple are nowhere to be found, and the priests of Israel have been replaced by the followers of Jesus.

---

28. The Temple is mentioned only in the temptation scene in Q 4.9. Jerusalem is mentioned only in Q 4.9 and 13.34.

4.8. *The Epistle to the Hebrews*

The appropriation of priestly discourse in the letter to the Hebrews is well known.[29] The portrait of Jesus in Hebrews is so dominated by this priestly Christology that references to his teaching and his miracles are absent, and his resurrection is mentioned explicitly only in Heb. 13.20.[30]

The priestly schema in Hebrews is constructed through a distinct interpretation of the Scriptures of Israel.[31] Ps. 109.4 provides the framework for this portrait (Heb. 5.6, 10; 6.20). This citation invokes the image of Melchizedek, and the priesthood of Melchizedek provides the structure for the argument that Jesus exceeds the priesthood of Israel. This exegesis demotes Levi, who, while in the loins of Abraham, pays tribute to a greater priest – Melchizedek. Passages from the prophets are used to criticize Israel's cult with its external offerings and to call for a spiritualization and internalization of cultic activity.[32] The death of Jesus is his priestly sacrifice, but it is also the act which validates his identity and sustains his ongoing ministry to God's people.[33] Jesus, for the community of believers, both realizes and transcends the priesthood of Israel. The new covenant actualized by the Son is eternal.[34]

Ironically, Hebrews roots this eternal priesthood precisely in the historical life of Jesus (Heb. 2.17–18; 4.15–16; 5.7–10). Jesus' temptation and suffering and his learned obedience provide the basis for both his identification with God's people and his qualification as the consummate priest. Christian and Jewish expectations are merged in him: 'Consider the apostle and high priest of our confession – Jesus' (Heb. 3.1).

In his role as the obedient Son, the holiness envisioned by the cult is realized in Jesus. This obedience is the basis of his exaltation. Jesus is not only the one who offers the offering; he is himself the sacrifice.[35] This spiritual transaction is unrepeatable, irrevocable, once for all. As the Levitical priests passed through the forecourt of the temple into the Holy of Holies, so Jesus has passed through the heavens (Heb. 4.14), allowing believers to draw near to the throne of power (Heb. 4.16).

The impact of this schema is crucial. The ancient covenant of Israel, with its Aaronic and Levitical priesthood, is set aside; it has been replaced by the type of Melchizedek, now realized in Jesus the Son. The result is redemption: 'Let us draw near with confidence to the throne of grace, that we may receive mercy and may find grace to help in time of need' (Heb.

---

29. The term ἱερεύς is used 15 times, with ten of them in reference to Melchizedek, while ἀρχιερεύς is used 17 times.
30. Schrenk, 'ἱερεύς' (2), p. 274.
31. Schrenk, 'ἱερεύς' (2), pp. 274–77.
32. Schrenk, 'ἱερεύς' (2), p. 275.
33. Schrenk, 'ἱερεύς' (2), p. 276.
34. Schrenk, 'ἱερεύς' (2), pp. 276–77.
35. Schrenk, 'ἱερεύς' (2), p. 280.

4.16). As a consequence of this new covenant, believers are called to ethical behaviour (Heb. 13.1–18). In this new typology the ancient traditions are superseded and a new identity is established: 'We have an altar from which those who serve the tabernacle have no right to eat' (Heb. 13.10).

5. *The Early Church and the Priesthood*

The replacement of Israel's priesthood continues in the thought of early Christianity. Jesus is understood as a priest not only in the letter to the Hebrews, but in Ignatius, Clement, the Martyrdom of Polycarp, Justinian, Clement of Alexandria, Origen and in the *Didache*.[36]

This conception is spread to the Christian community. The apostles are seen to be represented in the twelve bells on the garment of the high priest.[37] Hegesippus develops the image of James as a holy man – a Nazirite – who is the only legitimate heir to the priesthood of Israel.[38] Origen can speak of Christians as priests under the high priest Christ.[39] Various other patristic materials employ this concept.[40]

At the final stage Christian clergy are designated as priests. The *Didache* designates the prophets as 'our priests' (*Did.* 13.3), and various patristic references understand the clergy as priests.[41] This transition puts in place the concept which will dominate the larger sweep of church history: a Christian priest stands at a Christian altar offering to God a sacrifice in the form of the body and blood of Jesus. In the Protestant Reformation, Martin Luther reclaimed the priesthood for individual believers.

6. *The Historical Jesus and the Priests of Israel*

How should we locate Jesus within this line of development? Following the first principle of continuity, the historical Jesus must stand in some meaningful relationship, negative or positive, to the continuum which stretches from Israel to the early Church. The second principle of continuity is also important: while a historical portrait of Jesus cannot be irrefutable, it must be plausible, both in terms of the historical continuum and in light of the distinctiveness of Jesus' words and deeds.

---

36. Specific references may be found in Schrenk, 'ἱερεύς' (2), p. 283.

37. Justin Martyr, *Dialogue with Trypho* 42.1.

38. So W. Pratscher, 'Der Herrenbruder Jakobus bei Hegesipp', in P. Tomson, D. Lambers-Petry (eds.), *The Image of the Judeo-Christians in Ancient Jewish and Christian Literature* (WUNT, 158; Tübingen: Mohr Siebeck, 2003), pp. 147–61 (148–50).

39. Orig. *Exhortatio ad Martyrium*, 30.

40. Schrenk, 'ἱερεύς' (2), p. 283.

41. Schrenk, 'ἱερεύς' (2), p. 283.

6.1. *Jesus: A Disgruntled Galilaean*

While earlier portraits envisioned the Galilee as an isolated backwater which hosted various radical movements, a more balanced portrait has emerged in recent scholarship. Nevertheless, significant areas of conflict remain.

Chief among these is the presence of the Roman administration. Though the Galilee of Jesus was not occupied by the Romans, it was under their control. This meant not only the intrusion of Roman administration, but also the intrusion of Graeco-Roman culture. Sean Freyne notes that this intrusion is most evident in the imposition of Roman coins and in the building of Roman cities.[42] The discoveries at Sepphoris mean that Jesus lived next door to a thriving centre of Graeco-Roman power and administration and to the wealthy cultural trappings of the *Pax Romana*. Roman intrusion would bring economic, social and religious discomfort to the Galilee of Jesus.

A further discomfort would be evident in the relationship of Galilaeans to the Jerusalem temple and its leadership. Various cultic obligations would prove difficult for those who made their living from the land and in daily commerce. A trip to the Jerusalem temple was no easy matter. If there were priests in the Galilee, these common priests would live and work locally, commuting to Jerusalem for festivals and for their two weeks of annual service. They would be present more frequently in the synagogues. Some tension might exist between the urban and the rural ethos.

These two elements of conflict would combine in the office of the chief priests. They would be identified with Jerusalem, with the priestly oligarchy and with the temple cult. But they would also be identified with the Roman administration. Since the position of high priest was appointed by Roman leaders, at times on an annual rotation, collaboration with Rome was the norm. Beyond this, they would have been associated with the collection of the temple tax.

In the Gospels, Jesus' relationship with the ruling priests is marked by disdain and disengagement. The concerns of the priests, and the ruling priests in particular, are seen as largely irrelevant for the message and ministry of Jesus in the Galilee. It is probably significant that the traditions focused on Jesus' sayings – the Sayings Tradition Q and the Gospel of Thomas – have nothing to say of priests.

This presentation of Jesus as a disgruntled Galilaean locates him wholly within the ethos of his culture, place and people.

---

42. Freyne, *Jesus, a Jewish Galilean* (13).

6.2. *Jesus: More than a Disgruntled Galilaean?*

Are there elements which distinguish Jesus from this ethos and account for his enduring legacy? Was the tension between Jesus and the ruling priests unique? I wish to identity four plausible distinctions.

First, Jesus was a follower of John the Baptist. Luke implies that John stands in line to inherit a priestly office from his father Zacharias. Through Elizabeth his mother, John is one of the sons of Aaron. This double priestly line frames the heritage of John, but not his practice. John is not connected to the temple, and he exchanges a priestly lineage for a prophetic countenance. His place is the desert, his ritual is baptism, and his ethos is apocalyptic.

In each of the Gospels Jesus embraces the prophetic mission of John. From a historical perspective, Jesus was almost certainly a disciple of John. Luke furthers this connection when he suggests that Jesus is a relative of John through Mary. If so, Jesus may also be a descendant of Aaron. Though the Gospels labour to show the superiority of Jesus, his ministry echoes the ethos of John. Any priestly claim is exchanged for prophetic activity, and Jesus stands at a distance from cultic obligations, from dietary laws, from Sabbath limitations. Jesus preaches a coming kingdom and an impending disaster. Like John, he dies at the hands of the Roman occupation. This association with John and its impact on Jesus' ministry distinguishes him from the general discomfort which pervades the Galilee.

Second, Jesus embraced the role of an eschatological prophet. His prophetic ministry was only loosely tied to temple and to synagogue, and cultic acts were replaced by prophetic speech and deeds. While his view of the coming catastrophe was perhaps less apocalyptic than that of John, eschatology dominated his words and deeds. This eschatological world-view deeply impacted the mission of Jesus. In view of the coming kingdom, Rome is relativized. While the absence of criticism of Rome could be an apologetic device, particularly in Luke, Jesus appears to be genuinely unconcerned with the Romans. His parables seem to look over the head of the Roman power to another horizon: the approaching kingdom of God. In a similar way, the temple cult is relativized by this eschatological ethos. Since common duties and even such obligations as burying the dead are abandoned, there is little tolerance or concern for cultic obligations. Jesus' ministry is dominated by parables which elucidate the kingdom, by miracles which foreshadow its coming. In view of this inbreak, all foods are clean, the Sabbath is for human activity, and God's forgiveness is available to all. This eschatological projection would generate conflict both with the temple and with the Roman administration.

Third, Jesus practised a prophetic rhetoric. While his parables spoke of the near approach of God's kingdom, specific aspects of his speech envisioned the end of the temple and its cult. In doing so, he reflects prophets such as Jeremiah, who stood in the door of the temple to predict its demise (Jer. 26.1–24; Amos 9.1).

Several speech acts appear to be plausible historical accounts. The first is the accusation that Jesus threatened to destroy the temple. This charge is reported in three of the Gospels (Mk 14.58; Mt. 26.61; Jn 2.19). It is clear that this charge is troubling, and each of the three Gospels seeks, in its own way, to control the damage. The Gospel of Mark labels this as false testimony (Mk 14.57) and notes that even on this the witnesses could not agree (Mk 14.59). In the Markan account this charge has nothing to do with the condemnation of Jesus; he is condemned in light of his own confession of his identity (Mk 14.60–64). The Gospel of Matthew does not label the charge as false, but the tenor of the saying is blunted through a different technique: Jesus is not charged with directly threatening the temple, but witnesses note that he claimed to be able both to destroy and to rebuild it (Mt. 26.61). As with Mark, the condemnation is based on the self-confession (Mt. 26.62–65). The Fourth Gospel tells this saying as a part of the cleansing of the temple, which is placed near the beginning of Jesus' ministry. Here the saying is a direct quote on the lips of Jesus: 'Destroy this temple, and in three days I will raise it up' (Jn 2.19). The Johannine narrator intervenes to spiritualize the saying: 'But he was speaking of the temple of his body' (Jn 2.21).

Is it plausible that Jesus directly threatened the temple? The report of such a saying is present in three Gospels, and each takes care to redirect the charge. It is unlikely that three Gospel traditions would invent such a charge in different forms only to refute it. From a historical perspective, it is probable that such a charge was levelled against Jesus. While the emphasis on the third day may reflect a Christian reflection upon the resurrection, the claim that Jesus verbally threatened the temple is probably historical.

How does such a threat relate to the extensive prophecy against the temple narrated in the synoptic Gospels (Mark 13; Mt. 24; Lk. 21.5–36)? Is the discourse against the temple a construct based on the simple saying against the temple, or is the simple saying a condensation of the larger temple discourse?[43] Whichever way the literary development occurred, it is plausible that Jesus predicted the end of the temple and that this saying

---

43. It is noteworthy that a few manuscripts of the Gospel of Mark (D W it) insert the temple charge of Mk 14.58 at the end of the prophecy against the temple in Mk 13.2. As a consequence, Jesus predicts that not a stone will be left upon a stone, but after three days another temple, not made with hands, will be raised up. This appears to be a collation of the Johannine interpretation into the Markan discourse.

received renewed attention and development under Caligula (AD 40) and later in the aftermath of the first Jewish War.

Another saying tradition deserves attention. All four Gospels record a saying in which Jesus asserts that he has taught regularly in the temple, but was not arrested for this. The Synoptics place this saying in Gethsemane (Mk 14.49; Mt. 25.55b; Lk. 22.53), while the Fourth Gospel makes it a part of Jesus' trial (Jn 18.20). Furthermore, Luke takes this saying and uses it to conclude the story of the cleansing of the temple (Lk. 19.47). While Mark has the leaders respond to the prophetic act of cleansing the temple (Mk 11.18–19), Luke has them respond to the teaching of Jesus in the temple (Lk. 19.47–48). For the Fourth Gospel, Jesus' starkest critique of the Jewish leaders is delivered in the temple (Jn 8.1–59) and ends with an attempt to stone him.

These diverse compositions suggest that a strong connection existed between the teaching of Jesus, the temple and the process of his execution. While numerous Galilaeans may have been disgruntled with the temple and its leadership, Jesus is probably unique in the prophetic rhetoric which he directed against the temple.

Fourth, Jesus engaged in acts of prophetic symbolism; these had extraordinary impact and extreme consequences. The most significant of these is the cleansing of the temple. The Synoptics tell this story at the end of Jesus' ministry, where it is connected with Passover week and with the death of Jesus (Mk 11.15–17; Mt. 21.12–13; Lk.19.45–46). The Fourth Gospel places the story near the beginning of the narrative and uses it as a frontispiece for Jesus' ministry (Jn 2.13–23). In the Synoptics Jesus cites a combination of Isa. 56.7 and Jer. 7.11. In the Fourth Gospel, the disciples remember a verse (Ps. 69.10) which explains the zeal of Jesus.

Mk 11.18 directly connects the cleansing of the temple to the death plot by the chief priests and the scribes. The Gospel of Matthew softens this, connecting the anger of the chief priests and scribes to the healing of the blind and lame in the temple (Mt. 21.14–17). Luke connects the death plot, as well as the inability to seize Jesus, to his teaching in the temple and to the power of his words (Lk. 19.47–48).

Thus, each of the Gospels tells of Jesus' teaching in the temple, each tells of the cleansing of the temple, and each connects the opposition by the leaders to some aspect of temple activity. What is the most plausible explanation for these various narrative constructions? The best historical explanation behind these texts is that Jesus' teaching in the temple in the season of Passover brought to a head the conflict with the ruling priests. The most dramatic example of this is found in the prophetic act through which Jesus condemns the temple. Of all the scenes in the Gospels, only the cleansing of the temple provides plausible grounds for his arrest and execution. While numerous Galilaeans may have seen the temple as a place of corruption and collaboration, and numerous visitors may have been repulsed, particularly in the season of Passover, by the presence of animals, pagan coins and commercial exchange in the courts of the temple, the prophetic act of Jesus against the temple is distinctive. These seminal words and deeds can then be read back across the broad expanse of Jesus' story.

Further support for this line of development can be found in three literary patterns. First, no such priestly concern is found in the sayings collections of Q and of the Gospel of Thomas. Where there is no passion story, there is no priestly connection. Second, a concerted focus on anti-temple theology and on priestly Christology emerges only in literature from post-AD 70.[44] Third, the tenor of this Christian motif increases as the level of debate and separation from the synagogue increases.

7. Jesus in Continuum

By the time of Jesus' birth the high priest who controlled the temple and collected its taxes served as a compatriot of the Roman leaders and was supported by a priestly oligarchy in Jerusalem. If there were Galilaean priests, they received their office by ancestral privilege and served the temple for festivals and for two weeks per year. Such priests held common vocations and spent the majority of their time in the villages. The image of a Galilee disgruntled with the Jerusalem oligarchy and the temple elite is a historically plausible conception, and hints of this discontent may be found in Josephus and in rabbinical writings. Jesus emerged from this ethos of discontent, but he also stood out from it in a qualitative way. Jesus was a follower of John who had chosen prophetic expectation over priestly obligation. His prophetic eschatology relativized the Roman authority and challenged the dominion of the temple oligarchy. His prophetic rhetoric announced, over against Rome, a new kingdom in which God alone is sovereign. His parables offered God's forgiveness freely, without the intervention of cultic obligation, to tax collectors and sinners. This rhetoric was expressed most dramatically in Jesus' condemnation of the temple, which provides the grounds for his arrest and execution. In the season of Passover, another innocent Jew from the Galilee falls victim to Judaean collaborators and dies at the hands of the Romans.

It is possible that Jesus had only one significant engagement with the leadership of Israel.[45] The fall of the temple in AD 70 casts a new light upon the limited historical confrontation between Jesus and the priests of

---

44. There is no mention of the priestly conflict in the kerygmatic confessions or in the early hymns.

45. This would depend upon whether one accepts the single visit to Jerusalem in Mark or the multiple visits in the Fourth Gospel.

Israel. Some of Jesus' followers now see in the ruins of the temple the judgment of God and the fulfilment of Jesus' prediction.[46] For the Gospel of Mark, these events are a part of the new world in which the followers of Jesus live. The Gospel of Matthew shifts this conflict to the Pharisees in order to address the situation of a different community. Luke moves the conflict to a new level, suggesting in a new way that the priestly traditions of Israel are being replaced by the community of Jesus' followers. A full paradigm of supersession is reached in the letter to the Hebrews, where Jesus replaces the priests of Israel. This role is quickly transferred to the Christian community, then to its final resting place on the shoulders of Christian clergy.

At the centre of this continuum stands the historical figure of Jesus. Rooted in a world of common people, Jesus took part in the general discontent of the Galilee. Jesus' distinct conflict with the ruling priests is most plausibly rooted in his following of John the Baptist, in his eschatological proclamation of the approaching Reign of God, in his prophetic words and deeds. Jesus' vision of a kingdom where God's sovereignty is expressed in unmerited, unmediated forgiveness was most dramatically expressed in his symbolic attack on the temple. It was this act which led to his arrest by collaborators and his execution at the hands of Romans – events which placed him at the centre of the developing Christian story.

---

46.   In a similar way Hegesippus says the fall of Jerusalem was God's punishment for the death of James.

THE DEATH OF JESUS FROM A HISTORICAL PERSPECTIVE[1]

Ingo Broer

The cross on Calvary pales in the glaring
light of what happened in
Auschwitz.[2]

To speak on this topic at a scholarly conference without being able to present a new Gospel or at least a newly discovered source of a few canonical and apocryphal Gospels (for instance, a robber's Gospel that might describe Jesus' arrival in Paradise together with the one robber crucified at his side) seems somewhat audacious. Yet, scientific enquiry has the responsibility not only to make new discoveries, but also to deal with existing problems. In my view, this includes orienting such problems toward a convincing and thus widely accepted solution. In doing so, we cannot always put our hopes in new sources, even though these occasionally appear and provide entirely novel perspectives. Of course, this confidence in generally accepted solutions is, in a certain sense, naive, as even a brief glance at the practice of biblical exegesis, past and present, would demonstrate. Nevertheless, such solutions to the fundamental questions of our discipline – which should at least be a widespread, if not generally accepted view of certain basic assumptions – would seem inevitable if exegesis is not prepared to accept a thoroughgoing loss of influence (not to mention the consequences for the self-image of the academic discipline). Thus, despite the impression of naivety that might be evoked, it is necessary to work towards overcoming the widely divergent opinions, at least with reference to fundamental issues.[3]

With the following remarks, I do not intend to present an entirely novel view of the death of Jesus, a view that might, in the end, only seem convincing to me. Nor do I intend to attempt another reconstruction of the original form of Jesus' words on the destruction of the temple. And, as I see the current state of academic affairs in our discipline, it would not

---

1. Translated from the German original by T. la Presti and T. Broer.
2. O. Betz, 'Probleme des Prozesses Jesu', *ANRW* 2.25.1, pp. 565–647 (567).
3. On this, cf. also W. A. Meeks' splendid presidential address: 'Why study New Testament?', *NTS* 51 (2005), pp. 155–70.

seem advisable to focus on the connection between these words on the temple and Jesus' interrogation by the high priest, although the argument put forth by O. Betz was convincing at least for J. D. G. Dunn.[4]

My concern here is much more modest and yet, perhaps, also more demanding. As a result of the controversy involving R. E. Brown and J. D. Crossan,[5] at least five German-language publications have recently argued in favour of the *sole* responsibility of the Romans for the death of Jesus.[6] I would like to make a few remarks from a hermeneutical and historical perspective on this age-old hypothesis that was first put forth again in a new form in German-language publications by W. Stegemann.[7]

1. 'New' Arguments in the Debate on Jewish Participation in the Trial of Jesus

1.1. W. Stegemann's Position

The starting point for W. Stegemann's study is that point where any enquiry from a Christian and, above all, German perspective must begin – the legacies of the New Testament accounts of Jesus' death. From here, Stegemann rightly explores the correct formulation of the problem and in doing so rejects Mt. 27.25 and 1 Thess. 2.15 as sweeping instances of incrimination and as theologically and polemically oriented extreme statements that are not concerned with 'historically accurate descriptions of facts'. He then concludes that 'only a single issue' is 'pertinent to a historical inquiry: whether there was any historical Jewish authority that in some way participated in the crucifixion of Jesus as ordered by Pontius

---

4. Cf. J. D. G. Dunn, *Jesus Remembered* (Christianity in the Making, 1; Grand Rapids: Eerdmans, 2003), p. 633.

5. J. D. Crossan, *Who Killed Jesus? Exposing the Roots of Anti-Semitism in the Gospel Story of the Death of Jesus* (San Francisco: Harper, 1995). But cf. also the earlier books by Crossan, e.g. *Der historische Jesus* (Munich: Beck, 2nd edn, 1995), pp. 495–96, and their references to earlier publications. R. E. Brown, *The Death of the Messiah. From Gethsemane to the Grave: A Commentary on the Passion Narratives in the Gospels* (2 vols; New York: Doubleday, 1994).

6. W. Stegemann, 'Gab es eine jüdische Beteiligung an der Kreuzigung Jesu?', *KuI* 13 (1998), pp.3–24; E. W. Stegemann, 'Wie im Angesicht des Judentums historisch vom Tod Jesu sprechen?', in G. Häfner, Hj. Schmid (eds.), *Wie heute vom Tod Jesu sprechen? Neutestamentliche, systematisch-theologische und liturgiewissenschaftliche Perspektiven* (Freiburg im Breisgau: Katholische Akademie, 2002), pp. 23–52; P. Fiedler, '"... gekreuzigt durch Pontius Pilatus": Erwägungen zum Problem der Verantwortung für den Tod Jesu', in K. Märker, C. Otto (eds.), *Festschrift für Weddig Fricke zum 70. Geburtstag* (Freiburg: Alber, 2000), pp. 31–48; N. Rubeli-Guthauser, 'Er starb: Und die Gewalt seines Todes wiederholte sich', *KuI* 13 (1998), pp. 25–45. Cf. already before the publication of the book by Crossan, W. Reinbold, *Der älteste Bericht über den Tod Jesu: Literarische Analyse und historische Kritik der Passionsdarstellungen der Evangelien* (BZNW, 69; Berlin: de Gruyter, 1994).

7. E.g. W. Stegemann, 'Beteiligung' (6), p. 12.

Pilate'.[8] This claim is then worded more precisely in Stegemann's subsequent remarks as: 'In any case, the only issue to be considered is whether there was some indirect participation of the Jewish authorities of the time in the conviction of Jesus.'[9] There is no good reason to deny the fact that there is a widespread tendency in exegetical literature that considers the Gospel accounts of the action against Jesus to be basically correct and thus assumes some Jewish involvement in this course of action. According to Stegemann, this is, 'of course, due to the massive accusations against "the" Jews in the New Testament itself. Their persuasiveness is so great that even researchers who would not be inclined to pursue an anti-Jewish line of argument fall prey to it.'[10] For this reason, everything depends on the value of the Christian sources rather than those influenced by Christianity as historical testimony. One of these sources in Stegemann's view is the *Testimonium Flavianum*.[11] Stegemann considers all these sources at some length and relates six different arguments to them. We need not list all of them here, as they are fairly general in scope. So we maintain that our only sources on the death of Jesus are a) Christian, b) secondary sources not from eyewitnesses, which are c) theologically, polemically and apologetically oriented and thus are fictional texts with historical rudiments, texts that are not mutually compatible. Prominent among these theologically polemical or, with a view to the Romans, apologetic elements, Stegemann lists 'the accusation against "the" Jews or against Jewish authorities of being responsible for the death of Jesus'.[12] This, Stegemann maintains, reflects later experiences of early Christian communities with Judaism and is thus 'a backward projection of animosities experienced by the early "Christians"'.[13] In light of this fact and of the circumstance that the 'only relevant non-Christian testimony from antiquity on the death of Jesus',[14] that of Tacitus, says nothing about Jewish participation, the question arises '*whether there was any participation at all of some Jewish authority in the execution of Jesus by order of Pontius Pilate*'.[15]

Repeatedly, Stegemann stresses the idea that any details and the historical reliability of the sources in general must be subject to a 'meticulous historical analysis'.[16] His own historical-critical study, which

---

8. W. Stegemann, 'Beteiligung' (6), p. 6.
9. W. Stegemann, 'Beteiligung' (6), p. 8.
10. W. Stegemann, 'Beteiligung' (6), p. 7.
11. W. Stegemann, 'Beteiligung' (6), p. 9.
12. W. Stegemann, 'Beteiligung' (6), p. 11.
13. W. Stegemann, 'Beteiligung' (6), p. 10.
14. W. Stegemann, 'Beteiligung' (6), p. 12.
15. W. Stegemann, 'Beteiligung' (6), p. 12 (italics in the original).
16. W. Stegemann, 'Beteiligung' (6), pp. 10, 12. Cf. also the call for historical justice by E. W. Stegemann, 'Angesicht', p. 23.

Stegemann rightly limits to the Gospel of Mark, demonstrates that Mark's account is essentially kerygmatic in nature, contradicts regulations set down in the Mishnah, is in other respects historically implausible (the charge of blasphemy, the use of Christological titles), and exhibits an anti-Jewish tendency. In addition, the account in Mark is self-contradictory, as it allows the Sanhedrin to conduct a trial involving a capital offence, only to hand over Jesus to Pontius Pilate, who then begins his own investigation. Thus, according to Stegemann, the trial before the Sanhedrin fits effortlessly into 'the pervading tendency of this gospel to make the entire religious leadership of Israel responsible for the death of Jesus'. Furthermore, he maintains, 'for historical reasons, a trial before the Sanhedrin is extremely improbable'.[17] Only two other possibilities concerning Jewish participation in the trial can be taken into consideration: either the high priest or members of the leadership in Jerusalem handed Jesus over to Pilate to maintain the political order (a possibility not considered anywhere in the Gospels) or the entire matter was taken care of exclusively by the Romans. Stegemann does not explicitly and unequivocally state which of these two remaining alternatives he favours. But he does seem to be inclined to assume the latter possibility when he remarks that:

> The negative role of Jewish authorities is a structural element in the passion accounts of the gospels. But if this negative role is theologically motivated and is a polemical projection of early Christians' experience of rejection back to the time of Jesus, then it is certainly justified to question whether there was any historical participation of Jewish authorities in the trial at all.[18]

Of course, the essential point for Stegemann is that if there was any Jewish participation in the Roman course of action against Jesus, this was not due to *religious* differences between Jesus and the authorities,[19] but instead was solely attributable to the Jewish authorities' involvement in Roman hegemony.[20]

If the position held by Stegemann and others was correct, then the continuity between Jesus and earliest Christianity would have broken very

---

17. W. Stegemann, 'Beteiligung' (6), p. 15.

18. W. Stegemann, 'Beteiligung' (6), p. 20.

19. Similarly Fiedler, 'Pontius Pilatus' (6), p. 36, who summarizes what one might call the mainstream view in exegesis as follows: 'The conflicts provoked by Jesus on a religious level (in the area of the Law, i.e. the Torah) caused and confirmed the intention to kill in his Jewish opponents.'

20. On this cf. also E. W. Stegemann, 'Angesicht' (6), pp. 35–36, who, however, goes beyond his brother's views by excluding explicitly an intention to kill on the side of the Jews. For W. Stegemann this is only the indirect consequence of their lack of capital judiciary powers. On this cf. also Rubeli-Guthauser, 'Gewalt' (6), p. 32, who asks, regarding Crossan's hypothesis that Jesus' symbolic destruction of the temple was decisive for his imprisonment,

early. This is because following their view, early Christianity put Jesus' death, contrary to the actual circumstances and facts that surrounded it, in a completely new, anti-Judaic light, thus cutting several links between Judaism, Jesus and early Christianity. If on the other hand the traditional depiction of Jesus' death is correct, then the passion narrative is in correspondence to the actual facts and there is no break between Jesus' death and its depiction by early Christianity. This question thus goes to the heart of the problem concerning the continuity between Jesus, the Judaism that surrounded him and the post-Easter 'Christian' movement.

1.2. *Counterarguments: D. Sänger and A. M. Schwemer*

How do the critics respond to this position? I know of two responses in the German-language literature to Stegemann's argument: those of D. Sänger[21] and of A. M. Schwemer.[22] Both responses seem to have come about independently of each other, yet the argumentation is very similar – which is not surprising if we take Stegemann's own approach into account. If Stegemann emphasizes Tacitus' testimony with its exclusive mention of the Romans and rejects the accounts of the Gospels as historically inaccurate end-products of an increasingly anti-Jewish attitude, then the critics must question Tacitus' reliability and defend the accounts of the Gospels. Accordingly, both scholars evaluate the testimony of both Tacitus and Josephus in a way much in contrast with Stegemann's view.[23] Both scholars concur with R. Pesch and G. Theissen on the date of the oldest account of the passion and list several sections of the passion that seem to be based on historical fact. More explicitly, both Sänger and Schwemer maintain that a captive Jesus was handed over to the high priest, attribute some historical foundation to Peter's denial of

---

'if this ultimately religious explanation of Roman violence against Jesus does not preserve some of the old anti-Jewish reception structure (*Rezeptionsstruktur*), and (thus) historicizes a retrojection which we Christians for existential faith reasons don't want to miss'.

21. D. Sänger, '"Auf Betreiben der Ältesten unseres Volkes" (Iosephus ant. Iud. XVIII 64): Zur Frage einer jüdischen Beteiligung an der Kreuzigung Jesu', in U. Mell, U. B. Müller (eds.), *Das Urchristentum in seiner literarischen Geschichte* (Festschrift J. Becker; BZNW, 100; Berlin: de Gruyter, 1999), pp. 1–25.

22. A. M. Schwemer, 'Die Passion des Messias nach Markus und der Vorwurf des Antijudaismus', in M. Hengel, A. M. Schwemer (eds.), *Der messianische Anspruch Jesu und die Anfänge der Christologie* (WUNT, 138; Tübingen: Mohr, 2001), pp. 133–63.

23. Schwemer for example plays down the significance of Tacitus' account by pointing out that it is not based on an archive report, that it does not go beyond what was known to the Roman public servants of the second century and what Tacitus, just like Plinius, got to know as proconsul in the province of Asia, and that it also contains some inaccuracies (see Schwemer, 'Passion' (22), p. 135). She bases this view on H. Botermann. Cf. for a similar view also J. P. Meier, *A Marginal Jew: Rethinking the Historical Jesus*, vol. 1: *The Roots of the Problem and the Person* (ABRL; New York: Doubleday, 1991), pp. 90–91.

Jesus, and discover here a source supporting the historicity of the interrogation.

Whereas Sänger focuses on historical fundamentals in a more general way, Schwemer deals with numerous details of passages from the hearings before the Jewish authorities and before Pilate and considers a number of them to be historically reliable. In her opinion, the passion story in Mark is unequivocally under the influence of apologetics and serves to vindicate both Jesus and his disciples from the charge of political crimes. Yet, the complicated events have not 'simply been displaced by apologetics, polemics, and theological interpretation' in Mark, and in Schwemer's view are in no way simply fiction,[24] even though most likely not all the events took place in exactly the way described in Mark. Furthermore, she sees no fundamental anti-Jewish tendency in the Gospel of Mark. Thus, Schwemer takes at least the possibility of a formal death sentence by the Jewish authorities into consideration – not within the context of a preliminary interrogation by an *ad hoc* assembly called in to advise the high priest the night after the Passover, but, instead, at an earlier point in time.[25] In this view, the threat of destruction to the temple also appears to be historically accurate, as the difficulties for the early Christians to accept this saying are apparent in the Gospels and it inevitably raises the question of Jesus' messianic identity. Schwemer does not contend that Jesus' answer to this question (Mk 14.62) is historically accurate, but she does at least consider this section to be part of a very old tradition because of the early Christological position expressed by it. Jesus seems to have provoked the Jewish authorities by referring to his own messianic-judicial power.[26] Accordingly, Schwemer considers the reaction of the high priest described in Mk 14.63 to be 'quite realistic';[27] the high priests thought Jesus to be guilty and thus handed him over as a messianic claimant to Pilate. Pilate would not have come up with this charge against Jesus on his own. Schwemer concludes her argument with reference to the facts that Mark calls Peter an eyewitness who was nearest to the incidents themselves and that even the earliest Christians assumed that Pilate had clearly seen through the course of action undertaken by the Jewish authorities.[28]

In light of this controversy, the following remarks will focus on two issues: First, why is the issue of Jewish participation in the action against

---

24.   Schwemer, 'Passion' (22), p. 162.

25.   Schwemer, 'Passion' (22), p. 145. Cf. also Brown, *Death of the Messiah I* (5), pp. 362–63, 553–60.

26.   Schwemer, 'Passion' (22), pp. 150–51; here Schwemer cites M. Hengel. Cf. also A. M. Schwemer, 'Antijudaismus in der Markuspassion?', *TheolBeitr* 32 (2001), pp. 6–25 (13–17).

27.   Schwemer, 'Passion' (22), p. 150.

28.   The other side of more recent exegesis is represented e.g. by M. J. Cook's article, 'The Problem of Jewish Jurisprudence and the Trial of Jesus', in P. A. Cunningham (ed.),

Jesus of Nazareth actually so important that one group vehemently attacks it while another group just as vehemently seeks to defend it? Second, can the debate on the issue of Jewish involvement in the action against Jesus lead to a decision based on sound reasoning that perhaps is not beyond these 'front lines', but can mediate between them so that some sort of synthesis might come about?

2. On the Significance of the Possible Jewish Participation in the Actions Against Jesus

Both the studies undertaken by Brown, Crossan, Stegemann *et al.* and the prompt reaction to them indicate significant interest in this issue – not to mention their numerous predecessors in this debate. In light of the consequences of certain remarks about the Jews in the New Testament,[29] Stegemann's intention (which he does not only pursue with this particular essay)[30] is an honourable one.[31] But what are the motives of his

---

Pondering the Passion: What's at stake for Christians and Jews? (Lanham: Rowman & Littlefield, 2004), pp. 13–25. For him, Mk 14.55–63 is an echo of later church interests, and was not part of the old passion narrative. In this Mk 15.1 followed 14.53.

29.   On this, cf. the relevant passages in Mt. 27.25 and Jn 8.44. On the oldest passion narrative and the question of anti-Judaism, cf. Reinbold, *Bericht* (6), p. 322, who argues 'that the canonical passion narratives, ultimately based on their oldest predecessor, have become one, if not *the* main source of an anti-Judaism with specifically Christian motives. ... Until today only little has changed in this sinister history of effects (*Wirkungsgeschichte*) of the Christian passion accounts'. And above all p. 324: 'We shall hope that the historic insight, that already the oldest passion account was tendentious in that it shifted the responsibility for Jesus' death from the Roman to the Jewish side, can contribute to containing the partially anti-Jewish consequences of Christian passion accounts.'

30.   Among others, cf. already *idem*, 'Holocaust als Krise der christlichen Theologie', in *Holocaust als Krise der christlichen Theologie. Juden und Christen II* (Protokoll der Tagung der ev. Akademie Baden; Karlsruhe: Ev. Akademie, 1979), pp. 60–74, where he calls for a 'de-anti-Judaizing (*Ent-Antijudaisierung*) of the gospel', p. 63.

31.   However, one's view seems somehow distorted if one argues like Stegemann: 'Looking at the statements in the New Testament about Jesus' death in Jerusalem, it seems that their authors were certain about one thing: Pilate crucified Jesus because of a decisive collaboration of Jewish authorities. And just because blaming the Jews for their responsibility is so deeply anchored in the New Testament, this not only keeps being repeated, but is also the most important reason why both the churches and theology in general, including historical-critical exegesis, find it so difficult to distance themselves from this statement, which has become so disastrous for the Jewish people.' Given that, since Barnabas and Meliton of Sardes, reproaching the history of effects (*Wirkungsgeschichte*) of the New Testament for anti-Judaism is simply justified, the only result of the analysis, if the question is put like this, can be as the title suggests: The Jews did not take part in Jesus' death! However, Sänger rightly asked to do justice to the text and not to interpret it from the start on the basis of its history of effects. (Sänger, 'Betreiben' [21], pp. 10–12). Apart from this, one needs to take into account that in the New Testament we can find both critical and positive statements about Jews from one and the same author. Cf. on this and the concept of anti-Judaism,

opponents; why do they feel inclined or even forced to assert some form of Jewish participation in the trial of Jesus? Several answers seem possible here:

(a)   an interest in the historical reliability of the Gospels. Despite a discernible conservative evaluation of the sources at least in Schwemer's work, this motive does not seem to be a decisive one, since the lack of historical accuracy in the New Testament accounts on the whole is so manifest that this motive hardly seems plausible.

(b)   implying that anti-Judaism – despite the vagueness involved in this concept – would be the motive does not seem appropriate for well-educated German theologians, especially since it is evident that then my own interest in the issue would be subject to the same implication.[32]

(c)   interest in determining what really happened, or, in Ranke's words, 'how it actually was'. I suspect that the interest in a Jewish participation in Jesus' trial is somehow related to this motive. I assume that, in light of the conflicts between Jesus and Jewish religious teachers on the one hand and of the fact that only the Romans were able to enforce capital punishment, the biblical scholars find some form of cooperation between the Jewish and Roman authorities to be the most plausible explanation for the death of Jesus on the other hand.[33] Indeed, the death of Jesus must be explained somehow, since it is, after all, an undeniable historical fact. Nonetheless, this plausibility is probably not independent of familiar, habitual ways of thinking that should be taken into serious consideration.

Probably no single motive can be identified as the decisive reason; it would seem more likely that an entire ensemble of motives guide this exegetical work. Such an ensemble would probably comprise the historical reliability of the Gospels, which, indeed, should be upheld at least to a certain extent, as well as the interest in the historical events and habitual ways of thinking that, of course, do predetermine what is assumed to be plausible.

In more recent exegetical work on the New Testament, we seem to have lost sight of the differences between Jesus and Judaism. No longer does anyone write on this subject the way E. Käsemann did fifty years ago.[34]

---

chapter 4 in D. Sänger, *Die Verkündigung des Gekreuzigten und Israel: Studien zum Verhältnis von Kirche und Israel bei Paulus und im frühen Christentum* (WUNT, 75; Tübingen: Mohr, 1994).

32.   Cf. also Sänger, *Verkündigung* (31), *passim*.

33.   Cf. on this for example Sänger, *Verkündigung* (31), chapters 4.3 and 4.4.

34.   E. Käsemann, 'Das Problem des historischen Jesus', in *idem*, *Exegetische Versuche und Besinnungen I* (Göttingen: Vandenhoeck & Ruprecht, 3rd edn, 1964), pp. 187–214 (206–12). For a more recent discussion, cf. my article 'Jesus und die Tora', in L. Schenke *et al.* (eds.), *Jesus: Spuren und Konturen* (Stuttgart: Kohlhammer, 2004), pp. 216–54.

Does this not imply certain consequences for our understanding of the trial of Jesus? Can we still simply place the responsibility for Jesus' death on the differences between Jesus and the Jewish authorities? Is not Stegemann's evaluation fully in line with present trends in exegesis and must not it for this reason be considered more appropriate than the more traditional views? Why are we so affected by Stegemann's argument that we immediately react in a certain way?

I readily admit that what I am doing here right now stems from an impulse I had during the first reading of Stegemann's study. Do we react in this way because we are interested in (chance) historical facts? The motives behind the interest in this issue are, indeed, not really clear to me. Perhaps they will become more apparent in the course of further discussion.

3. *Where Do We Go from Here?*

Obviously, it is typical of academia that the same issues are raised again and again, but that the attempts to resolve such issues vary. In its own right, this need not present a problem and, instead, could simply indicate the difficulties involved in dealing with such issues. But this does become a problem if none of the attempts to deal with the issues is without precedent and analogies. For this reason, one can gain the impression that the very same questions are constantly being worked through.[35]

The method employed by Sänger and Schwemer, whose analyses attempt to extract historical facts from individual sections of the passion, is typical of our discipline and presents no cause for objection. Yet, it apparently does not make any headway against the general charge levelled by Stegemann *et al.*, because these scholars can already look back on the results of similar, earlier studies, but are not willing to accept them as being reliable and in accordance with the historical facts.

Stegemann's evaluation of the relevant exegetical facts cannot really come as much of a surprise since there are recent analyses of the oldest passion which maintain that the earliest accessible source of Mark's passion has a polemical anti-Jewish bias[36] and that even the author of this

---

35. Note that most of the critical points that Schwemer and Sänger put forward against Stegemann's positive judgment on the reliability of Tacitus' account were already discussed by Blinzler! Cf. J. Blinzler, *Der Prozess Jesu* (Regensburg: Friedrich Pustet, 4th edn, 1969), pp. 49–52.

36. Cf. Reinbold, *Bericht* (6). The author already associates the oldest passion account, which precedes the Gospel of Mark, with the (at least at first sight) very polemical passage 1 Thess. 2.14–16. Cf. e.g. pp. 324, 205 and 318: 'The oldest account of the passion of Jesus that we can reconstruct is already guided by the interest to free Jesus of any *crimen* that might have been relevant for the Romans, to pass instead the actual burden of guilt on to the Jews. This tendency ... has caused the Roman responsibility for the killing of Jesus to be

earliest version no longer had any historically reliable information about
the death of Jesus. Thus, we must acknowledge that this debate has led to
the following result: *in light of the disparate assessments of confirmed New
Testament sources on the part of biblical scholars*, no unanimous decisions
on the exact circumstances surrounding Jesus' death can be expected. In
other words: the conclusions of various groups of biblical scholars on the
historical facts of the passion contradict each other to a significant extent,
and in light of the widely divergent appraisals of the sources, such
appraisals being preliminary to the actual exegetical work, this contradiction is inevitable.[37] For this reason, our attempt to arrive at a solution
here cannot proceed from the analysis of individual passages of the texts
or from individual arguments following from such analysis, but, instead,
must be conducted at a different level. It remains to be shown whether this
attempt can meet with success. Certainly, in light of the familiar biases
and predispositions, some scepticism is called for. But here, even at the
outset, one point that has been referred to not only by J. D. G. Dunn is
especially important: 'In recent questing it has been more widely
recognized that a test of any hypothesis' viability is whether it provides
a satisfactory answer to the question, Why was Jesus crucified? To be
"historical" the historical Jesus must have been crucifiable.'[38]

This other exegetical procedure, which sets aside the various appraisals
of actual New Testament sources, can only be one that employs the
fundamental historical principle of analogy to draw conclusions from
secular sources about how the occupying Roman forces carried out
executions in Palestine around the time of Jesus. In doing so, we will not

minimized, while that of the Jews was maximized.' Cf. also A. Garsky, 'Jesus vor Pilatus: Die
Barrabaserzählung und ihre Aussage über die Verurteilung des "Königs der Juden"', in S. H.
Brandenburger and T. Hieke (eds.), *Wenn Drei das Gleiche sagen: Studien zu den ersten drei
Evangelien* (Münster: LIT, 1998), pp. 152–70 (157–60).

37. So here even calling for greater scientific accuracy etc. wouldn't help! One can
demonstrate these different viewpoints very nicely for example with Mk 14.65. According to
Stegemann the maltreatment of Jesus reported there is 'almost unimaginable' (W.
Stegemann, 'Beteiligung' [6], p. 14; cf. also Crossan, *Jesus* [5], p. 514). But Schwemer sees
this completely differently and uses similar accounts by Paul, Bar Kochba and Menachem
ben Hiskia to back up her claim (Schwemer, 'Passion' (22), pp. 153–54). Cf. also the
assessment by F. Avemarie, 'Die Juden oder die Römer?', *Zeitzeichen* 4 (2004), pp. 8–10 (8),
regarding the availability of sources: 'There are good sources.'

38. Dunn, *Jesus* (4), p. 784, who references other authors; cf. also C. Tuckett, 'Sources
and Methods', in M. Bockmuehl (ed.), *The Cambridge Companion to Jesus* (CCR;
Cambridge: Cambridge University Press, 2001), pp. 121–37 (136), who points out: 'It is
perhaps one of the strongest criticisms to be brought against many of the nineteenth-century
liberal Protestant lives of Jesus that they made Jesus into such a "nice chap" that it becomes
virtually impossible to conceive how anyone could have taken exception to him. Any
proposed reconstruction of Jesus has to be a Jesus who was so offensive to at least some of
his contemporaries that he was crucified.'

be able to totally ignore New Testament sources, but they will play not nearly such a significant role as they have thus far had in the refutation of the studies put forth by Stegemann *et al.*

But before we undertake this attempt, let us first examine Stegemann's argument on Tacitus' *Annals* 15, even though this argument is expressed in only a few sentences. This is necessary because Stegemann casts, so to speak, a general suspicion of an anti-Jewish bias on the New Testament sources, whereas he appraises Tacitus' text in such a positive way that this text becomes the major testimony for an exclusively Roman course of action against Jesus.[39] Certainly, Stegemann is right in assuming that the historical reliability of the Gospels must be critically assessed in reconstructing the life of Jesus. But the question remains whether the positive assessment of the detail mentioned by Tacitus is justified.

3.1. *The Testimony of Tacitus as a Source Supporting an Exclusively Roman Execution of Jesus*

The reliability of Tacitus' text[40] has been a subject of controversial debate in the relevant literature for quite some time.[41] In this sense, the debate on the testimony of Tacitus between Stegemann on the one hand and Sänger and Schwemer on the other has an extensive tradition. As early as Goguel,[42] for instance, the testimony of Tacitus was attributed to a pagan source, that is, to one that was influenced neither by a Christian nor by a Jewish standpoint; the contention that Tacitus' text was fundamentally dependent on the conditions prevalent at the time the work was written[43] can already be found in Renan.[44] The same applies to the opinion that Tacitus' account of Christ came from Christians he had dealings with as governor of the province of Asia[45] or to the assertion that Tacitus' text is

---

39. Although he points out the reliability of this text in one sentence only, cf. W. Stegemann, 'Beteiligung' (6), p. 7 (and also p. 19).

40. Regarding the text-critical problems, cf. H.-W. Kuhn, 'Die Kreuzesstrafe während der frühen Kaiserzeit: Ihre Wirklichkeit und Wertung in der Umwelt des Urchristentums', *ANRW* 2.25.1, pp. 648–793 (696 n. 284).

41. Cf. the completely opposing judgment by H. Botermann, *Das Judenedikt des Kaisers Claudius: Römischer Staat und Christiani im 1. Jahrhundert* (Hermes Einzelschriften, 71; Stuttgart: Steiner, 1996), pp. 177–78: 'The denigration of the Christian sources makes one think that with the historian Tacitus we finally gain some firm ground under our feet.' Tacitus enjoys 'a reputation, which he does not deserve for his accounts of the first Christian martyrdom ... I am talking about his failure as a historian.'

42. Cf. Blinzler, *Prozess* (35), p. 52 n. 52 and more recently Tuckett, 'Sources' (38), p. 123.

43. Cf. Schwemer, 'Passion' (22), p. 135.

44. Cf. Blinzler, *Prozess* (35), p. 50, who already quotes Renan for a similar view. Cf. also Schwemer, 'Passion' (22), p. 135.

45. Cf. Schwemer, 'Passion' (22), p. 135.

dependent on Pliny.[46] The fact that in this context nearly every detail is controversial is a relief to the biblical scholar, as it demonstrates that such seemingly irresolvable controversies do not only occur in the field of New Testament exegesis. In addition, the debate also shows that the reliability of this testimony cannot simply be assumed – although Stegemann does precisely that.

Since several commentators have convincingly argued that Tacitus employs an anachronism in calling the governor a procurator[47] and is not well informed about the origins of the Jesus movement (he envisages it as having already existed before Jesus),[48] Stegemann is ill-advised to place such considerable emphasis on this testimony. This is also true because his argument results primarily from his negative assessment of the reliability of the Gospels, based on their presumed anti-Jewish bias and other considerations, and, in this sense, would not have had to depend on Tacitus' testimony. Sänger's remark that Tacitus would have had 'no reason whatsoever' to 'mention Jewish participation in the trial, even if he had known of such involvement',[49] seems to be significant for assessing the historical reliability of Tacitus' comment. Indeed, we should not even stop there, since the remark on the execution of Jesus under Pontius Pilate obviously serves the purpose of presenting the early Christians in as negative a light as possible, so that the label of superstition subsequently applied to this movement and its link to the horrors and atrocities common in Rome do, in any case, become more plausible. Attributing the execution to 'the Jews' or mentioning their involvement in it would have directly detracted from this intention, because this would have diminished the negative effect that Jesus' execution precisely at the hands of the Romans had for the Christians. For these reasons, such a comment here would be totally unexpected, as it would directly contradict Tacitus' intentions. But this means that the lack of a reference to some Jewish involvement in the trial of Jesus here is not at all so significant that it could be considered a major piece of evidence in favour of a purely Roman execution. Such a reference at this point in Tacitus would damage his more comprehensive intention within the larger context.

---

46. Cf. Blinzler, *Prozess* (35), p. 51 and Cornelius Tacitus, *Annalen Bd. IV Buch 14–16, erl. u. mit einer Einl. versehen v. E. Koestermann* (Heidelberg: Winter, 1968), p. 234. Reinbold, *Bericht* (6), p. 301, alternatively supposes information from Pliny or due to his own governorship.

47. Cf. e.g. Schwemer, 'Passion' (22), p. 135, who relies on Botermann, *Judenedikt* (41); Meier, *Marginal Jew* (23), p. 100 n. 8; Kuhn, 'Kreuzesstrafe' (40), p. 677 n. 153.

48. Cf. Meier, *Marginal Jew* (23), and Botermann, *Judenedikt* (41).

49. Sänger, 'Betreiben' (21), p. 24.

3.2. *Jesus Died on the Cross – The Political Dimension of Jesus' Execution*
All the critics do at least agree that Jesus died on the cross. For this
reason, this insight can function as a starting point for a tentative attempt
to arrive at further insights with which both groups of scholars could
concur. According to the rule 'the more general, the more trivial', the first
stipulation to be deduced is a very simple one: The crucifixion was carried
out by the Romans. Despite the fact that there are also records of
crucifixions conducted by the Jewish authorities, there is no need to go
into further detail on this point,[50] since precisely this aspect is emphasized
by those critics who maintain that there was no Jewish involvement in the
action against Jesus.[51] But there is a further ramification here, namely,
that the execution of Jesus took place for political reasons or for reasons
having to do with preserving the political order. Although it is not
generally tenable that the Romans did not interfere with religious matters
of the Jews, since, for example, between AD 6 and 41 the high priest's
ceremonial robe was kept by the prefect and only handed over for special
feast days, and the high priest's tenure in office was dependent on Rome's
goodwill, this interference with the Jewish religion was not of a religious
nature, but, rather, of a political one. Even though Josephus often neglects
to mention the reasons,[52] it is apparent that the high priests were not
installed in or removed from office because of their religious or theological
views, but because of their political conduct or the trust the Romans
placed in them or withdrew from them.[53] The Romans did not interfere
with internal (religious) matters among the Jews[54] – and they probably
had no deep understanding of such matters. In any case, the comments in
Tacitus and Cicero are characterized neither by goodwill nor by
knowledge of Jewish religious customs,[55] and the fact that Philo actually
mentions that Petronius had some rudimentary knowledge of Jewish

---

50. Cf. P. Egger, *'Crucifixus sub Pontio Pilato': Das 'Crimen' Jesu von Nazareth im
Spannungsfeld römischer und jüdischer Verwaltungs- und Rechtsstrukturen* (NTAbh, 32;
Münster: Aschendorff, 1997), pp.173–74, who not only points out the 800 crucifixions under
Alexander Jannaeus, but also two further references from the Mishnah and the Midrashim.

51. Cf. also J. B. Green, 'Crucifixion', in M. Bockmuehl (ed.), *The Cambridge Companion
to Jesus* (CCR; Cambridge: Cambridge University Press, 2001), pp. 87–101 (88), who argues
that no fact in the life of Jesus 'is more incontrovertible than his execution on a Roman cross
by order of Pontius Pilate'.

52. Cf. *Ant.* 18.34–35; 18.90–95; 18.120–23.

53. Cf. e.g. E. M. Smallwood, *The Jews under Roman Rule: From Pompey to Diocletian*
(Leiden: Brill, repr., 2001), pp. 277–78, 349, who characterizes the high priests appointed by
the Romans: The aim was to guarantee 'that Jewish leadership remained in the hands of
politically acceptable men'.

54. Cf. for example, Acts 18.12–16.

55. Tacitus, Histories 5.5; Cicero, *Pro Flacco* 67; cf. also Tacitus, *Annals* 15.44 about the
Christians.

philosophy and piety shows that this was not something to be taken for granted.[56]

The following factors are in favour of the stipulation that the reasons for Jesus' execution at the hands of the Romans were political reasons: his execution as a robber and alongside other robbers, the Roman elimination of the eschatological prophets, and the crucifixions conducted by the Romans in the period up to the outbreak of the Jewish war. But this must now be substantiated.

3.3. *The Elimination of the Eschatological Prophets*

If we examine Josephus' references to the killing of Jewish prophets and pseudo-prophets who were not brought to trial before the prefect, but were done away with by the military action of a division of soldiers, we notice that these persons often considered themselves prophets and promised miracles that they expected among the 'last things', but that it was not for this reason, but because of the concomitant uproar that they were killed by the Romans.

3.3.1. *The Samaritan Prophet*

This is the case with the Samaritan prophet (*Ant.* 18.85–87), whom the masses[57] wanted to follow – not only taking up arms – to Mount Gerizim to find the holy artefacts ostensibly buried there by Moses. The Samaritan councillor explicitly informed the Syrian legate that these masses were not in uproar against the Romans, but that they had moved to Mount Gerizim to protect themselves from the hubris of Pilate. Here, the weapons and the explicit defence against rumours of revolt indicate that this matter did in any case have certain political connotations and that misunderstandings suggested themselves.

3.3.2. *Theudas' March to the Jordan* (Ant. 20.97–98)

Similarly, the march of a large multitude[58] to the Jordan under the leadership of Theudas in AD 44–46 is hardly to be thought of as a peaceful outing. There is no mention of arms here, but it is stated that the people took all their possessions along. In and of itself, the march does not indicate hostile intentions against the Romans, but the emigration of such a large number of people was certainly also politically significant,

---

56. This statement holds despite the fact that Judaism was attractive to pagans, and that for instance in Damascus a significant number of women were attracted by Judaism (*War* 2.559–61).

57. Josephus speaks of ὡς μεγάλῃ πλήθει.

58. While Josephus even talks about a ὄχλος πλεῖστος here, according to Acts 5.36 only 400 men were involved, a number probably sufficient for a Roman military mission.

unless, as implied in *Ant.* 20.118–36, direct anti-Roman goals were being pursued in any case.[59]

3.3.3. *The Marches into the Desert and the Egyptian Prophet*

The report of the large crowd led into the desert by swindlers at the time of Felix, recounted twice by Josephus (*Ant.* 20.167–68; *War* 2.258–60), contains unequivocally political elements, at least in the presentation in the Jewish War. For here the crowd is promised 'signs of *liberation*' in the desert and from the march the governor Felix gains 'the impression that this is the first step toward an upheaval' (*War* 2.260). We find a similar situation in Josephus' account of the Egyptian prophet (*Ant.* 20.169–72; *War* 2.261–63). Here, too, in the account in *Antiquities* only the eschatological context is manifest, whereas in the Jewish War not only is the number dramatically increased, but also the political dimension of the whole incident is emphasized. From the Mount of Olives and 'with the help of his *armed companions*', the Egyptian could have 'made his way into Jerusalem *by force, taken the Roman occupying army* by surprise, and set himself up as the *ruler of the people*'. Much the same applies to another march into the desert led by a γόης, again with promises of salvation and of the end of the prevailing evils, that is only referred to in passing by Josephus (*Ant.* 20.188). Such evils need not necessarily refer to the oppression under the Romans, but such a connection does at least seem plausible.

3.4. *The Slaying of Jesus in the Light of the Slaying of the Eschatological Prophets*

The slaying of the eschatological prophets demonstrates that political motives were decisive in their elimination at the hands of the Roman occupying forces. In each case, the prophets are characterized by promises of eschatological signs and by a mass following,[60] and the Romans attack on their own initiative. In this context, Josephus mentions no cooperation with the Jewish authorities. Regardless of the fact that Jesus did not die on the battlefield in the midst of some military skirmish, but as a result of some sort of trial, anyone assuming that the Romans were solely responsible for Jesus' death and wanting to support this claim would have to enquire whether there were circumstances in Jesus' life that were similar to these mass movements and might have led the Romans to believe that Jesus was comparable to, for instance, Judas the Galilaean and was, therefore, to be eliminated. Historically speaking, the only mass

---

59. Apart from the views mentioned by Egger, *Crucifixus* (50), p. 88 n. 239, cf. also Smallwood, *Jews* (53), p. 260.

60. Cf. B. Wander, *Trennungsprozesse zwischen frühem Christentum und Judentum im 1. Jh. n. Chr.* (TANZ, 16; Tübingen: Francke 1994), p. 76 for a similar view.

phenomenon[61] in the Jesus tradition that could have caused offence to the Romans would probably have been the entry into Jerusalem.[62] Yet, up to this point, the supporters of an exclusively Roman responsibility for Jesus' death have not suggested that this was a decisive reason for the action against him.[63] Of course, in the relevant literature there are indeed references to the entry into Jerusalem, and it is assumed that this was at least part of the reason for the action against Jesus.[64]

As much as it is the obligation of our discipline to understand the sources better than the authors of the Gospels did, just as much is it necessary to point out that the New Testament authors saw no basis for the actions of the Jewish or Roman authorities[65] against Jesus in the form of his entry into Jerusalem and that those commentators who affirm a historical foundation to this story limit its symbolic significance to the disciples and make special note of the substantial difference to the

61. This seems to be the crucial point with the eschatological prophets mentioned by Josephus. Egger, *Crucifixus, passim*, e.g. pp. 191, 175, on the other hand, thinks that as for the Romans, 'eschatological-prophetic acts are seen as subversive *in principle*' (italics mine). Cf. also the assessment of eschatological prophetism among Jews by C. Burchard: 'It was not an offence to spread eschatological hopes, to threaten the temple or to promise a new one, to pretend to be a representative of God's kingdom or the messiah, and to fill people with enthusiasm for this' (C. Burchard, 'Jesus von Nazareth', in J. Becker *et al.*, *Die Anfänge des Christentums: Alte Welt und neue Hoffnung* [Stuttgart: Kohlhammer, 1987], pp. 12–58 [54].

62. Cf. on this most recently U. Luz, 'Warum zog Jesus nach Jerusalem?', in J. Schröter, R. Brucker (eds.), *Der historische Jesus: Tendenzen und Perspektiven der gegenwärtigen Forschung* (BZNW, 114; Berlin: de Gruyter, 2002), pp. 409–27 (419) and Dunn, *Jesus* (4), pp. 640–42. On the zelotic interpretation of the entry by Brandon and others, cf. the references in Egger, *Crucifixus* [50], p. 184 n. 196. Egger himself (see *Crucifixus* [50], p. 152 and n. 22; cf. also pp. 166–67), refers to Jn 11.48 and 7.31ff., where he finds expression of concern by the Jewish authorities about a possible widening of Jesus' followers to a messianic movement that could lead to a Roman intervention similar to those against other eschatological prophets. Much as such a consequence may seem conceivable from the point of view of the Jewish authorities, Josephus never mentions any cooperation between them and the Romans in his corresponding passages. Egger also does not consider the Johannine character of the motives (doing signs; believing in him).

63. Even E. W. Stegemann, who agrees with his brother's opinion in principle, does not refer to the entry in Jerusalem in isolation, but incorporates Jesus' whole behaviour in Jerusalem, a behaviour which somehow appeared to be a threat to public order, into the case for a possibly Jewish arrest (E. W. Stegemann, 'Angesicht' [6], pp. 40–41).

64. Cf. for example, J. Gnilka, *Das Evangelium nach Markus. 2. Teilband: Mk 8,27–16,20* (EKKNT, II.2; Neukirchen-Vluyn: Neukirchener Verlag, 1979), p. 119, who also points out that the lack of consequences from Jesus' entry into Jerusalem has been seen (for example by Klostermann) as an argument against the authenticity of the entry, at least if the entry happened as described. Wander, *Trennungsprozesse* (60), p. 71, points out that neither the entry nor the cleansing of the temple 'raised any attention by the Roman authorities – only Jewish authorities saw this as a danger'. Of course, this statement comes from an assessment of the sources completely different from that performed by Stegemann and others. Cf. also Wander, *Trennungsprozesse* (60), p. 76, and Avemarie, 'Juden' (37), p. 10.

65. Cf. Wander, *Trennungsprozesse* (60), p. 76.

militant, Zealot messianic claimants.[66] Thus, the grounds for the elimination of Jesus solely at the hands of the Romans can hardly be sought in his entry into Jerusalem, however triumphal this may have been. And in any case, even if the entry into Jerusalem presented a possible reason for the intervention, it would not be at all certain that such action was taken only on the part of the Romans and not of the Jews, since the Jews were most definitely the authorities immediately responsible for the internal stability of the state, as Egger has demonstrated.[67] Indeed, according to the Gospels of Mark and Luke, a hostile reaction on the part of the authorities does follow the Cleansing of the Temple, whatever action provides the basis for this story (Mk 11.18). But characteristically enough, no reference is made to the Romans, only to the high priests and scribes, even though there are records of interventions on the part of the Roman soldiers within the temple complex.[68]

Thus, the Roman military actions against the eschatological prophets recounted by Josephus shed no light on the Roman course of action against Jesus that could make the sole responsibility of the Romans seem plausible. Rather to the contrary: Jesus differs significantly from the prophets described by Josephus and for this reason analogous measures taken against him on the part of the Romans are not very likely.[69]

If maintaining public order was the decisive factor in the elimination of the prophets and the masses following them in Palestine during the first century, this is also true for the crucifixions that are recorded to have taken place during this period and should now be examined more closely. We can disregard both the notorious crucifixion of 800 rebellious Jews under Alexander Jannaeus around 90 BC and the crucifixion of 80 women by the Pharisee Shimeon ben Shetach mentioned in the Mishnah,[70] since we are more specifically concerned with how the Roman occupying forces,

---

66. Cf. R. Pesch, *Das Markusevangelium. II. Teil: Kommentar zu Kap. 8,27–16,20* (HTKNT, 2.2; Freiburg: Herder, 1977), p. 188; L. Schenke, *Das Markusevangelium: Literarische Eigenart – Text und Kommentierung* (Stuttgart: Kohlhammer, 2005) p. 265: 'That the parade and cheering continued within the doors of Jerusalem and in the streets is not reported, and also not assumed by the author. The whole activity is limited to the group around Jesus. One could say: The king of Israel comes to Jerusalem, and nobody notices.'

67. Cf. the summary of his results in Egger, *Crucifixus* (50), pp. 133–36.

68. Cf. for example, *War* 2.223–27 and Acts 21.27–36.

69. Luz, 'Jerusalem' (62), pp. 414–15, finds parallels between Jesus and the aforementioned prophets. In doing so he refers to the prophetic aspects, but neglects completely the significant differences between the prophets mentioned by Josephus and Jesus. Saying that the operation reported by Josephus in *Ant.* 18.85–87 against the intention of its originators got out of hand is, according to Luz, only one of many possible interpretations, which incidentally doesn't seem to be strengthened by the fact that the participants were armed.

70. Cf. *War* 1.97–98; 1.113; *Ant.* 13.380–83; 4Q169 Frag. 4 + 3 points out how unbelievable this event was for Jews; m.Sanh. 6.5.

who from AD 6 on had the right to administer capital punishment, actually went about doing so.

3.5. Crucifixions in Palestine under Roman Hegemony[71]

3.5.1. Crucifixion under Varus
The first crucifixion to be examined here took place under Varus. There are three records of this crucifixion, although one tradition, the Assumption of Moses, is only a very general source.[72] Regardless of certain differences in detail, both testimonies in Josephus concur that this was a crucifixion of the leaders of a rebellion in 4 BC.[73]

3.5.2. Crucifixion under Tiberius Julius Alexander
Much the same applies to the crucifixions of James and Simon under the procurator Tiberius Julius Alexander, a nephew of Philo of Alexandria. Josephus cannot directly accuse these two of rebellious actions, but in an indirect way he puts them into such a context by introducing them as sons of Judas the Galilaean, of whom he explicitly says that he wanted the people to rebel against the Romans.[74] He also makes a direct reference to his own preceding account of this rebellion (in *Ant.* 18.4).

3.5.3. Crucifixions under Ummidius Quadratus and Felix
In reference to crucifixions under Ummidius Quadratus (AD 48–52), Josephus also mentions in both passages[75] that the people involved were rebels. This is also the case in his accounts of the arrest of Eleazar and the crucifixion of some of those involved in the same conspiracy under the procurator Felix (AD 52–60). In *The Jewish War* (2.253), Josephus calls Eleazar a leader of a gang of marauders (ἀρχιληστής), who had ravaged the land for 20 years; he calls those who were crucified robbers.[76] In the parallel passage (*Ant.* 20.161), Josephus also uses the term robbers, but here he mentions that Eleazar was even responsible for the formation of the gang (Ἐλεάζαρον ... τὸν συστησάμενον τῶν ληστῶν τὸ σύνταγμα).

---

71. Cf. on the following, Kuhn, 'Kreuzesstrafe' (40), pp. 706–19, as well as Egger, *Crucifixus* (50).

72. *Ant.* 18.295 par. *War* 2.75; cf. also *Apoc. Mos.* 6.9.

73. According to *War* 2.75 the army looks for the τοὺς αἰτίους τοῦ κινήματος and Varus orders the αἰτιωτάτους to be killed. According to *Ant.* 17.295 the army looks equally for τοὺς αἰτίους τῆς ἀποστάσεως.

74. *Ant.* 20.102.

75. In *War* 2.235 Josephus uses the words ληστρικός and στασιώδης to describe the mass of people, in *Ant.* 20.129 he talks about νεωτερίζω and ταραχή.

76. On this term cf. also O. Michel, O. Bauernfeind, *Flavius Josephus, De Bello Judaico/ Der jüdische Krieg: Griechisch und Deutsch I* (Darmstadt: Wissenschaftliche Buchgesellschaft, 3rd edn, 1982), p. 443 n. 133.

3.5.4. *Crucifixions under Gessius Florus*

Finally, we can comment on the crucifixions that took place under Gessius Florus[77] and were already a prelude to the Jewish War, that these occurred within the context of a Jewish revolt.[78] This final example is also of interest because here there was some interaction between the Jewish authorities and the procurator, but in this case the high priests, the elite and those held in high esteem were at pains to defend the people before Gessius Florus.

3.5.5. *The Trial of Jesus in Light of the Crucifixions Recounted by Josephus*

It should now be clear that, due to the lack of analogies between the marauder revolts described in the sources and the Jesus movement, there is no route leading from here to a direct execution of Jesus at the hands of the Romans. In the accounts of the Jesus movement we do find mention of a sword (Mk 14.47 par.), but on the whole it seems that the movement was more typically peaceable than violent. In this sense, these considerations seem to cast no light upon an exclusively Roman crucifixion of Jesus, and no parallel presents itself. In any case, the last accounts of Roman crucifixions in Palestine mentioned above deal with *hearings before the procurator*, if at all, only extremely briefly. If such a hearing is mentioned, Josephus restricts himself to a single word such as διάκουσας (*Ant.* 20.129), φωραθείς (*War* 2.253) or ἀνήχθησαν (*Ant.* 20.102), whose actual appearance in the manuscript is uncertain.

4. *Conclusions and Corollaries*

4.1. *Conclusions*

In my opinion, the foregoing remarks result in three perspectives for the issue at hand:

1. There are no parallels between Jesus and the incidents referred to by Josephus that led to Roman military actions against the Jews and to crucifixions. Thus, from the reasoning provided by Josephus in comparable cases, an exclusively Roman (!) course of action against Jesus is not at all intelligible. In the final analysis, of course, the teaching of Jesus may have had a political dimension. But this dimension does not seem to have been very prominent in his actions and was perhaps not even clear to the world around him. Even the authors of the Gospels do not take recourse to the charge that Jesus was politically dangerous. In any case, we have no record stating

---

77. *War* 2.293–308.
78. Cf. *War* 2.295, where στασιασταί are mentioned.

that Jesus was labelled as politically dangerous, as is the case with
the prophets in Josephus.

2. All the actions documented by Josephus had an unequivocally
    political dimension.[79] There was mention of weapons, revolts and
    robbers. This suggests that Jesus was also crucified for such
    reasons,[80] and this is supported by the fact that he was crucified
    alongside robbers (Mk 15.27; cf. Mk 15.7).[81] Another point that
    supports this claim is the idea that Jesus' crucifixion was most likely
    a result of the charge that he was 'King of the Jews' as the title on
    the cross says.[82] This obliges us to seek to explain Jesus' execution
    as a political one. If, as we have just seen, Jesus' deeds were not
    political in this sense, then his execution must have been based on a
    misunderstanding, and we are obligated to at least indicate how this
    misunderstanding may have come about. In light of the killings by
    the Romans without Jewish involvement mentioned above, it is not
    probable that this misunderstanding originated solely on the part of
    the Romans.

3. Stegemann lists the following points that, in his view, are in favour
    of his stipulation that Jesus was 'arrested by the Romans and
    brought before the prefect':

    • This hypothesis can be explained without taking recourse to
       further hypotheses.

    • The crucifixion itself also reveals the reason for the execution,
       namely, an uprising, and allows for certain conclusions about
       Jesus' capture by Roman auxiliary troops.

---

79. Cf. the summary expression in Kuhn, 'Kreuzesstrafe' (40), pp. 724–25: 'From the
beginning of Roman rule in 63 BC apparently only rebels, or those taken for rebels or
sympathizing with them, were executed in this way.' Cf. also p. 733.

80. Cf. on this also Kuhn, 'Kreuzesstrafe', p. 733, who argues that the crucifixion as a
rebel followed already from the practice of punishment by crucifixion in the Palestine of this
time.

81. Cf. on this also A. Strobel, *Die Stunde der Wahrheit: Untersuchungen zum
Strafverfahren gegen Jesus* (WUNT, 21; Tübingen: Mohr, 1980), pp. 114–15; J. Clabeaux,
'Why was Jesus Executed? History and Faith', in P. A. Cunningham (ed.), *Pondering the
Passion: What's at Stake for Christians and Jews?* (Lanham: Rowman & Littlefield, 2004), pp.
27–40 (35–36), who thinks that '... for the Romans they were some kind of rebels'.

82. The authenticity of the inscription on the cross also belongs to the hotly debated
topics in New Testament scholarship, often pleaded for and against; cf. again Reinbold,
Bericht (6), p. 274. He sees the discussion of the authenticity of the title on the cross as part of
the duties of historical critique, which is not meant mainly methodically, and points out that
in the (few) comparable cases there 'was obviously a personal element, or the intention to
humiliate the accused', that played a role. But how did the evangelist or the 'poet' of the
passion account hit on this in the first place, if there were only very few cases? From a
historical point of view, according to Reinbold, Jesus was sentenced to death on the cross by
Pilate alone, without any proceedings in front of the Sanhedrin, because of a political offence
(causing public revolt), *after Jerusalem's priestly aristocracy had had him arrested* (Reinbold,
Bericht [6], pp. 308–11).

- The reason behind Jesus' arrest is then related either to his preaching or to some 'possible' symbolic rite carried out in the temple that might have led to a mass disturbance, which, in turn, was then the reason for the arrest by the Roman occupying forces (cf. the analogous arrest of Paul in Acts 21).[83]

These points must be confronted with the following argument: The instances of slaying both in the context of military actions of the occupying forces and through crucifixion apply to persons who caused political unrest or participated in a revolt, and thus were 'robbers' as Josephus saw them. Although Jesus was also executed as a robber, we must maintain that it is not at all apparent how and why the *Romans* identified him as such. Nor do we know how the arrest by the Romans, as stipulated by Stegemann, actually came about. Neither do we know of a prophet who was killed by the Romans solely because of his teaching nor do we know of one who was crucified by the Romans because of some minor symbolic prophetic rite. Analogy, one of the most reliable means for determining historical facts, is lacking here, and this is not in favour of the reconstruction suggested by Stegemann.

4.2. Analogies of Cooperation Between Jewish and Roman Authorities
Though we have no records in Josephus of a Jew being 'eliminated' by the Romans for religious reasons, two cases are known in which religious 'offences' did lead to execution by the Romans and thus can be considered analogies. The first case is that of Jesus ben Anania, one that has often been discussed in the recent literature. Ben Anania's prophecy of the destruction of Jerusalem and the temple led certain 'well-situated Jews' to arrest and mistreat him and subsequently prompted the Jewish authorities to hand him over to the procurator, who had him whipped to the bones only to announce that he was apparently a madman and for this reason set him free (*War* 6.300). This is a clear case of cooperation between Jewish and Roman authorities for religious reasons, based on a prophecy of the destruction of Jerusalem and the temple. There is no mention of a mass movement in this particular case.[84] Interestingly enough, the

---

83. W. Stegemann, 'Beteiligung' (6), p. 19.

84. Egger, *Crucifixus* (50), pp. 143–44, wants to understand the expression δαιμονιώ-τερον τὸ κίνημα τἀνδρός in the sense of an 'uprising movement', 'revolt' and 'rebellion' and demonstrates this impressively by Josephus' use of language. But how does he then want to understand this passage – does he consider it as a more-than-human, godly rebellion? And is the outcry 'a voice from the east, a voice from the west, a voice from the four winds; a voice against Jerusalem and the sanctuary, a voice against the bridegroom and the bride, a voice against all the people' meant to cause revolt? Cf. also the listing of Josephus' use of κίνημα in K. Rengstorf, *A Complete Concordance to Flavius Josephus vol. 2* (Leiden: Brill, 1975), p. 502. And what about the reference to the prophets Isaiah and Jeremiah (Egger, *Crucifixus* (50), p.

Romans only intervened after the prophet had been handed over to them by the Jewish authorities. Despite their obvious presence in the city, they seem to have seen no reason to take action against the prophet on their own initiative. It seems quite questionable whether the action of the Jews in this case can be explained simply with their interest in preserving political stability. It is certainly an oversimplification if the Roman actions against the prophets recounted by Josephus are related to the prophets' 'prophetical and eschatological acts'.[85] Most likely, the decisive factors for the Romans were not the promises of recovering temple artefacts or the parting of the Jordan, and so on. Instead, the mass movements based on such promises and actions, some of them described with explicit mention of weapons, provided the Romans with a justification for their military intervention. Precisely this aspect is missing in the account of Jesus ben Anania, and thus it seems quite questionable whether this case can be readily compared with the others. It is hardly surprising that in this case the Romans only began to play their rather dangerous role after they had been requested to do so by the Jewish authorities.

Furthermore, crossing the boundary to the inner temple court,[86] which was clearly marked by a stone wall that was three yards high, an offence for non-Jews that was punished with the death penalty,[87] might also have necessitated cooperation between the Jewish and the Roman authorities. This is, in any case, the view of K. Müller, who also asserts that in such cases the Jews were able to pronounce the death sentence, but could only impose it after formal confirmation by Roman proceedings.[88] If this interpretation of the Latin and Greek inscriptions were to be preferred to

---

142)? Incidentally, Egger's analysis points in the same direction, despite his different assessment of the Jesus ben Ananias episode, and comes to the conclusion that Jesus was arrested by the Jewish authorities.

85.   Cf. Egger, *Crucifixus* (50), *passim*, e.g. pp. 144–45, against other authors. Cf. otherwise also Egger, *Crucifixus* (50), e.g. p. 210, for the parallelization of Josephus' prophets and Jesus, which ignores the decisive difference concerning the mass phenomenon and the rebellion character.

86.   Cf. *War* 5.193f.; 6.124–26; *Ant.* 15.417; *Leg. Gai.* 212; m.Mid. 2.3.

87.   'No foreigner is to enter within the balustrade and embankment around the sanctuary. Whoever is caught will have himself to blame for his death which follows.' This translation as well as the Greek text can be found for instance in Josephus, *Antiquities VIII: Books XV–XVII with an English Translation by R. Marcus* (LCL, 410; Cambridge, Mass.: Harvard University Press, 1963), p. 202 n. d.

88.   Cf. K. Müller, 'Möglichkeit und Vollzug jüdischer Kapitalgerichtsbarkeit im Prozess gegen Jesus von Nazareth', in K. Kertelge (ed.), *Der Prozess gegen Jesus: Historische Rückfrage und theologische Deutung* (QD, 112; Freiburg: Herder, 1988), pp. 41–83 (68). Müller argues explicitly against the hypothesis put forward, for instance, in O. Michel, O. Bauernfeind, *Flavius Josephus, De Bello Judaico/Der jüdische Krieg. Griechisch–Deutsch 11.1: Buch IV–V* (Darmstadt: Wissenschaftliche Buchgesellschaft, 1963), p. 251 n. 64, of a spontaneous justice by the people. In any case Josephus does not talk about a collaboration between Romans and Jews at this opportunity. According to Wander, *Trennungsprozesse*

the widespread view that in such cases the death penalty either was carried out by a lynch mob or was imposed solely by the temple priests, then here we would have more evidence of cooperation between Jewish authorities and the Roman occupying forces on the basis of a religious offence.[89]

4.3. *The Accounts of Josephus and the Criminal Conviction of Jesus*

Josephus' reports on military actions against eschatological prophets and on crucifixions of rebels are not in favour of a view that places Jesus' arrest and execution solely at the hands of the Romans. In Jesus' case, neither a mass following nor any other indications of political unrest are detectable – precisely those elements that were mentioned in the descriptions of Roman action against Jewish prophets and robbers. In light of the fact that for certain religious offences there was, indeed, some interaction between Jewish and Roman authorities, such cooperation, as described by the Gospels, is not as unequivocally out of the question as Stegemann *et al.* think. For if we do not simply wish to relinquish every possibility of historical reliability in the Gospels – and in view of his evaluation of the sources, such relinquishment would be the ultimate conclusion of Stegemann's work – then we will be able to gather from them that Jesus was a religious prophet who, during his own lifetime, had already gained a small number of followers. But how then should his crucifixion solely at the hands of the Romans have come about? From everything that we can learn from Josephus, some form of cooperation between Jews and Romans does explain, in particular, Jesus' arrest and his designation as a robber much better than any exclusively Roman course of action. This does not necessarily mean that the Jews were the driving force[90] behind such action, but neither can the opposite assumption be proven. In view of the non-biblical sources that were the main basis of our analysis, this result is not at all surprising. Since Jesus' activity was hardly blatantly political, the various statements made by Josephus point more in the direction of a Jewish initiative than in that of exclusively Roman action. In particular, on the basis of the accounts in Josephus, no reason for direct Roman action against Jesus is detectable. Thus, it might very well be that the Jewish authorities intervened, handed Jesus over to Pilate, and subsequently had no more to say in the further proceedings. In any case, for the reasons mentioned above they do not

---

(60), p. 78, there were many cases where the Jewish death penalty was reconsidered by the Romans; on p. 57, however, he references for this Strobel, who lists exactly one case, namely Acts 18.14–15.

89. Cf. P. Segal, 'The Penalty of the Warning Inscription from the Temple of Jerusalem', *IEJ* 39 (1989), pp. 79–84 and the preceding footnote.

90. Cf. Brown, *Death of the Messiah I* (5), p. 379.

seem to have been fully uninvolved in the course of action against Jesus.[91] In conclusion, we might note that the scenario of Jewish participation in the trial of Jesus of Nazareth postulated here was an inner-Jewish trial that certainly had its parallels later in proceedings of Christians against Christians.

---

91.   I do not know whether in the light of this finding it is still necessary to point out with L. Schottroff: 'If in my historical argumentation I come to the conclusion that there was a Jewish participation, then I need to point out plainly that this does not legitimize how Christians have, through the centuries until today, talked about Jews. I have to also make clear that there is a historical connection between the German concentration camps and Christian anti-Judaism' (L. Schottroff, 'Die Schuld "der Juden" und die Entschuldung des Pilatus in der deutschen neutestamentlichen Wissenschaft seit 1945', in *idem*, *Befreiungserfahrungen: Studien zur Sozialgeschichte des Neuen Testaments* [TBü, 82; Munich: Kaiser, 1990], pp. 324–57 [357 n. 124]). Actually, one should take the content of this sentence as self-evident.

INDEX OF AUTHORS